MARTIN CLASSICAL LECTURES

MARTIN CLASSICAL LECTURES

These lectures are delivered annually at

OBERLIN COLLEGE

on a foundation established in honor of

CHARLES BEEBE MARTIN

Pindar and Aeschylus

MARTIN CLASSICAL LECTURES

VOLUME XIV

BY

JOHN H. FINLEY, JR.

PUBLISHED FOR OBERLIN COLLEGE

BY

HARVARD UNIVERSITY PRESS

CAMBRIDGE: MASSACHUSETTS

1955

73380
884.5
F513p

DISTRIBUTED IN GREAT BRITAIN BY
GEOFFREY CUMBERLEGE
OXFORD UNIVERSITY PRESS
LONDON

LIBRARY OF CONGRESS CATALOG CARD NUMBER 54-11110
PRINTED IN THE UNITED STATES OF AMERICA
AT THE PRESS OF THE OBERLIN PRINTING COMPANY
OBERLIN, OHIO, U. S. A.

THE MARTIN CLASSICAL LECTURES

Volume XIV

The Martin Foundation, on which these lectures
are delivered, was established by his many friends
in honor of Charles Beebe Martin, for forty-five
years a teacher of classical literature and classical
art in Oberlin College.

FOREWORD

These chapters spring from lectures delivered on the
Charles Beebe Martin Foundation at Oberlin College in
February 1952. They carry vivid gratitude for unforgotten acts of kindness and hospitality by many friends in
Oberlin, not least by the Chairman of the Committee on
the Martin Lectureship, Professor Charles T. Murphy,
whose kindness has loyally continued to the book in manuscript. I am grateful also for the saving advice of three
other friends who kindly read the manuscript, C. H. Whitman, J. A. Moore, and H. C. Bennett, and am greatly in-
debted to Mrs. C. H. Whitman for reading the proof and
preparing the index. I cannot forego stating, though in-
adequately, my gratitude to two Pindarists, the latter of
whom I did not know: to Sir Maurice Bowra, who by long
and generous friendship as well as by his writings has
shown me much in Pindar, and to L. R. Farnell, whose
admirable edition of Pindar has offered a companionship
that has seemed almost friendship.

CONTENTS

CONTENTS

PART ONE

SYMBOLIC THOUGHT

PINDAR and Aeschylus were born within a few years of each other in or about the late twenties of the sixth century. Both saw at close range the massive events that led in the great age of Greece, and both intensely felt the breath and movement of the times. Having gone in youth from Thebes to Athens for his musical training, Pindar could have known almost as well as Aeschylus the temper of the recently and painfully founded democracy. He seems even to have had ties with the family of Cleisthenes, the founder.[1] The two young men presumably knew each other in these years, though there is no information that they did. Pindar felt continuing admiration for Athens during her period of glory in the Persian wars and for a time thereafter,[2] but the paths of the two men already diverged with the wars, Thebes having submitted to Persia with resultant loss, shame, and lingering need of self-justification. Both visited Sicily during the 470's for performances of their works at the invitation of the Syracusan dynast, Hieron. Aeschylus, who seems otherwise to have passed his life and produced his some ninety plays[3] in Athens, died on a second visit to Sicily in 456/5. Pindar must have traveled throughout Greece and the islands, possibly to Cyrene in Africa, as performances of his choruses dictated. Besides our four books of odes for athletic victors, he left thirteen books,[4] chiefly of works for religious festivals, such as paeans, dithyrambs, and hymns, and to a less extent, of poems for individuals, such as threnoi and enkomia, of all of which only fragments remain. He survived Aeschylus by at least a decade, during which time the military expansion of Athens evoked by her success in the Persian wars and begun during Aeschylus' lifetime reached its height. The Athenians overran Pindar's

native Boeotia during the decade from 457 to 447, and a
year earlier invested the island city of Aegina, where Pindar
was much at home and for which more of his extant poems
were composed than for any other state. The divergence,
somewhat masked at the start, between the innovating
temper of Athens and the conservative spirit of Thebes and
the other Greek oligarchies grew starker with each year
after Salamis. If much in theme and cast of mind and style
unites the two men, the currents of their times served equally
to divide them.

Ancient commentators more commonly ally them on
grounds of style than, with their sharper historical sense, do
modern scholars. Eduard Meyer confronts them in a fine
passage as spokesmen respectively of a dying and of a growing culture,[5] and this judgment expresses the usual view.
The two emerge almost Hector and Achilles. "Strong was
the man who fled but still stronger he who pursued him behind." On historical grounds the appraisal is just. The future was on the side of the progressive spirit of reason and
independent inquiry which Athens embodied and Aeschylus
deeply felt, and tragedy, the vehicle which he created, was
the vehicle of the future, in the sense that it presents characters in their inner independence and responsibility, trying
to grasp and deal with their fates. His lonely and innovating Prometheus has no counterpart in Pindar. If it is held
a chief achievement of the Greeks to have reached a view
of man as obedient to reason and through reason molding
nature and society, Aeschylus is by far the more creative and
prophetic figure.

Yet this historical judgment is one-sided. It weighs too
little those elements of response to life which show less
openly in history. It is true that of all the well-known Greek
writers Pindar has been the least understood in modern centuries. Only Milton, Marvell, and Gray greatly reflect him;
even Pound, who might have been expected to respond to

him, mysteriously fails,[6] perhaps because at first glance
Pindar seems chiefly an apologist for the established order.
The surface reasons for this neglect are clear enough; the
latent reasons are harder to catch. The athletic setting of
his poems can seem alien and even trivial. His language
can be imperious, steep, and on occasion private, but not
more so than Aeschylus' language, which is more understood.
A more essential difficulty is that he speaks, and evidently
thinks, through an elaborate set of symbols, partly figures
from the heroic tradition such as Achilles or Ajax, partly
divine figures or, so to speak, momentarily divine figures,
such as Hesychia, Quietude, at the opening of *P.* 8 or Theia,
The Bright One, in *I. 5.* His gods and heroes are of course
well known, and most of these divinized abstractions appear
in Hesiod's *Theogony* and in other writers. The difficulty
is really not in these figures themselves but in the train of
thought that they carry. Pindar is beyond compare the symbolist among Greek poets, not in conscious rejection, like the
French symbolists, of common logic or in any ascetic effort
to reach a more absolute plane of being, but because these
heroic or religious figures are his natural way of stating the
relationships and meanings of life. This is what is meant
by those who speak of his prelogical way of thinking.[7] A
state of being evokes to him another plane of completer being on which the gods or heroes move, and in speaking of
the one he soon passes to the other. But legends are naturally imprecise and inclusive. The Ajax of one poem, for example, is not quite the Ajax of another. Even in the same
poem, he can include several meanings. "The greater mass
of men is blind of heart," Pindar writes in *N.* 7. "Could it
see the truth, brave Ajax furious from the armor had not
driven the smooth sword through his chest." (vv.24-27).
The scene is Ajax's suicide after the dead Achilles' arms had
been awarded Odysseus rather than himself. But what does
the crowd's blindness precisely mean? Is Pindar defending

himself against specific recent criticism, or making a more general claim that in the confusions of life the poet discerns true grounds of excellence as the crowd does not? Or does the figure of the suffering Ajax include, as it does in two other poems (*I. 4, N. 8*), the Dorian ideal of the man of honor and endurance, and thus look in part to the victor, not to the poet? It is often impossible to define Pindar's exact implication. This is so because of the inclusiveness of symbols, notably his. They cover several facets of a state of being which to him is the essential meaning of an occasion and the true ground of his poem. The difficulty of understanding him is not in his boldness of language or use of myth or cult, but in the weight of meaning which his mythic figures carry.

This is one difficulty; a second may go deeper. Aeschylus reflects the rational and innovating temper of Athens in his characteristic use of the sequence of three plays, the trilogy, by which he expresses time and development. Even the darkest of the extant plays, the *Seven Against Thebes*, concludes its trilogy, if not with progress, at least with emergence from error and violence. The other plays, except the unique *Persians*, have to do with evolutions, which, to be sure, transcend analytical reason in the sense that they involve suffering and experience, yet culminate in reason since suffering and experience bring a higher order. Aeschylus has enormous hope in the world. He believes in the possibility of progress, though it is not an easy progress and must be won by something like Aristotle's cleansing of the heart as applied to a whole society. His thought expresses itself so to speak in a line; Pindar's in a point. Through his conservative Theban background, but in large part certainly through his visionary temperament, Pindar is not interested in social change. His concern is for absolute being, a state which he feels men rise to in great moments and which alone sheds meaning on life. To follow him is chiefly to penetrate the various meanings which he attaches to this absoluteness and to see its relationship to ordinary life. Such a vision causes him to reject certain gross or violent myths about the gods; "leave war and every strife remote from the immortals." (*O. 9*. 40-41) In this sense he can be said to share Aeschylus' innovating outlook. But the impulse is different. His world is basically static, whereas Aeschylus' is evolutionary; hence the previous comparison to the point and the line. To compare them with their contemporaries, Pindar verges toward Parmenides, Aeschylus toward Heraclitus; the one toward unity and rest, the other toward change and movement. It is of course true that movement implies goal, and though Heraclitus sees the upward and downward balance of the world, he approves the soul's ascent to the final fire. Similarly the movement of Aeschylus' trilogies culminates in rest and order finally achieved. This vision of a final order beyond change is the bond between the four men, not least between Aeschylus and Pindar. It is astonishing that so violent an age as theirs could have produced this striving for ultimate harmony. Or perhaps highest energy has an affinity for rest and one should find parallels in Michelangelo's neo-Platonism or the sense of transcendence in Shakespeare's late comedies. But however that may be, Pindar and Aeschylus rise to this sense of order at very different stages, Pindar from the immediate events of common life, Aeschylus through an historical vision of the painful ascent of society as a whole.

Pindar is difficult, then, through both the method and the object of his thought. His method is the symbolism whereby he evokes a kind of ideal counterpart of known reality, static and timeless, inhabiting a lucent region like Olympus in the *Odyssey*, "which is not shaken by winds nor ever wet with rain nor does snow draw near it, but the clear air spreads cloudless, and light courses flashing." His object is to lay hold on the repose of this ideal realm, since he feels that self-transcendence, the flash of the gods in this world, is the only thing that gives it value. It could be said that this difference between the two is simply the difference between lyric poetry, the poetry of mood, and dramatic poetry, that of movement and conflict. This is of course true but does not alter the fact that each found or partly created a form appropriate to himself. The two forms, as suggested, also reflect two societies, the static regimen of the oligarchies and the evolving order of Athens. This is an important fact which bears even on the character and growth of these forms, and we shall return to it. But it is not, as an historical judgment suggests, the fact of final importance in our understanding of the two men. In every human life, even the most energetic and progressive, there must exist feeling for static form. If it were lacking, there could be no sense of the identifying essences of things: spring as contrasted to winter, youth as contrasted to age, all the apprehensible orders of existence through which at any given moment the world takes shape and repose. The fact of final importance about Pindar is not his oligarchic origins, though these may have inclined him to this way of thought, but the way of thought itself. If Aeschylus has been more relevant to Western political history since the Renaissance, and if his processes of mind have been easier for modern centuries, the fact does not diminish Pindar's relevance. It stands essentially outside of history and intellectual change, in the sense that response to the reposed shapes of life and feeling for a momentary or lasting harmony in things are themselves apperceptions which defy change.

Since a chief problem in understanding Pindar is his symbolic cast of thought and, despite some differences, a similar outlook shows in the great Aeschylean figures, it may be well to start with this outlook. The word symbol is ambiguous. In one sense every word, every sound, signifies something beyond itself. Certainly the attempt to express sensory impressions through words ends by conveying something quite different from the object originally perceived; and this something different is both less and more, less because it cannot convey the original object in its own completeness, more because it also conveys feelings about the object. Since feelings are thus involved even in sensory images, it follows that the most seemingly casual image in speech or writing tells something about the observer's attitude as well as about the observed. Homer's "Hector of the glancing helmet" or "wine-dark sea" evoke not only a man or the sea, but convey a certain nobility in Hector as warrior and a certain expanse and dark majesty in the sea. But if it is thus impossible to distinguish exactly between an image and a symbol, symbols seem to bear a heavier weight of meaning and to exist proportionately less for purposes of objective description. Their main burden, if one may put it so, is of categorization. They lift the thing or act which they describe largely out of its own existence into something significant of a larger setting. Symbols have especially to do with the observer's feelings. Granted that images carry such feelings also, their main function is toward the object. The emphasis of symbols is more intellectual. Though they do not break the sensory bond with life but express the mind's categories through the involvement of the senses, they yet chiefly convey meaning and significance. At the start of the *Agamemnon* are two passages about eagles. In the first they shriek vengeance for the young which have been stolen from their nests. In the second Artemis is angry because they kill a pregnant hare. Malraux sees in the age-old motif of beak and talon expression of the world as will and violence.[8] This feeling is here. The first eagles are the Atreidae's just violence against the adulterer Paris; the second eagles are the evil involved in this just violence, which destroys peace and interrupts order and fertility. In killing Iphigeneia in order to calm the

winds and let the army embark, Agamemnon acts with the
second as well as with the first eagles. When Orestes describes himself in the *Choephoroe* as the eagle's son (v. 247),
he falls heir to this fearful involvement of just with unjust
violence, which is the subject of the trilogy. The word symbol as used here will mean such a description of something
only in part for itself, but chiefly for its overtone of judgment or categorization.

This method of expressing meaning, not by open statement and analysis, but through the refraction of the senses,
is of course native to the arts in all periods. But it has a
special quality in the verse which comes into existence before
the development of prose as an opposite and competing
form. Prose forces poetry to mark off its own ground. The
French symbolists consciously rejected processes of thought
suitable to logical inquiry and reasoned choice, in favor of a
more intuitive and direct apperception of being. A cardinal
point of John Dewey's was that reason exists to solve problems, and though it would be untrue of much philosophic and
speculative prose, not to mention the prose of fiction, to say
that it has no concern with the sphere of being but only with
that of Dewey's problem-solving, the sphere of action, yet
the growth of prose has tended to relegate verse to the former sphere. These distinctions are elusive. Verse in trying
to catch the nature of things of course looks to action also,
since awareness of reality is the premise for action. What
is involved seems something like the distinction between pure
and applied science. Each has its characteristic emphasis,
but it is hard to say where the one begins and the other ends
or whether they are ever quite distinct. Similarly, awareness of life simply in itself precedes and surrounds any specific plans for life. Prose being incomparably the vehicle for
the latter, verse in realizing itself has tended toward the former, increasingly in the last century. The point now being
made is that in the early Greek centuries, as in the first stages

of other literatures, this was not the case. Prose did not exist as a literary medium, evidently because the rational and empirical outlook which is at the heart of prose had not yet developed. One may therefore be justified in speaking, with Vico,[9] of an age of feeling which expresses itself in particulars (the mythic figure) as contrasted to an age of reason which expresses itself in generalization (philosophic or scientific law) or in adopting the terms of Brooks Adams,[10] age of faith and economic age. There need be no implication that feeling withers as reason grows. The continual redefinition of the arts asserts feeling's perpetual youth. But the opposite is what concerns us here — in Vico's terms, the undisputed reign of feeling before the rise of reason. Part of the charm of Greek literature is that it traversed these phases and their complex subdivisions with pristine response to each.

It is accordingly possible to speak of two main periods of Greek literature, which may be called the periods of symbolic and of conceptual thought. The point of division between the two, earlier in Ionia, is in Athens about the middle of the fifth century. This is the age of Anaxagoras and Protagoras, of Socrates' early manhood and Thucydides' youth, of the first enthusiasm for physical and historical inquiry, of nascent logic and political theory, and of the beginnings of serious interest in prose style. This is the turning point that leads to Aristotle and to the conceptual analysis of the arts and sciences which is the groundwork of Western thought. What is meant by the term conceptual thought is clear enough. It is the search for categories behind the sensuous play of image, for rational simplification underlying apparent variety. The term symbolic thought is less clear. It too seeks order and simplification, but not by evading the play of image which instead of being a source of confusion and hindrance is the very language by which it speaks and even sees.

What is implied in the term symbolic thought may be clarified by the example of the *Odyssey*. Odysseus in his travels goes through three main kinds of experience. The first is inward and moral. The lotus-eaters are languor and drowning of the will; Circe's arts are evidently the sensual pleasures; the Sirens' song is the intellectual pleasures. (The Sirens offer a Faustian vision; they explain history and nature. "We know all that the Argives and Trojans suffered by the gods' will in broad Troy; we know whatever comes into existence on the all-nourishing earth" [12. 189-191]). Odysseus' visit to the underworld and speech with the dead, though akin to the Sirens' song as satisfying the mind, are more intimate and emotional as related to private memories and fears. Calypso at first glance resembles Circe, but her essential meaning is different: the Olympian possibility of life clear of death and age, though at the price of family, home, and the bonds of common humanity. These adventures comprise a kind of inward travel. A second category has to do with kinds of society. The Cyclopes live in primitive loneliness without ships or agriculture, dependent on their flocks. ("They have neither counselling assemblies nor established laws, but inhabit lonely caves on peaks of the high mountains. Each rules over his children and wives, and they have no regard for each other." [9. 112-115]). They are as far below the social and inventive Greeks as the almost godlike Phaeacians are beyond them. In the latters' country it is perpetual spring. Their magic ships cross the seas without the work of helmsman or oarsmen. They live at ease in wealth and grace, and the very gods at times dine with them. They are slightly soft. ("We are not good boxers or wrestlers, but fast runners and unrivaled oarsmen. We love banquets, the lyre and the dance, changes of clothing, warm baths, and the bed." [8. 246-249]) The Cyclopes and the Phaeacians are evidently primitive and Utopian extremes. A third class of adventures is geographical. Odysseus sees the island from which the winds come, the land where the sun pastures his cattle (clouds in the early form of the myth, whether or not consciously so to Homer), the famous strait with whirlpool and reefs, essence of the sea's danger, and the country "where a sleepless man might earn two wages, as herdsman and as shepherd of the white-fleeced flocks; so close are the paths of day and night." (10. 84-86) It may be added that Odysseus himself is a not less representative figure, dominated as he is by the opposite desires for knowledge and for home, placelessness and place, uncommitment and commitment, life as idea and life as choice.

The query is, how conceive the cast of thought behind this story. Are the adventures allegorical? The answer is certainly no, if by allegory is meant the conscious dressing of a concept in sensuous form, for example, Bunyan's Vanity Fair for Temptation, Dante's Virgil for Reason, or Prodicus' two goddesses for the virtuous and the profane life.[11] Not only is the story too translucent for such a purpose and the adventures too clearly on one plane, but Homeric Greek lacks words for such abstractions as sloth, the sensual pleasures, the intellectual pleasures. The generation of the sophists first fully elaborated these and similar terms, and Socrates' famous difficulties in the Dialogues had a double cause: not only that abstractions are elusive but that the very words for them had to be coined or recast. Prodicus' story of the two goddesses, just mentioned, seems the first clear example of allegory in Greek. To repeat, this definition of allegory assumes that the intellectual abstraction is already in the narrator's mind and that he invents the sensuous terminology to give the abstraction color. But if Homer lacks such abstractions, is his narrative simply an adventure story like a thousand others? The answer is again no, since otherwise posterity would hardly have found in Odysseus' travels the obvious meaning that they contain, nor would Odysseus have kept for later ages his character as the adventurer in experience. He is not a random adventurer like Sinbad but one whose voyage is felt to be analytical of experience generally, or at least of masculine experience.

How then conceive a process of thought which seems to have no need of concepts, yet deals with what is later recognized as their substance? The answer is no longer simple. It apparently calls for two assumptions: first, of sensuous feeling for experience so strong and so fresh as to suffuse whatever judgments the mind makes, with the result that the judgment and the experience become intertwined, each invoking and expressing the other; and second, of some confinement and limitation not so much of experience as of the accepted means of expressing it, through ritual or dance or cycles of stories about known characters. This latter assumption may be slightly retrospective, positing such traditions because they are seen to have existed. Yet it is not in fact hard to imagine stories getting started in a simpler and more comprehensible society and then accreting other stories, so that cycles would come to be formed which would perpetuate themselves because they remained relevant. These would comprise, so to speak, a common denominator of the varied experience of individuals, but would be capable of change as new talent and fresh conditions prompted. Parry's analysis of the methods of oral poetry,[12] though not directed to this question of the way in which an unlettered poet sees reality, is nevertheless relevant in describing a tradition which keeps familiar forms of expression because they are both functional to the singer and known to his hearers, yet which is continually hospitable to changes that a new singer brings and other singers, as well as audiences, learn from him and make their own. As said, it is not hard to understand the growth of such stories about known characters in accepted situations, or to see how they could comprise a kind of chart of common experience, on a more exalted and wider plane, to be sure, but basically proportionate to experience because it was their function to interpret it. This was our second assumption, of a vocabulary of character and situation so familiar that the poet phrases all his major insights and judgments through its sensuous medium, indeed himself thinks through its medium. This thinking through a sensuous medium was our first assumption and remains the harder. Yet exactly this assumption is necessary if, until the age of Socrates and the sophists, or a little earlier outside the mainland, the Greeks did not begin to rely on conceptual analysis for those central interpretations of the world, the state, moral standards, and the relationships of social life which reason was later to furnish through its medium of prose. As suggested, poetry still supremely expresses our existential awareness of all these relationships, though in rivalry now with a conceptual prose which is not always and only directed toward problem-solving, but rises to visions of reality also. Even prospective poets today go to school to Aristotle's reason, not to Homer's symbol, and learn habits of conceptuality which they must later unlearn. The present passionate rejection by poetry of anything but directest feeling partly signifies intuition's struggle against our universal schooling in concept. Yet all societies depend on some widespread common view of reality. Intuition grasps the fuller meanings and the imperfections of these accepted schemes, and the emergent symbols of the arts portend revisions which will later be rationally grasped and incorporated. But all this is easier to understand in societies in which analytical reason already partly clarifies the reigning view. The progress from the rank jungle of primitive folk tale to Homer's lucid poems was mysteriously won not by conscious reason but by the intuitive refinement of myths. Recent writers are helpful who reject the Thomistic and Kantian breach between sense-impression and reason, holding that, even in early childhood, we do not perceive the world as an undifferentiated flow of impressions, but already sort out one tree as like another and a second dog as like a first.[18] This is to say that analytical reason does not alone divide experience into categories but that the senses from the first play their part. Or it is at least to say that we should not recognize as categories only those which reason finally sorts out, but that we achieve these categories also by the joint play of mind and sense. Admitted that, in this intense region where mind and sense jointly grasp the world, emotion enters also and a child can feel a tone of joy or sorrow as well as almost a personality in a plaything or piece of furniture. Yet to define truth as only that which reason isolates comes near assuming a life free of emotion and the senses, as if these were liabilities and not part of our equipment for apprehending the world. All these are ours simultaneously and if we do not understand how they operate indissolubly in the symbols of art, yet these symbols remain statements of inclusive truths because truths most fully representative of our consciousness. The poet always works with them, the early poet more easily and naturally because he does not have to unlearn reliance on reason only. Circe is simultaneously a person, a category of experience, and a quality of emotion. She has this inclusive meaning, because to Homer ways of seeing reality, separate to us, are not yet separate.

So much for the working of symbolic thought, little though these explanations may have lightened its mystery. The early poet's sense of not knowing how his insights came to him seems what is expressed in his appeal to the Muses and in the character of Apollo as an unpredictable god whose presence or absence cannot be foreseen.[14] Such statements are particularly characteristic of Pindar and seem to imply a kind of intent waiting, not for any rational scheme, but for images and stories to form in his mind which would illuminate the present and contain its special meaning. The clear fact in any case remains that, before Socrates, the Greeks received from the poets alone their central interpretations of reality. This period of symbolic thought begins with Homer, notably includes Aeschylus and Pindar, and extends to Sophocles as its last complete spokesman. It came to an end only when the philosophers succeeded the poets as classifiers of experience and purveyors to society of the main relationships of things.

Homer's symbolic world is less complicated than those of Pindar and Aeschylus. Odysseus sees among the dead exemplars of social and family life, and if the great moments of the *Iliad* and *Odyssey* transcend such common categories, these experiences of Odysseus in the underworld remain characteristic of the poems. Achilles asks of his son; Agamemnon talks of his wife; Odysseus sees his mother; Ajax is a former friend, now an enemy. The heroines with whom Odysseus speaks are those who had union with the gods and became the means whereby something godlike brightened their mortal offspring. Tantalus, Ixion, and Sisyphus, by contrast, were too confident of their mortal powers and ended in futile pain because these powers were in fact less than godlike. Here is a clear world of orderly categories, with suggestion of its wonder and hints of its limits. Add to these the further categories of the travels, inward or of the world (though both, as we have seen, are on the same plane in Homer), and something like an outline of life emerges. The world of the *Iliad* is similar, if less simply presented. On a first stage are natural objects, each possessing its own characteristic color and enjoying almost a life of its own: the wine-dark sea, the shadowy mountains, the stars, roaring waves, stubborn cliffs, the seasons, animals (each in its character, so that in the similes lions are comparable to attackers, wolves to a fierce, wasps to an angry, sheep to a broken company[15]), also man-made things, the swift ship, the sharp bronze. All these describe a stable

world of clear recurrent forms. At another stage are the
kinds and conditions of men or, since a human being is inseparable from the role in which life casts him, the kinds and
conditions of fates: Thetis as a mother, Briseis as a disap-
pointed girl, ignoble Thersites, laboring and somewhat limited Ajax, managerial Odysseus, the three old men, Nestor
still intensely immersed in life, Phoenix now beyond it (almost Aristotle's distinction between practical understanding,
phronesis, and wisdom, *sophia*[16]), and Priam, the essential
figure of age, as once fortunate, now close to submergence.
These and the many other characters comprise a gallery of
recurrent attitudes representative of sex, age, endowment,
and fortune. The greatest figures rise beyond these commoner categories, and Achilles in his intense and visionary
loneliness merges with the fearful brilliance of war itself, as
contrasted to Hector, whose life is the peaceful ties of city,
family, and settled duty. The fire of war attends the one as
a motif, the water of peace attends the other. If Achilles is
the greater, it is because he will not solace and distract himself with social bonds, however benign, but rises through intensity of spirit to awareness of the spirit's limits, beyond
which are the timeless gods, each in his due realm. Achilles
thus resembles the Odysseus of the *Odyssey*, except that the
actual world is good enough in the latter's eyes to draw him
home from Calypso's offer of escape from common life,
whereas Achilles returns to his mortal limits with sorrow
and resignation, if with new mercy also.

The purpose of the foregoing was not to discuss the
Iliad or *Odyssey*, a world in themselves, but to suggest their
cast of symbolism. As compared with, say, Polynesian folk
tale, Homer's poems are intensely intellectual. External nature, even human beings and inward states of mind have
their identifiable and recurrent forms. There is order in the
world which the mind can grasp. Aristotle's rational analysis of experience is potentially already present. In that sense,

the lucidity of the Greek vision of life begins with Homer. But as compared with Pindar, he seems less aware of what he is doing, less conscious that what he tells of Troy or Odysseus is essentially analytical. He of course makes clear that the great events of his poems happened in a remote past, when men were handsomer, richer, stronger, and closer to the gods. Hector lifted a stone, "which two men, strongest of the people, could not easily pry from the ground onto a cart, such as mortals now are." (12. 447-449) The tradition of Homer's blindness (which may reflect the fact and was at least common in singers, as Demodocus in the *Odyssey* and the reference in the *Hymn to Apollo* show) is memorable because it catches his attitude of peering with the eyes of the mind into a vanished past. Yet this sense of their pastness does not make his heroes the less real to him or prevent his describing their every action in detail. Here we are back at the point made earlier about a fixed set of characters and situations. So thoroughly do these possess Homer's imagination that, though he is in fact describing nature and experience, he does so entirely through the traditional medium of his heroic theme. Pindar stands more consciously at some remove from the heroes. He too expounds reality through the legendary figures, and partly also through his divinized abstractions, but he is more fully aware than Homer that these comprise an ideal world. He does not think, as the sophists and philosophers were to do, through abstractions, but familiar shapes of gods and heroes preside for him over existence giving it meaning and order. His intelligible world too is a world of symbols. Yet he realizes, as Homer seems not to, that something more than years separates these figures from ordinary reality. They are the theme of Muses and poets, the means by which the gods inspire knowledge; they are the substance of his *sophia*, wisdom, which is what he calls his poetry. The mystery of Homer's symbolic clarification of the world is greater, because he seems unaware that he is telling anything beyond the acts of his heroes, whereas in fact they embody a lucid and intelligible order. Pindar is more nearly at the threshold of conscious reason, and his figures, who to Homer fought on the dusty plain of a real Troy or before an actual Thebes, have now partly risen out of history, like cloud-shapes standing clear of the horizon. This is not to say that they have ceased to be historical to Pindar, but that they have somehow become existential also.

Aeschylus differs in these same ways from Homer and also in his sense of time. The echo of the great events in Athens during his life and his intense awareness of social change endow Aeschylus' personages with the quality of belonging to a series in time. This evolution may take place within one figure, as evidently in Prometheus in the lost later plays of the trilogy, but even in our one play Prometheus carries innovation and struggle with him. Most Aeschylean figures exist in this way on two planes, as themselves and as stages in a process. Agamemnon's decision for the army and against Iphigeneia looks to his death; his death to vengeance by his son; the latter's punishment by the Furies to the establishment of a new order by Athene through the Areopagus. This sense of time and process is at the core of Aeschylus' thought and, as a revolutionary idea, may surpass even his creation of tragedy. Certainly it is the motive force behind it. His sense of time is prefigured in Hesiod's *Theogony* in the account of the painful ascent from primal chaos to the Olympians' bright sway, but the *Works and Days,* if it is in fact by the same author, knows nothing of this ascent as applied to men. On the contrary, we have fallen from the gold to the iron age, and for all human purposes, the stern round of the seasons and the laws of labor and morality are fixed and changeless. This is Homer's tacit assumption also, though he looks to far more than the farmer's round. As we have seen, his shapes are the static forms of sea and land, animal and artifact, man and woman, youth and age, wisdom and folly, repose and violence — a thousand attitudes of life, recognizable, recurrent, suffused with a kind of six-o'clock-in-the-morning light, the reflection of their beauty and vitality. Homer's world could be serenely orderly, were it not for the at once shattering and irradiating entrance into it of passion, heroism, and death. With these, a further, uncertain dimension is given the world, which opens now upon the gods and something akin to them in the heroes. Pindar shows this feeling both for static forms and for something still brighter but disturbing beyond them. His difference from Homer, we have also seen, is that he is more fully conscious that the heroes represent a higher kind of meaning. Aeschylus differs from both in that no forms are static to him, unless it be the final vision of order that he catches, for example, in the rule of justice begun with the Areopagus. And since his personages are thus involved in time and change, they come nearer expressing ideas. The conflicts of characters on the stage obviously take meaning from more general conflicts, and it was his sense of these that inspired Aeschylus' great creative act. In both his sense of time and new vehicle of the stage, he moves away toward conscious concept and action based on reason. Yet, needless to say, he too sees the world through his personages. Why otherwise present the figures of gods and heroes on the stage? It was Plato who devised, though Euripides in moments foresaw, the drama of ideas. In their reliance on symbol rather than on concept, Pindar and Aeschylus remain true contemporaries, though the one saw life as participation in changeless being, the other as involvement in changing process.

Two lines of thought have been pursued so far. The first, concerned with poetic symbolism, saw in Pindar and Aeschylus, as well as in Homer, minds for whom reality was chiefly comprehensible through heroic figures and situations, not through ideas. Though artists continue to see life in this way (and all people in so far as reality comes to us in the senses' clothing), the early age of Greece, when prose did not yet exist, gained its main clarifications by this means. The fact chiefly explains the classic, if by classic is understood the lifting of the specific to the representative and the assumption of order and meaning in these representative forms. The second point had to do, not with the means, but with the temper of Pindar's and Aeschylus' thought. As Aeschylus' trilogies treat evolutions, so they show a new absorption with process and a mind morally concerned with change. Are morality and social change the roots of reason and science? The definition of reason as problem-solving would seem to say so, and in fifth-century Athens the social revolution bred and accompanied the intellectual revolution. The old myths no longer sufficed to explain a greatly enlarged and quickly changing world, and sophists and philosophers leapt to supply by reason the clarifications once given by myth. Aeschylus comes far nearer than Pindar toward taking this portentous step. Needless to say, he does not take it. He is too deeply immersed in his characters and in the complex meanings which they carry. But his temper is partly moral, whereas Pindar's is religious. Aeschylus is so absorbed with change that he risks losing that final sense of rest and participation that alone gives value to any moment of life. He struggles toward a receding future; Pindar accepts a perpetual present. But this is only to repeat what was said at the start, that if Aeschylus has been more comprehensible to modern times, Pindar's response to pure being is outside history.

PINDAR, LIFE AND POETIC FORM

THOUGH it is possible to relate the odes to Pindar's life and trace changes of outlook and emphasis, the final impression is of how constant he stays. No clear parallel suggests itself to so long a poetic life (the earliest dated ode, *P.* 10, is from 498, the latest, *P.* 8, from 446) that changes so little. There seem several explanations. Unlike the tragedians, who worked in a new form, he fell heir to a very ancient choral tradition. Those Greeks who in remote times left the homeland for Ionia eventually sang of heroes and even gods who were in effect equally uprooted, and the word hero in Homer means simply a fighting man. But the Greeks who stayed behind continued to feel in hill and valley the voice of tradition magnified by cult. To them a hero was a sacral figure, the possession of the community, one whose grave they could see and on whose help they could count. Even in the years when Homer and other Ionian singers were coming to see in the heroes a gallery of representative men and fates, there must have existed in the homeland very different traditions about these same figures, varying from place to place through local piety and cantonal mood. Song and dance, the communal act of worship and festival, were the medium of this place-rooted feeling. When with the wakening and prosperity of the seventh century the city-state took on its characteristic form, intensely and increasingly stimulating Greek localism, choral poetry rose as its setting rose. It corresponds in literature to the temple in architecture. As the temple honored the local god, who if worshipped elsewhere was felt to be especially at home there and in fact had certain local peculiarities, so citizens or their sons or daughters proclaimed their inheritance in the local heroes, noted the heroes' ties with the gods, held up their example, and imprecated their favor. In Alcman all these acts are to be seen. Is it fanciful to feel in the ordered dancers a likeness to the ordered columns? The individualistic sixth century extended this communal poetry to embrace notable men. This is the century of signed vases, of verse similarly signed by Theognis or Phocylides, of the monodic poetry of Sappho and Alcaeus, of the sayings of the seven wise men, of tyrants and lawgivers, and of the founding of all the great games except the Olympian, the hunting ground and test of ambitious athletes, usually men of means and connections also. Simonides, a third of a century older than Pindar, is said to have invented the epinician ode, which like the enkomion and threnos expresses this new individualism. But it is worth repeating that the greater part of Pindar's poetry was sacral, which is to say, in the old communal manner. If our odes perpetuate Simonides' innovation, their spirit is far more ancient, and the meaning of the victor's deed to Pindar is in its relevance to his city with its gods and heroes.

Pindar is usually called an international poet, as he was in the sense that he wrote for members of virtually all the chief Greek states at home and abroad or, in the case of cult songs, for the states themselves, including the aloof and hardly penetrable Sparta. He moreover wrote a kind of intercantonal Greek reflecting the general literary heritage and free from those heavy tinges of dialect which had originally marked choral poetry and still marked that of his contemporary, Corinna, if in fact she is his contemporary.[17] Yet when he is in any given state, he writes as if he were a citizen of it, invoking its heroes, appealing to its past, and intuitively adopting its tone and mood. This is the sure mark of his allegiance to the older communal tradition, and helps explain the relatively unchanging nature of his verse. The same fact is also his chief source of trouble. He sees himself in the traditional way as the interpreter "sent alone to the community," (O. 13. 49) the exponent of its standards and meaning. Yet he moved increasingly as he grew older in worlds of myth burningly clear to himself, hardly so to his hearers. Hieron replaced him by the less visionary but lucid Bacchylides, and he struggles with his chagrin in *P. 2.* In two Aeginetan odes (*N.4, N.7*) he complains that he is misunderstood. One feels a sense of mission always risking disillusionment. The sense of mission is the old assumption of the choral poet as illuminator and guide of the community. The risk of disillusion springs from the new intensity and inwardness of the age working in Pindar despite himself and forcing a complexity of vision which endangers the simpler older assumption. It has been said of the lonely and individualistic thought of Heraclitus that at first glance it implies the decay of the community, but in fact results in a new vision of it.[18] Pindar's development seems precisely the opposite. He never doubted the mission toward the community on which his poetic form rested, yet unconsciously verged to those realms of lonely and private insight which tended to become incompatible with this form.

What has been called Pindar's *Programm* is another cause, related to the first, of his relative unchangingness.[19] By *Programm* is meant the various duties of an epinician poet toward the victor's triumphs, present and past, to his close kinsmen and their triumphs, even at times to his trainer. It also includes duties toward the victor's city, and here touches the social role of the choral poet just described. The gifted writer Schadewaldt lists with insight the many traits of Pindar's language which follow from these obligations. The poet proclaims or carries a message or comes with the gift of the Charites; the victor receives a due reward which is like rain after drought or a drink from a mixing bowl; the city's past glories solicit the poet, but the joyful present later recalls him; his testimony is true and lasting. Transitions from one part of the ode to another invoke high phrases, for example, on ending the myth, "check the oar; quickly rest anchor on the earth" (*P.* 10. 51), or in reverting to the present, "but ancient favor sleeps and men are unremembering." (*I.* 7. 16) These and a thousand other phrases are functional, enabling the poet to treat the themes expected of him. They resemble a vase painter's decorative motifs as at once pleasing and serviceable in marking areas. But here again ambiguity and conflict creep in. Pindar's personal statements, his "I," can imply only this formal, bardic tone as he makes a transition or breaks off a theme which he feels too long, or they can on the contrary carry quite personal feeling, even in conflict with his expected theme. He is so identified with his song that his "I" can sometimes mean the chorus. Schadewaldt somewhat mystically finds a resolution between this formal Pindar and this personal Pindar in a third and higher state when, as master of his medium and lifted by its power, he feels no conflict between the two selves, but the personal "I" merges with the formal "I" to give an ease and authority beyond either. There is truth in this view, which broaches the mysterious nature of any great style in its curious mixture of the personal and impersonal. But for present purposes, it is enough that the canons, *thesmoi,* of his epinician task joined with the older interpretative role of the choral poet to give similarity of phrase and movement even to poems written decades apart. This is not to say that the *Programm* need be followed with a fixed emphasis or in a constant order or even completely. Nor is it to say that Pindar's most formal phrases are not his own. Bacchylides has analogous devices, occasionally very close, but for the most part in his own gentler and more pictorial style. To judge by the youthful *P.* 10, Pindar adopted his own heady and driving manner early in something like completeness, and he never changed it because it was bound up to him with a social view of his role which he continued to hold in spite of the intense strains imposed by his inward and visionary temperament.

Yet if his form stayed fixed, his outlook changed. The Alexandrian scholars evidently had lists only of the Olympian and Pythian victors, or at least collated only these lists with the odes, with the result that the *Nemeans* and *Isthmians* are undated.[20] Even the dates given for the *Olympians* and *Pythians* can be corrupt or conflicting. Hence, despite long discussion and what seems a certain achieved area of agreement, some uncertainty lingers and new dates are occasionally offered for one or another poem. At bottom, the reasons for uncertainty are those already mentioned, the natural imprecision of symbols and the formal sides of Pindar's style. He says surprisingly little that is concrete of any victory. One may reflect with amusement that athletes too are stylists and could have wished in Pindar a sharper eye for manoeuver in the pankration or tactics in a race. His usual clients, if not the princes like Hieron or Arkesilas, must have been men of very concentrated purpose, best with a horse or an opponent. But if such were their wishes, he sovereignly neglects them. In thinking of the actual event in relation to Pindar's ode, one is reminded of certain red-figured vases displaying an athletic scene on one side and a musical scene on the other. Ideally, as Plato later felt, these two sides, music and gymnastic, implied each other and Pindar's impulse was faithful to this tradition. The lithe athletes of the Aeginetan pediments represent scenes from the Trojan wars. They are the present lifted into the greater and more meaningful past very much in his manner.

Granted a lingering uncertainty of date for some odes, three periods of outlook and attitude seem clear. *P.* 10 and 6 and, with somewhat less certainty, *O.* 14 and *N.* 5 and 6 illustrate the first period, which extends through the Persian wars. In 498, the date of *P.* 10, even Marathon was unforeseen, much more the shattering events of the great invasion. Pindar was in his early twenties and was writing,

as had Anacreon and Simonides, for one of the powerful
governing and land-owning families of Thessaly. He
patently feels the fortune and brilliance of these, to all ap-
pearances, quite secure people, who have as much, he says,
as men may aspire to. "To their lot has fallen no small
share of the pleasant things of Hellas; may they meet no
vengeful vicissitudes from the gods." (vv. 19-21) Only
a god is free from pain. A man is happy who has won the
highest prizes and sees his son victorious. "He cannot climb
the brazen sky but, in those glories that our mortal breed
lays hands on, reaches farthest sail." (vv. 27-29) He compares Perseus, a hero worshipped in Thessaly,[21] who by the
gods' help reached the blessed country of the Hyperboreans,
Apollo's people. "The Muse is never absent from their
haunts. On all sides throbs the dance of girls, the cry of
lyres, the ring of flutes. They wreathe their hair with golden
laurel and dine in felicity. Illness and hated age touch not
their holy breed. From wars and battles clear, they live
escaped from too just Nemesis." (vv. 37-44) The land of
the untroubled Hyperboreans is a projection of Thessaly,
and its joy an extension of the present joy. The difference
is that their happiness lasts, while men's is tentative. Yet
the resemblance is as important as the difference. A god led
Perseus, but a god's hand is also in the present victory. This
feeling for the golden moment that cancels past toil and almost cancels coming loss is wholly Pindaric and recurs with
complex variations. But the mood is more material now,
more satisfied with what the stable present offers and more
confident of this present. Pindar, so to speak, casts outward
on the world desires for order and harmony which he will
later recognize as partly beyond the world, in music and inner order. He yields to gayety and opulence, and if the
poem is young, it is in the degree of his surrender to these
lucky and attractive people. Though the poem has high
moments, there seems something overdone and slightly pro-

vincial about it. *P. 6*, to the young Sicilian prince Thrasy-
bulus, shows similar virtuosity and similar overstatement.
He seems not yet aware that what he seeks is not easily possessed by any group of people, even people so fortunate as
these patrons, but is in himself and in his poetry, in the keeping of the invisible Muses rather than of the visible
Thessalians.

The marvelously fresh *O.* 14 and *N.* 5 equally convey
the security of a known world, and with less strain as written
for families in neighboring cities of the kind that he knew
well, rather than for distant and slightly alien magnates. But
since an attempt has recently been made to date both poems
later,[22] they will be deferred for the moment. The invasion
of 480-79 with its shocking consequences for Thebes inaugurates the second period, which is that of Pindar's middle life
and greatest productivity. The security of those who had
enjoyed no small share of the pleasant things of Hellas was
now less easily taken for granted, and Thebes' wretched
stand in war destroyed something of the old assurance between man and man leaving suspicion at home and some
wish for apology abroad. In *I.* 8, written for an Aeginetan
soon after the war, Pindar fervently invokes the legendary
ties between the two sisters, Aegina and Thebes, bonds evidently weaker now. "Quit of ills beyond our coping let us
sing something glad even after pain. The rock of Tantalus
over our head some god has turned away, toil beyond Hellas'
daring — Treacherous years overlie men, twisting life's
track. But even these things can be healed, so there be freedom." (vv. 8-16) This freedom is not only from Persia
but freedom to return to an earlier repose and confidence,
things less easily regained. The myth of the poem has ex-
trinsic interest in supplying a chief theme in Aeschylus's
Prometheus, the secret that Thetis will bear a son stronger
than his father. But here the secret is told her august pursuers, Zeus and Poseidon, in order that they may stop their

rivalry and end the fears of worse conflict with some
stronger future son. The price of their reconciliation is that
Thetis shall marry a mortal and bear Achilles, who for all
his brilliance will die in battle. Discord, its painful healing,
death in battle as the price and memory of the healing, these
are very different themes from those of before the war. And
as if Pindar now felt that harmony eluded any actual present
and was to be found only in the longer vision of poetry, he
gives as precedent for his ode the song which the Muses sang
at Achilles' pyre. (vv. 65-66) The shock of events both
turned him to more sombre themes and taught him that
order was not so much in events as in poetry or at least could
be shed on the one because it existed in the other.

Soon after the war he wrote what may have been his
best known poem, the dithyramb for the Athenians, of which
we have the fragment, "shining and violet crowned, by poets
sung, Hellas's stay, brilliant Athens, god-inspired city."
(fg. 64) But *P*. 9, performed in 474 at Thebes, shows that
praise of a long-standing enemy even when her great acts
were fresh was looked on with small favor at home, and he
feels compelled to reaffirm his devotion to Thebes. Yet such
tensions might have slackened and something like the old
composure returned, had he not gone to Sicily late in 476 to
celebrate various triumphs in the Olympian games of that
year, chiefly the tyrant Hieron's victory in the single-horse
race. If the war had damaged the old assurance that excellence was almost tangibly present in a certain code of life
and state of luck, this visit to a new world completed his
emancipation. Perhaps emancipation is the wrong word.
There remains in all the poems for people of the familiar
Greek cities a tone of ease and at-homeness which the great
Sicilian odes lack. It is a pity that these lead off the Olympians and Pythians and are read first, because the impression
tends to arise that they reflect Pindar's normal manner
rather than an intensification of it, in some ways a thorough

departure from it. Someone has said that the history of every Greek poetic form is of steadily increasing secularization, and if so, the Sicilian odes show the process in Pindar himself. Lacking the ritual setting for his poems which existed at home, without the sacral overtones of local myths, in fact without local myths, but singing as a paid performer at a banquet, perhaps even as a lone performer and not through the medium of a chorus (as two passages suggest),[23] he was torn from known assumptions and cast wholly on himself. He supplies by virtuosity what the occasions lack in meaning or, rather, discerns a meaning quite unlike that of such occasions at home, in that it sprang from himself and not from local myth. Accordingly he emerges now quite consciously as the spokesman of the Muses, the discerner of the lasting but, at any given moment, obscured and confused truth, and as one who, because he sees this truth, grasps the just meaning of the present. The ground for this authority is inspiration. He now repeatedly states his dependence on the gods for an insight as mysteriously given the poet as is strength or wisdom the athlete or king. These statements mark his emancipation from any fixed setting and his acceptance of himself. When he returned to Greece, he resumed the familiar and no doubt infinitely more congenial role of the choral poet in the setting of a community, but with a difference now. Having once stood apart, he could never completely return, in the sense of merging fully again in any community or any present, but was willing to recognize that what he saw was above the present, even above the past, a set of shapes giving meaning to each.

Examples of this new confidence toward his poetic role will be given presently. The poems of this middle period comprise the great majority of the odes. He was at the height of his success on his return to Greece, and the relatively untroubled years between then and slightly after 460 coincide with his maturity. He repeatedly visited Aegina, for which in addition to the epinicians he composed a cult song for the temple of Aphaia,[24] the pediments of which date from these years. If the occasion of the poem was the re-dedication of the temple, the fact would fix a final kinship between the tense athletic sculptures displaying the acts of Aeginetan heroes at Troy and Pindar's vision of these same heroes as prototypes of athletes. Herodotus (VIII 64.2, 83.2, 93.1) tells how the contingent from Aegina, judged the finest at Salamis, just before the battle sent back a trireme to take on board the sacred images of Aeacus and his descend-ants. It is such a sense of relationship to the heroes, partly sacral, partly political, partly expressive of a code of action and even of an ideal of physical strength, that inspires both the pediments and the odes. He was close also to Delphi. The most nearly complete of the poems that have been re-covered from papyri is a paean for the Delphians, which he says he composed, "obeying his heart as a child its mother" (fg. 40. 11-13), because a chorus for the occasion was for some reason lacking. He apparently attached mystic mean-ing to his birth in the month of the Pythian festival (fg. 183), and was a votary of Apollo beyond any god except Zeus. Zeus seems to have conveyed to him the inaccessible, almost intolerable brilliance of the gods, like the sun in O. 1 blazing at noon in the empty sky, but Apollo was closer to men — "he who from heavy sickness offers men and women cures, who brought the lyre, and gives the Muse to whom he wills, inducing warless harmony in their hearts, and holds his secret mantic seat." (P. 5. 63-69) If far from capable of being counted on or predicted, as Pindar's almost tremu-lous prayers for divine help make clear, Apollo was neverthe-less more accessible to men, and his brilliance crowned achievements rather than dazzled and overpowered them. Pindar composed in these years for virtually all parts of the Greek world except the newly liberated cities of Asia Minor and the colonies in the region of the Black Sea: for Abdera

on the Thracian coast and the king Alexander of Macedon,
for the islands Tenedos, Samos, Rhodes, Delos, and even
Ceos, the home of Bacchylides, for Arkesilas the tyrant of
Cyrene in Africa, for Locri in South Italy, and at home
chiefly for Aegina, Argos, Corinth, Eastern Locri, and his
native Thebes. He maintained his ties with Sicily, compos-
ing *P.* 1 and the consolatory *P.* 3 for Hieron after his return, as well as the dark and intensely personal *P.* 2. *O.* 6 to
Hieron's adviser and general, Agesias, is also of this time, as
is the second poem, *N.* 9, to the tyrant's brother-in-law,
Chromius.

Dispute and misunderstanding were mixed with the success of these years. In the paean for the Delphians just mentioned, his partisanship for Apollo was so strong as to make
him see the god's avenging hand in the death at Delphi of
Neoptolemus, Achilles's son who had finally destroyed
Apollo's city, Troy. Nothing makes clearer the patriotic
and religious involvements of cities with their heroes than
the offense felt at Aegina at this version of the legend, and
Pindar elaborately attempts amends in *N.* 7. *N.* 4 contains
what seems a reply to those who disliked the complication of
symbol and myth through which he saw the world. He first
hesitates to attempt the myth, saying that the canons of the
epinikion forbid long tales. Then he yields: "Yet by a love-
charm my heart is drawn to touch this new-moon rite."
(v. 35) This touching of the festival means seeing it in the
mythic light familiar to him. For he rejects the criticism of
a competitor who "with jealous eyes revolves in the dark his
hollow thought that falls to earth," and goes on in the wonderful lines of recovered self-trust which Milton follows in
the sonnet on his twenty-third year: "What virtue Fate the
lord has given me, I know well, creeping time will complete
destined. O straightway then, sweet lyre, in Lydian tones
weave this song too, beloved of Oenone [Aegina] and
Cyprus, where Teucer distantly rules, the son of Telamon

. . .." (vv. 39-47) The rival had objected precisely to Pindar's flight into the more than historical regions of his myths;
for it is to these that he returns as he regains confidence.
Whether by the rival's unsoaring thoughts one should understand a manner, like Bacchylides' in certain poems, which
leans on moralistic proverbs and attempts no such symbolic
statement, is less clear. What is certain is that Pindar realizes that his own visionary understanding is not shared by
everyone, and a sense of standing apart, hard for him because he sees his role as social and communal, appears in repeated statements that the true poet is not taught but inspired, an eagle among daws.

This leads to a final point on his outlook in these middle
years. If the war and the experience in Sicily had taught
him that his vision was beyond events and not contained in
them, he remained attached to the world by the standards of
success which he acknowledged. If a god's hand is in mortal
greatness, whether a king's, an athlete's or a poet's, brilliance
at time floods the world. Even if the irradiation dies and
we cannot keep it, still its occasional presence has shown
meaning and order. Pindar has not the tragic vision, or does
not yet have it, which sees this meaning and order as wholly
in inner experience and unconnected with, even in conflict
with the ordinary order of life by which men win or lose,
govern or are governed. Only Sophocles' Oedipus has sight
of this lonely truth which annihilates society, but when both
he and Philoctetes return in Sophocles' late plays to participate in history, even they attest to a connection between inner experience and the outer world of institutions. Still more
does Aeschylus in his optimism believe that inner gains
are translated into society's gains. Thus Pindar's attitude
in these years of approving institutions as at least the vessel
and recipient of an order given by the gods and fully embodied only in them is what all Greeks must have felt who
found meaning in society. But Pindar goes somewhat farther

and tends to feel that, where any brilliant success exists, the
hand of the gods is visible. This comes near to approving
success as such. His oligarchic background inclined him to
established things, and he did not yet wholly reconcile two
conflicting sides of success: as the gods' revelation and blessing of excellence or simply as the luster attaching to anything
that emerges on top. He wanted to believe that victory always implies excellence, hence that the social order is just
and meaningful. Yet he is forced at times to see that excellence fails and the world is out of joint. In *I.* 4, the Theban
family for which he writes had lost four men in one day,
evidently at Plataea and on the Persian side, and their hopes
had commonly failed even in athletics; in *N.* 9, the admirable
Amphiaraus and Hector die at Thebes and at Troy in hope-
less causes. This troubling vision that success may not be
god-given is what haunts him in *P.* 2, when he struggles to
accept Hieron's preference of Bacchylides. The epinikion of
course celebrated happy occasions, and every outer influence
turned him against a tragic view which would rob place and
achievement of their moral value. One should perhaps be
less surprised that Pindar wanted to see success and meaning
in life than that Sophocles was willing to see failure and lack
of meaning. In any case, the poems of this period do not
face the question of evil and failure, if they sometimes catch
peripheral sight of it. Pindar religiously wants the vision of
order, and if he knows that order is essentially with the gods
and not with men, he sees its working in men also, perhaps
too blandly.

Soon after 460 the Athenians began the great surge of
expansion in mainland Greece which eventually collapsed, but
meanwhile carried their fleets around the Peloponnesus, overpowered the Corinthians and Aeginetans on land, giving
them Aegina, Megara, and Pegae, and in the battles of
Tanagra and Oenophyta in 457 first matched the combined
Spartans and Boeotians on even terms and then defeated the

Boeotians alone, opening the Boeotian cities to them.
Though we are least informed on these middle years of any
part of the fifth century, it appears that the Athenians did
not occupy Thebes, contenting themselves with minor towns
where democratic sentiment may have favored them. They
lost Boeotia though not Aegina in the reverses of 447-446,
but meanwhile revealed, if Marathon and Salamis had not
adequately revealed already, what eruptive power had issued
from the democratic revolution in Athens. Pericles accepted
the verdict of this decade as final and henceforth consoli-
dated Athens' sea power in the Aegean, but the dream of
territorial conquest in Boeotia continued to haunt the Athenians, until it shattered at Delium in 424. We are probably
justified in reading back from Thucydides into these years
the bitter struggles in many towns, partly economic as between the established and the rising classes, partly political
as, for instance, in Plataea's hatred of Theban control, which
contributed to Athens' revolutionary strength and weakened
the authority of the landed families. Pindar was in his early
sixties at the start of this upheaval, and four poems are usually taken as marking his darkened mood, *N*. 8 from about
459 or a few years later, *I*. 7 from after Tanagra and
Oenophyta of 457, *P*. 8 of 446 when Boeotia had been liberated but not Aegina, and *N*. 11 which is close in mood to
P. 8. It has been urged with characteristic insight by C. M.
Bowra[25] that *P*. 11 also belongs among these poems, closely
following *I*. 7 and reflecting the period when the Athenians
were in Boeotia.

In all these poems Pindar's confidence in any tangible
excellence or order in events is all but gone. The apocalyptic
close of *P*. 8 states this sense of the vanity of things most
clearly. He recognizes the young victor's exultation in his
triumph but now as something personal and fugitive. "He
who has won some beautiful new thing in his great luxuriance
soars in hope on the wings of his strength, his heart beyond

wealth. In a little time men's happiness waxes. So also it
drops to the ground, by some checking purpose shaken." This
purpose, which is hostile to continued brightness, seems to be
in events, but it infects a man's hopes also. He goes on,
"Ephemerids. What is one? What is he not? A mortal
is shadow's dream. But when the Zeus-given radiance comes,
a blazing glory rests on men and a honeyed life. Dear
mother Aegina, in freedom's course lead on this city through
Zeus and ruling Aeacus and Peleus and brave Telamon and
through Achilles." (vv. 88-100) The shadow and insub-
stantiality of life are transformed only as the gods' brilliance
passingly touches them and clarity and happiness briefly return. In the final prayer for Aegina it is as if the city itself
took on being only through the touch of Zeus and its heroes.
We shall return to the mystic imagery of this passage, but
here it may be taken simply to mark an almost polar contrast
to the Hyperborean passage in the youthful *P.* 10. The contrast is not quite complete since, however brilliant and desirable the life of the feasting Thessalians had once seemed,
it did not reach that of Apollo's ageless and changeless people, and now, though life is shadow, it can still catch the
gods' flame. Pindar's age as well as the blow given his political assumptions is no doubt to be read in the change. He
writes *N.* 11 for a victor from the small island of Tenedos,
who though successful in nearby contests had never ventured
afield to more testing games. Pindar on the whole approves; for though he sees promise in the young man and in
his ancestry, the insecurity of all hopes weighs with him more
heavily. "No certain sign from Zeus attends mankind. We
nevertheless set foot on proud acts, desiring multitudinous
ends. Our constitutions are prisoner to shameless hope. But
the rivers of foreknowledge lie remote. Seek limit in gaining. In unattainable loves are the sharper madnesses." (vv.
43-48) Pindar had not been one to counsel moderation;
only the just-quoted *P.* 8 gives similar caution. Who had

believed more than he in the flash of success? Its power
over him still speaks in the line on the madnesses of unattainable loves. But the line carries more than the mere love of
victory, extending indefinitely to the brilliance and fulfillment which he had always wanted to see in the world and
of which athletic success had been only a sign. The caution
of this poem resembles the visionary close of *P*. 8 in taking
from life the warmth of this hope.

The three periods of his work[26] thus mark a progression
from outward to inward, from meaning seen as tangibly embodied in an existent social order to meaning seen as private
and in a man's feeling. The boy's golden mood in *P*. 8 is
felt as only his own, a sudden flooding joy which lifts him
beyond wealth but which Pindar knows will pass. He even,
in the lines just preceding those quoted, feels sympathy for
the boy's four beaten rivals, "on whom no laughter sweet
shed happiness as they sought their mothers, but they shrink
down alleys alone from enemies, gnawed by failure." (vv.
83-87) This new inwardness is not always melancholy. On
the contrary, he feels new weight now in friendship, a life of
honor toward his time, and the prospect of leaving a good
name to his children. If there is (to one man's taste at
least) a poem more evenly admirable than others, it is *N*. 8,
usually taken as from just before the fall of Aegina. It begins with an extraordinary meditation on youth, which carries his thoughts to the youth and first beginnings of Aegina,
when even Athens and Sparta sought and accepted the leadership of Aeacus. This happier vision yields fresh assurance
that only the prosperity which the gods give is enduring, and
he finds in the award of Achilles' armor to the quick Odysseus
rather than to the brave and reserved Ajax and in the latter's
suicide the example of the world's injustice. He would not
have, he says, such a mind, but if others want gold or land,
would die approved of his fellow citizens, having praised
what was admirable and spoken blame of the corrupt. "Vir-

tue grows like a vine in green dews lifted in the wise and just to the liquid sky. There are manifold uses of friends, in pains the chief, but joy too seeks to give pledge of itself before their eyes." (vv. 40-44) After saying that he cannot recall the victor's father from death, he yet states the power of verse to exorcise sorrow, a power which it had even before Adrastus attacked Thebes. This hint of coming war at the end confirms the vision at the start of Aegina's once-acknowledged place and dignity and the sense of present change in the bitter and intensely felt account of Ajax's death. Yet personal honor and friendship remain untouched, and in the opening metaphor of the lines just quoted, the liquid sky and green dew nourish virtue as they do the vine, as in the course of a deeper natural order. These inner securities are translated into poetry through the need which is expressed at the end of the quotation, joy's need to share itself. The security which in his early period he found in a materially brilliant society and which even in the more emancipated middle years he still admired in gifted and successful people, now returns to the world only from inner experience. Poetry is the outer witness to this inner joy, and imparts to the world rather than takes the world's reflection. This is a stage not unlike that reached by the tragedians, except that Pindar reaches it still holding in sight the brightness, however changed now, with which he started.

This process of growth and change in Pindar's outlook could have been followed in much greater detail, and the result would have been something like a biography reconstructed from the poems. Wilamowitz first attempted this task, and others have interested themselves in the stages of Pindar's life.[27] But there are weaknesses in this approach, partly from the uncertainty that still haunts the dates of some poems, partly because we have after all only four and some fragments of the seventeen books, but chiefly because such a method tends to seize on what changes rather than on what stays constant in the odes. The latter element is surely the more characteristic and the more elusive, and we shall return to it now.

Nearly every poem of Pindar is a metaphor, the terms of which are the victor and the heroes. The likeness is never fully pressed, since to say openly that contemporaries resemble demigods touches impiety. Yet this metaphor is pervasive, not only because each community felt itself in its heroes, which were at once its past, its bond with divinity, and its moral and even physical exemplars, but because Pindar saw reality through such mythic means. As men, yet direct or remote offspring of gods, the heroes imply the gods, and a third dimension thus enters the metaphor. At one extreme, heavily involved in life, stand the victor, his family, his city, the memory of his past efforts, and the shadow of coming efforts. At the other extreme stand the gods, clear of time and struggle, radiant with a completion of which victory catches a momentary glint. The point where the two extremes meet is in the moment when the gods' timelessness touches time and change. The heroes stand at this middle point exemplifying and expressing what the victory implies on both parts: on the part of men, effort, endurance, honor, all the high traits which the heroes themselves embodied and with the further implication that these denote a man's city and heritage as well as himself, since the heroes likewise denote the city; and on the part of gods, the touch of self-transcendence and unforeseen power, with which they had given final elevation to the lives of heroes and which was the sign of their acting in the world. The two terms of the recurrent theme are thus uncertainty, continuation, action, courage — involvement, that is, in time — and achievement, rest, vision, and (in its meaning to Pindar) harmony—escape from time. The one is process; the other, being. The heroes have a hold on both worlds. The immortal Muses sang of the dead Achilles, and after a life of labor Heracles, in the splendid

line of *I.* 4, became "a king of golden halls and Hera's son."
(v. 66) The force of the tacit metaphor gives men too a
hold on the second world of pure being, insofar at least as
their acts reveal a self-transcendence like, if less than that
revealed in the heroes.

Before giving examples of this scheme, one may pause
on the metaphor as such, since nothing is more characteristic
of the age or more fundamental to both Pindar and Aeschylus. It is a truism that the simile, not the metaphor, is
Homer's natural device. He composed in what is not far
from the simplest of all styles, the so-called *lexis eiromene*
or strung style, the character of which is to note separate
events in a string of equal clauses. The account in the first
book of the *Iliad* of Odysseus' journey to return Chryseis to
her father may be an extreme example. "But when they
came inside the very deep harbor, they furled the sails, and
set them in the black ship, and they lowered the mast to the
mast-holder letting it down with the forestays quickly, and
they rowed her forward to the mooring-place with oars. And
they threw over the anchor stones, and made fast the ropes,
and themselves went forth in the breakers of the sea, and
they took forth the hecatomb for Apollo the far-darter, and
forth Chryseis went from the sea-travelling ship." (*Il.* 1. 432-
439) Each act has its clause, and if other passages lack this
entire simplicity, yet it is obviously through means close to
these that Homer catches his matchless variety of things,
each complete in itself and owning its moment of entire attention. The simile is the medium of such a mind, since it
compares two things, each of which is grasped separately and
fully. "As when storm-flooding rivers down mountains running into a meeting of valleys cast their mighty water from
great springs in a hollow ravine, and far off on mountains a
shepherd hears their crashing, so from them [the armies]
joining rose cry and labor." (*Il.* 4. 452-456) He does not
call the two armies rivers, as would a metaphorical style,

though the ferocity of streams in spate or storm-driven waves is often evoked to him by battle. Rather he holds the rivers and the battle strictly apart in their own existence; in fact, he here holds apart the rivers and the listening shepherd, with the result that each is felt alone and space intervenes between them. This sense of space then imparts itself to the battle, and the plain of Troy is for a moment remote and seen as a whole. Homer's tireless objectivity and the sense which he gives of seeing a thousand details with sharpest clarity but at some remove reflects a mind which does not assert itself against things but, so to speak, waits on them, finding due place for each. Such a mind sees an endless series of presents. It is absorbed in the moment, can easily digress, and tends to make its effects by the sheer mass of the things that it successively sees rather than by choice and elimination. The style perhaps owes part of its power to the fact that the consciousness likewise receives impressions of separate things, for instance, light coming in a window, or a shadow by a tree. The intellect, by contrast, relates impressions in its own structures and by so doing saps their vitality and vividness, substituting its own. Hence one could perhaps call the Homeric style the style of consciousness as contrasted to intellect, or, since the *Iliad* and *Odyssey* also have order and structure, it might be better to speak of intellect deeply embedded in consciousness and not yet struggling to fight clear. In the *Phaedo,* Socrates repeatedly speaks of the mind's desire for pure idea free of sense impression. This would seem the opposite of Homer's wish, if the thought could have occurred to him. He, on the contrary, remained unweariedly absorbed in the sight of things, and the separate existence of the parts of his similes, like his separate clauses throughout, follows from this absorption with identity and distinctness.

The fact that most poems of Pindar are only an enlarged metaphor and that his report of victory, for example, can be

variously water or wine or a beacon or can board a ship or
be brought from the Muses' garden, obviously betrays a deep
change of outlook. The mind was now more aware of itself
as a motive force. Men felt the origin of judgments and
emotions to be within them rather than from the gods' inspiration. Such an outlook is admittedly more visible in
tragedy than in the odes, since Pindar continues to feel in
victory the gods' sovereign touch, and his precise tone is
harder to catch than is Aeschylus'. Yet it is clear that both
feel a new and exalting sense of the mind's power, and
though the political and military events of the period are
sometimes given as explaining the common traits of their
bold styles, the cause goes deeper and lies somewhere in this
realm of the mind's heady pride in itself. Perhaps this ambiguity in Pindar is only another case like that described in
the poems of his middle period in which he simultaneously
recognizes order and meaning as beyond the immediate social order, yet wants to see them in the social order. Just
so, the processes of his thought show that he feels in the
mind a great uniting power which brings things together,
sees them in each other's light, and even merges them
through metaphor so that they become part of each other.
Yet unlike Aeschylus he does not press this new sense of
power to its conclusion in a new and terrifying sense of responsibility, but is content in Homer's fashion to see the
hand of the gods in great human acts. Or perhaps despite
all that has been said so far about his seeing life through
myths, they continue elusive, and the gods' acts through
heroes and victors may be only a way of stating these men's
greatness and responsibility. Certainly the gods help only
those who help themselves. But however one may try to
express Pindar's sense of these final matters, the fact is clear
that, as compared with Homer, he brings the balance away
from the outer world and toward the ordering mind, away
from things seen in their separate particularity and toward a

uniting vision which the mind imposes on things. Thus he also moves away from Homer's simple style and from the Homeric simile to a far more complex style and to the metaphor. To choose from innumerable examples one already cited, when he says in *N*. 8, "virtue grows like a vine in the green dew lifted in the wise and just to the liquid sky," virtue and the vine are curiously mingled. The liquid sky which nourishes the growing vine with dew is felt to nourish virtue also in such a way that both share in a natural process which is benign and encompassing. He unites what Homer would have divided, and in this act of uniting, which is the metaphor, lies a new exaltation in the mind's simplifying and synoptic power.

This is not to say that either Pindar or Aeschylus fully adopted an organic style in place of Homer's perpetually successive manner. One way of grasping the classic in Sophocles is to see it as the triumph of the organic. Oedipus and Antigone have a concentration and centrality and imply an elimination of detail without earlier parallel. The term late archaic as applied to Aeschylus and Pindar signifies a stage just prior to this full grasp of organism. They simultaneously feel the uniting force of a great central idea, yet are drawn aside from it by a competing love of detail almost suggestive of Homer's. Few greater simplifying shapes have been conceived than Prometheus. He towers over the play, uniting the action and giving it his own scope. The sympathy of the chorus of Oceanids, spirits of harbor, shore, and seascape, conveys the very earth's sympathy for him.[28] Yet though they have this meaning, the Oceanids begin by telling how in their ocean cave they heard the clash of iron when Prometheus was fixed to the rock, and how in their haste and curiosity they forgot their slippers. They go on to recall the joyful wedding song at his marriage and, with frightened thoughts of themselves, deduce that one should not marry among the rich and exalted. In all this they are simply girls, wonderfully fresh and unspoiled in their transparency of feeling. But the contrast between their meaning as Oceanids and their character as girls is the contrast between Aeschylus' sense for organic idea and his competing attraction to detail. The parallel is clear to late archaic statuary in its stiff nobility of shape coupled with its minute attention to the rendering of hair, ornament, and dress. It is as if two intense forces were at play, the one towards life as idea, the other towards life as variegation. The immense vitality of the late archaic is in this struggle of impulses, the one simplifying and reducing to form, the other complicating and leading out to a thousand responses to the world. The same conflict is quite as strong in Pindar. The central tacit metaphor of the likeness of victors to heroes refracts into the vivid colors of an immediate present or imagined past, but the tension of the odes is not so much between present and past or actuality and myth as between Pindar's guiding vision of an occasion and the countless attractions which he feels toward specific images. If the metaphor is his medium as the simile is Homer's, he has not mastered it as fully as will Sophocles. The exaltation of the style is in its sense of the mind's power to simplify and relate, a power the more exalting because it is always being jeopardized by an opposite attraction to multitudinousness.

To return to the central metaphor, let us consider it in two poems, *N*. 5 and *O*. 1, though many others would serve as well. *N*. 5, the first of three odes (the two others being *I*. 6 and *I*. 5) for Pytheas and Phylacidas, sons of the Aeginetan Lampon, is usually dated as from the untroubled period just before Salamis. *I*. 5, the last of the three, is vividly inspired by the battle, and hence seems to fall soon after it. A less natural dating which would put all three poems after 480 and the battle-inspired *I*. 5 some years after has lately been revived on grounds of resemblance of phrase between *N*. 5 and a poem of the late 470's, *I*. 2.[29] These echoes are quite clear, but to accept them as decisive for the later date has the difficulty of forcing one to imagine both Pindar and Bacchylides (who composed his 13th ode for the same occasion as *N. 5*) as not only failing to mention the battle soon after it but as writing in a tone of settled confidence and repose. One can no doubt imagine reasons either for this strange silence or for the echoes between *N. 5* and *I. 2*, but the lingering uncertainty well exemplifies the problem of dating some of the odes. In any case, Pindar's mood is untroubled, and no poem breathes more freshly than *N. 5* the sense of faith in the world that has seemed characteristic of his earliest period.

Nemean 5. This is a poem of the sea, of movement, and of places beyond the sea. If one could hypothecate two kinds of rest, the one before testing and adventure, the other after them as realization of their beauty and meaning, the sea is the interspace between these rests, leading out from the one to the other. "I am no statuary that I make idling images on their same bases planted. No, by every merchantman and skiff, sweet song, take voyage from Aegina with announcement that Lampon's son, broad-sinewed Pytheas, at Nemea won the pancratiast's coronal, not showing on his cheeks the summer yet that brings the grape-flower soft." (vv. 1-6) The ode ends with a like command to raise sail. This sense of the opportune sea and of reaches beyond it gives tone to the myth, how the sons of Aeacus prayed by the altar of Zeus Hellanios that Aegina might one day be famous for bravery and for ships. "And warrior heroes, Aeacids from Kronos, Zeus and golden Nereids sprung, he honored, and his city, land beloved of guests. Which once, by Zeus Hellanios' altar standing, lifting their arms together to the sky, Endais' storied sons and the king Phocus prayed might be great in men and famed for ships." (vv. 7-12) There follows a curious passage about Phocus, Seal, son of the nymph Psamathea, Sand, and born on the sea beach, the half-brother of Peleus and Telamon. Legend held that his brothers killed him, hence had to leave Aegina, a story that evidently explains their life elsewhere. Perhaps it also conveys the victory of civilization over the primitive waste of beach. But Pindar will not mention this evil past. "Sharp truth revealing whole her face is not more profitable, and silence is often wisest for men to ponder." (vv. 16-18) A similar unwillingness to accept the evil in myths appears in *O.* 1 and several other poems. The cause seems partly social: as heir to the choral tradition, he feels himself the expositor of standards and would see only good in heroes and gods. But it is also because these figures are at the core of his own thought. The line of Aeacus is to him Aegina, just as in *P.* 9, when he feels that his loyalty to Thebes has been questioned, he cries, "Dull is the man who swathes not Heracles with his speech or fails to celebrate ever the streams of Dirce, that reared him and Iphicles." (vv. 87-88) The patron heroes are more than personifications of their cities. They are living presences in contemplation of whom the past and present become meaningful. Thus in *O.* 9 he protests that Heracles could not have opposed the gods. "O lips, reject this statement. To vilify gods is bitter wisdom, and senseless boast is folly's obbligato." (vv. 35-39) In each of these passages, what one says of the heroes involves how one thinks as a man. The heroes are in the very process of Pindar's thought, and the fact explains why he hints here at Phocus' unhappy fate only to turn silent about it. His thought follows the traditional story until it reaches a dilemma, at which his higher view asserts itself. He could not simply have omitted the story, because it was involved with figures and events which were in effect his train of thought.

But after this troubled hesitation he takes heart. "Eagles fly beyond the sea." (v. 21) The sea beyond which Peleus traveled and beyond which the boy went for his victory stretches also for Pindar. It is the sparkling unknown, the place of challenge and uncertain response, the end of rest in the familiar, offering a second rest on the other side only to the eagle's wings. The myth is as relevant to Pindar as to the boy, since the sea for both demands a form of self-transcendence. This is what Peleus obtained in distant Magnesia through his merits and Zeus's mercy. No symbol is more central to the odes than that which follows of Peleus' attainment of the sea nymph Thetis. It recurs with constant elements: the ineffable presence of the gods at the wedding, the sound of the ultimate music of Apollo and the Muses, the flash of gold, Pindar's most constant single mark for the divine. "Gladly for them on Pelion sang the Muses' fairest chorus, and waking in their midst with golden quill his seven-tongued lyre Apollo led forth sacred strains of every kind." (vv. 22-25) In *P*. 3 he links with this wedding that of Cadmus and the divine Harmonia as the two highest examples of mortal fortune. "Of mortals they are said to have found highest bliss, who heard the gold-diademed Muses singing on the mountain and in seven-gated Thebes, when the one gained ox-eyed Harmonia, the other Thetis, storied child of Nereus sage. And gods dined with both, and they beheld Kronos' royal sons on golden chairs, and received wedding gifts." (vv. 88-95) The music, the gold, the calm Olympian presences convey the rest which is on the farther side of struggle and timelessness briefly rising upon time.[30] That music accompanies such moments points again the relevance of the myth to Pindar as well as to his victors. We shall return in the next chapter to this theme of harmony. Here it is related that Peleus achieved his ineffable fortune through reverence for Zeus Xenios and consequent respect for his host, the king of the Magnesians, whose wife made advances to Peleus in the time-honored fashion of Potiphar's wife. Zeus heeded this act of reverence and, together with Poseidon (he with whom Zeus quarrels for Thetis in *I*. 8), con-

ferred her on Peleus — Poseidon "who often from Aegae
seeks the bright Dorian isthmus, where glad bands with the
flute's cry greet the god, and vie in hardy strength of limb."
(vv. 37-39) At the end the joy of the occasion carries tones
of Peleus's joy, which is as high as men can reach, and like
his, it has hints of the gods' presence in the success which has
crowned effort and the music into which struggle has been
raised. The sea of this poem is a summer sea, conveying life
as open to possibility. In some other poems it is dark and
submerging. But here Peleus attains the nymph, the prayer
that Aegina be famous for ships is confirmed, the boy has returned from across the water with victory, and Pindar's
poem has both come from beyond the sea, in the sense of
having caught sound of the gods' music, and will travel out
again on ship and skiff, in the sense of becoming famous.

   Olympian 1. *O*. 1, the first of the odes to Hieron, is at
first glance a much more complicated poem. The previous
N. 5 ends, if one may trust an emendation, with the boy offering his wreath of victory at the shrine of Aeacus. The
shrine in any case is clear, and the chorus is to be imagined
as singing near the image of the hero whose line the poem
glorifies. In Hieron's court by contrast Pindar stood unsup-
ported by tradition or cult and, as suggested, the coruscation
of the poem is the measure of his aloneness. His communal
role has become a personal role, and his sacral art an act of
virtuosity. Yet these new circumstances served to clarify as
well as to complicate, and *O*. 1 states with exceptional care
Pindar's basic metaphor involving victors and heroes. To
omit for a moment the famous opening, he begins much in
the manner of *N*. 5 by broaching a story only to turn away
from it. This is the fearful tale that at a banquet once offered the gods by Tantalus, the Olympians cannibalistically
ate his son Pelops, repairing him magically later on. For the
existence of this tale Pindar sees two reasons, the false charm
of a deceptive but exciting poetry and the jealousy which

makes men believe evil, especially of the great. Both points
illuminate what seems a new self-awareness in him. He sees
his function as not merely or chiefly to give praise, but to un-
cover the hidden through inspired insight and to reveal
truths which the future will confirm, though they are concealed by the uncertainties of any present as well as by common rancor. "Wonders are many and, on occasion, tales
devious with embroidered lies bewitch mortal speech beyond
the true assertion. And Grace, who fashions all delight for
men, confers her glory and contrives that even the unbeliev-
able commonly be believed. But sequent days are wisest witnesses. It befits a man to speak well of the gods; the blame
is less." (vv. 28-35) The true account which he gives of
Tantalus is quite different. "If ever the watchers of Olympus honored a mortal man, this man was Tantalus. But di-
gest his great felicity he could not, but from his pride got
massive desolation, so incompassable a stone the father hung
above him, fain to fend which from his head he wanders
from his bliss. He lives this helpless life of fixed anxiety,
fourth torment among three, because he stole from heaven
and gave the boon fellows of his youth the nectar and am-
brosia with which the gods made him deathless." (vv. 54-
64) The gods are not cruel. On the contrary, they offered
their favorite a happiness like their own, only to see it rejected for the ties of common gregariousness. Tantalus' motive resembles Adam's in sharing the apple with Eve rather
than endure a lonely glory in Eden.

Two extreme positions have thus been marked out, both
of which Pindar rejects. The first is that the gods are savage and care nothing for us; this is the brutal story of the
banquet. The second is that we may aspire to quite godlike
happiness; but this is impossible since Tantalus could not
stand his dizzy height. He now goes on to expound a third
position which he accepts and which is the burden of the
ode. Poseidon had loved Pelops and carried him to Olym-

pus. When his father Tantalus was cast out, he too returned
to mortality. Yet the god continued loyal to him, and when
as a young man he took courage to try to win Hippodameia
from her formidable father in a chariot race, Poseidon answered his prayers. "Drawing near the gray sea alone in
the darkness he called to the loud-crashing god of the hand-
some trident, and he appeared close at his side." (vv. 71-74)
Pelops tells of the thirteen suitors of Hippodameia whom
her father had hitherto outraced and killed. "But great danger takes no supine man. Since we must die, why should one
crouch in the dusk, cosseting to no end a nameless age? This
trial shall come to me. Do thou give dear completion."
(vv. 81-85) The god gave him his golden chariot and
winged horses. He won the race, the girl, and the Peloponnesus, and in death was buried at Olympia, where his tomb
is tended with heroic honors. Something of his brightness
surrounds all victors, and Hieron's success, like his, reveals
a god's favor. Pindar hopes some day to celebrate a chariot
victory by Hieron, the highest triumph, which would complete the resemblance to Pelops. These resemblances are
tacit. As said, it would be presumptuous to express the analogy outright. But Hieron's fortune matches that of Pelops
at every step, as prince, as victor, and as favored by the gods.
Above all, the main truth of Pelops' life applies to Hieron,
that we are neither in a godless world nor can be gods, but
occupy a middle ground in which, whatever the rancorous
may say or however confusing the present may be, courage
can receive that validation by the gods which is success and
glory.

To return now to the celebrated opening, few lines of
Pindar are better known, but their brilliance dazzles interpretation and they resemble Milton's Jehovah in remaining
dark with excessive bright. "Water is excellent, and gold
like blazing fire stands clear at night above imperious wealth.
But if of feats you would sing, my heart, seek than the sun

no hotter radiant star by day in the vacant sky. Nor let us sing a contest nobler than the Olympian, whence the sounding hymn is flung around poets' wits, to chant the son of Kronos as we reach Hieron's rich felicitous hearth." (vv. 1-11) Three things are described in sequence: water, gold like fire at night, and the sun by day in the vacant sky. The sun stands in relation to the Olympian games, and these in turn to Zeus, since it is to Zeus that poets' minds turn in contemplation of Olympia. The scholiasts tend to be distracted by the four elements as established by Ionian physics, earth, water, air, and fire, and notably by the chief element according to Thales, water. But Pindar elsewhere shows no sympathy for such ideas, which are certainly irrelevant here. One scholium comes closer in saying that Pindar chooses the three things judged best by man, an interpretation which resembles that of most modern scholars.[31] It has been justly said that Pindar is describing things bright and lasting. The *reclame* of Olympia and Hieron's pomp as monarch evoke images of transcendent things. But the question remains why he chooses precisely water, gold, and the sun. It is here suggested that these symbols have a relation to the poem as a whole, which, as we have seen, expresses a basic attitude of Pindar's towards the relationship of men to gods. More precisely, it is suggested that water is inspired by his view of poetry, gold by his view of the heroes, and the blazing sun by his view of the gods.

As for water, its likeness to poetry occurs to him repeatedly. There are the streams of the Muses (*N.* 7. 12), the sounding streams of verse (*I.* 7. 19), the soft dew of songs (*P.* 5. 99); he pours poetry like a libation (*I.* 6. 9) and sprinkles men with praise (*I.* 6. 21). Two preludes take up the figure: "Joy is the best physician of finished toils, and songs, wise daughters of the Muses, touch and exorcize them. Even hot water wets not the limbs so soft as praises married with the lyre" (*N.* 4. 1-5), and in a poem written just before he left for Sicily, "Great use for men exists in winds, exists in the waters of the sky, rainy children of cloud. But if with toil a man fare well, honey-voiced hymns, prelude of later praise, are paid and sworn security to mighty acts." (*O.* 11. 1-6)   In the present poem water can hardly help carrying these overtones.   One may therefore translate water as excellent rather than as best, though the shading is minor and Pindar would not be above calling water as associated with contemplative repose and harmony the best of things.

As for gold like fire in the night, this is one of the tangled metaphors mentioned earlier, in which each element colors the other.   He does not, as Homer would, hold fire apart as seen by itself in the night and then compare it to gold, but the gold shines out of darkness like fire and has a quality of sudden illumination.   *I.* 5, the poem on Salamis, has an extraordinary opening not unlike this passage.   "Mother of the Sun, Theia of many names, through thee mankind deems gold of mighty strength beyond all else.   Yes, and ships upon the sea contending and horses at chariots through an honor, queen, from thee grow things of wonder in swift-whirling races." (vv. 1-6) Theia is listed in the *Theogony* (371-374) as a primal goddess, child of Earth and Heaven, and mother of the Sun, Moon and Dawn.   She is evidently no actual goddess of cult, but possesses Pindar's imagination as a principle of brightness behind all radiant things, not only gold but the flash of oar and chariot and the physical exaltation which also implies gold to him.   This mystic view of gold is in the present passage.   One thinks of Apollo's golden lyre at Peleus' wedding and the gods on golden chairs or of the golden chariot with which in this poem Poseidon gave Pelops victory.   It seems fair to say that the glint of gold characteristically marks for Pindar those moments when the divine transcendence touches this world.   Even the gray olive of the Olympian wreath is called golden when it means victory (*O.* 11. 13; *N.* 1. 17), and the green laurel of the Hyperboreans' crowns is gold because it is near immortality. (*P.* 10.40) But if gold carries this meaning of transcendence, its opposite, darkness, evokes things uncertain, characterless, and transient. Pelops cries to Poseidon out of the darkness and rejects for himself a life spent in shadow and a nameless old age. In the visionary close of the late poem, *P.* 8, Zeus's blazing light momentarily invests men's shadowy lives when they rise to victory. The two other apparitions like that which occurred to Pelops, Apollo's appearance to Iamus in *O.* 6 and Athene's to Bellerophon in *O.* 13, both similarly occur out of darkness. In this passage, then, the gold which flashes like fire out of night is the god-given emergence of glory out of transience, a brightness such as crowned the life of Pelops, which would have been passed in shadow except for his courage and Poseidon's help.

Finally, as for the blazing sun alone in the sky, it has to do with Olympia and Olympia with Zeus. In several passages Pindar expresses the forbidding, dazzling, and almost negating side of the gods. He has moods when the gods' timeless brightness is blinding, and the gulf between them and men nearly complete. He warns the victor's father in *P.* 10 that he cannot climb the brazen sky, and the phrase recurs in the impressive opening of *N.* 6, his most formal statement on the gods. "One is the origin of men and gods, and from a single mother we both draw breath. Yet potency utterly distinct divides us, so that the one is nothing, but the brazen sky remains a seat secure forever. Yet we are a little like the immortals in great mind or form, though we know neither by day nor through our nights to what goal fate has written that we run." (vv. 1-7) We shall not dwell on the passage here except to note that it is full of jerks and hesitations because at every suggested likeness of men to gods some reservation seems necessary. A similarity exists and it is the subject of most of the odes, yet it must always be hedged around with dissimilarities, which at times seem

overwhelming. What is man that Thou art mindful of him?
The burning radiance of the lonely sun in the present passage
resembles the brazen heaven of the two other poems. It is
in the spirit of the dizzy eminence that Tantalus could not
endure. If Pindar began by thinking of Olympia, his mind
moved quickly to Zeus, and the blazing sun in contrast to the
fire by night is the difference between Zeus's perpetual day
and the illumination which Pelops got out of his mortal night
and which, or something like which, now rests on Hieron.
It may be added that when Pindar recurs to this passage at
the close of O. 3, he mentions water and gold but not the
sun. Water and gold, poetry and triumph, are germane to
any celebration, but the sun has symbolic relevance only
when, however great men's golden triumphs may seem,
thoughts of the gods' dazzling eminence intervene to put
them in their place.

It has been asserted that images such as those of water,
gold, and the sun in this poem or of the lyre in P. 1 formed
unconsciously in Pindar's mind, and that it is these which
guided his imagination.[32] There seems truth in this view,
if one add that the heroes are Pindar's main symbols and
that such images as those which we have just considered attach themselves to them. Or perhaps it would be fairer to
say that such images attach themselves to his total view of
life as embracing gods, heroes, and men. Water here or the
lyre in P. 1 connotes poetry, which in turn implies to him a
vision of the divine order and its revelation through myth.
To think of him as merely entranced with bright images is to
take from him that absorption with pure being which is as
much his identifying trait as El Greco's light or Aeschylus'
sense of space. A minor example or two in this same poem
may serve as illustration. The erotic motif which explains
Poseidon's later loyalty to Pelops is a way of expressing the
gods' intervention in the world. It recurs in two superb
poems, P. 9 and O. 6, which have to do with Apollo's love

for a mortal woman. We shall turn to these in the next chapter, but the point to observe here is that the motif does not stand by itself in any of these poems but to Pindar is bound up with his general view of gods and men. It may have been a weakness of the Greeks through their response to the world to have brought the gods excessively into it, and a fastidious impulse in Heraclitus and Xenophanes and even in Pindar objects. Yet the opposite problem of aloof gods who cared nothing for the world would be as great, since there would then be no means of conveying the flash of the divine in things. Hence though he would purge the ancient myths, he was instinctively forced to accept them as conveying with all their excesses the brilliance in the world which he sought. Again, he says that he will praise Hieron with the Dorian lyre, which is to say that he wishes to see in the tyrant's rule some Dorian legitimacy. This wish is more thoroughly expounded in *P*. 1, but the Dorian lyre here already carries overtones of a regimen going back to the heroes and, to Pindar's eyes, giving sanction and meaning to Hieron's otherwise raw power. In short, the mind which catches in the Dorian lyre or in Poseidon's love for Pelops sight of a more final order is the same mind that sees in universal things, water, gold, and the sun, similar suggestions of import beyond themselves.

THE ODES

"WHAT god, what hero, what man shall we proclaim?" Pindar asks at the beginning of *O. 2.* This chain of participation whereby heroes in their great moments share something of gods, and men something of heroes runs through the odes and is the most characteristic thing about them. It was described earlier as a metaphor, a way of seeing things together. It was also called a set of symbols, figures spanning the interval between time and timelessness. The victors are fully involved in time and place; the heroes are partly thus involved through their ties with certain cities and the fact that they were once men; the gods stand clear above all and could be quite beyond events if they did not look to the world almost as much as the world looks to them. The whole system, if anything so fluid and iridescent may be called a system, is strangely complete. It includes not only the exterior sphere of time, place, and history, but the inner sphere of character and state of mind also. This symbolic and mythological cast of thought characteristically looks both outward and inward at the same time, or rather, so objectifies the inward that it appears side by side with the outward. Strictly speaking, a myth means a divine happening, for example, the birth of Athene from Zeus's head or the fact that the sun has cattle — which is to say, the judgment that the purest emanation of Zeus is intelligence or the natural fact of clouds in the sky. Legend relates historical happenings, foreign war at Troy or domestic war at Thebes. Folk tale has to do with representative attitudes of life: in the earlier example, Circe's enchantments, which are sensual, as contrasted to the Sirens', which are intellectual, or the motif in the *Iliad* that Achilles must choose either a long and inglorious or a short and glorious life, a choice expressing

the brevity of anything intense. Folk tale thus has largely
to do with inner states, legend with outward events, myth
with both. But though one may mark off these spheres, they
in fact coalesce, and Peleus, for example, as Pindar conceives him, is a figure from all three. The presence of the
gods at his marriage to Thetis is mythological, as catching
one phase of connection between men and gods; his ties with
Aegina and Magnesia are legendary; his resistance to the
blandishments of the queen of the Magnesians is from folk
tale. But to note this mixture is simply to restate the simultaneously external and internal character of such symbolic
thought. The stories told of the heroes were an immense
projection of possible motives, states of mind, and responses
to the world, all tied to known scenes and places but also
transcending scene and place because, being connected also
with the gods, they verged on the changeless. It is because
any victory starts such a train of connection in Pindar's mind
that the victory itself ceases to be the main subject of an ode,
but is only the first step in a series of relationships, which is
in fact the subject.

We shall now take up certain corollaries to the central
axiom, main associations, that is, which for Pindar gather
about the chain which leads from men to heroes to gods.
The procedure is well short of ideal and may be no better
than the chronological method, imperfect as that is. The
difficulty is that associations evoke each other, with the result
that, though an ode may chiefly concern one theme, it wakes
cognate themes as well, like a bell rousing murmurs from
the rest of the chime. Hence one cannot simply state the
main themes and assume that the odes divide themselves
among them. Yet Pindar's is a formal art, and it would be
a worse error to suggest that each ode stands by itself reflecting chiefly a particular occasion. This suggestion is the
main weakness of the chronological method. On the contrary, the occasion is fitted into a system and outlook as dis-

tinctive as a painter's style. The occasion partakes of the
style, not the style of the occasion. These themes, to give
inadequate names to them, are vicissitude, harmony, attainment, and essence. The terms obviously mean little in themselves, nor do they comprise the only possible such list. Yet
certain odes turn chiefly on each theme, and each in turn
carries a characteristic complex of symbols and ideas. With
due sense of the difficulties involved, we shall therefore take
up the odes under these themes.

i VICISSITUDE

Olympian 2. The term is particularly inadequate to
O. 2, the splendid ode of 476 to the aged Theron, tyrant of
Akragas, and Pindar's one extant poem on the after life.
O. 3 was the public ode for the celebration of Theron's
chariot victory. Like *O.* 10 for the colonial city, Western
Locri, and indeed like *O.* 1 for Hieron, it tells a legend from
Olympia, evidently for want of local legends in the western
cities. As Hieron was brought into connection with Pelops
in *O.* 1, Theron's victory is seen in *O.* 3 as the gift of the
Dioscuri, sharers with Heracles in the first games and now
publicly worshipped by Theron in thanks for his triumph.
O. 2 by contrast seems for Theron's ear alone. Nominally
an epinikion, it is in fact a consolatory poem and a meditation on death. Pindar's role as prophet and visionary is as
visible here as in *O.* 1. The old tyrant had met recent troubles, though it is unclear exactly what they were. His daughter Demareta had been married to Hieron's older and
greater brother Gelon, the founder of the Deinomenid
tyranny in Syracuse and conqueror of the Carthaginians at
Himera in 480. At his death in 478 she had passed to the
third of the brothers, Polyzalus, who as guardian also of her
son seemed marked as Gelon's heir. But Hieron emerged
in power, and the resulting strain between him and Polyzalus

extended through Demareta to Theron also. An unfortu-
nately corrupt scholium[33] further suggests that Theron's son
Thrasydaeus, who held power at Himera, took sides still
more violently with Polyzalus against Hieron. These dynas-
tic relationships were a form of political allegiance. Hieron
had accordingly appeared earlier in 476 with an army before
Akragas, where peace was made evidently with humiliation
to Theron and at the price, the scholium suggests, of estrangement from his son Thrasydaeus. The poet Simonides
is named as the negotiator of this truce. The fact that on
Theron's death in 472 Thrasydaeus openly attacked Hieron,
was defeated and sent into exile, strengthens the view that
the old man was now not only humbled but left uncertain of
his dynasty's future. Some such recent background explains
the consolatory tone of the poem and Pindar's brooding on
the wave-like alternations of life.

Whatever Orphism was, whether a body of fairly fixed
practices or merely an outlook involving belief in the trans-
migration of the soul, successive existences, and the need for
purity,[34] it was accepted by Theron and seems to have flour-
ished at Akragas. The philosopher Empedocles, who led
the democratic party there after the fall of the dynasty, left
as one of two chief works a book entitled *Purifications,*
Katharmoi, the fragments of which show close parallels to
this poem. It is usually held that the views presented here
are Theron's only and not Pindar's, and it has been justly
said that, if pressed, he would have found it hard to reconcile
the series described here of six transitional lives, three on
either side the grave, with his usual statements that the
heroes through virtue won direct immortality.[35] As for ordinary men, it is still less clear that he accepted any such belief.
He often speaks of forebears in another world taking pleasure in their descendants' successes, but nowhere else in the
odes, as contrasted to a few fragments similar in tone to this
poem, expounds such a scheme of successively tested lives.

Yet to deny kinship in these views to Pindar's normal outlook is curiously unsatisfactory. Peleus and Cadmus, who in other poems endure pain and disappointment, yet reach the golden moment of their marriage to goddesses, appear here in the land of the blessed, as does Achilles. They have only stepped over without inconvenience into this new scheme. The blaze of gold which marks this land is the gold which elsewhere shines in moments of transcendence. Above all, the process whereby after six good lives the virtuous escape the wheel of change only exalts and schematizes Pindar's usual feeling for vicissitude. He characteristically sees in success a combination of forces: a man's own stamina and excellence, a god's favor, and a certain mysterious tide or gravitation toward excellence in a man himself or his forebears or both. This gravitation can seem to stop, even to turn, but it shows in the end and to Pindar flashes visibly in the moment of triumph. But this usual attitude closely resembles the present mystic scheme of tested lives, which only projects into another world what Pindar accepts for this world. In this poem and elsewhere, to judge by the fragments, he was notably uninterested in those who failed the test. He would have understood the hope and vigor of Dante's *Purgatory,* not the despair of the *Inferno.* As he waits for the moment when this life crowns struggle with fulfillment and something timeless irradiates time, so he emphasizes in the Orphic scheme the analogous stage of fulfillment. If he accordingly cannot be said to have shared these views, he could enter into them imaginatively because they in many ways complemented his own. Religious emotions are perishable, and Homer can mock gods in one scene whom he feels as awful powers in the next. The mood here resembles that of Plato's myths on the after life. What is said in both transcends but is harmonious with their commoner views, as lines projected from a geometrical figure form like but larger relationships above the first.

The poem begins with the famous lines quoted at the
start of the chapter. God, hero, and man correspond complexly to the sun, gold, and water in the first lines of O. 1.
After praising Theron's justice and hospitality and the toil of
pioneering forebears who founded Akragas, holy habitation
by the river, he prays that the future may be as kind as the
past. Theron's fresh wounds, notably toward his son
Thrasydaeus, seem implied. "Of acts once done in justice
or unjustly not even Time, father of all, can make the reality
undone. But oblivion through a favoring lot may follow.
By noble joys dies the inveterate sorrow overcome when a
god's destiny summons aloft high bliss." (vv. 15-22) The
wavelike movement of the poem is begun. Theron's
victory is taken both as a joy in itself that cancels pain and
as a sign of the longer drift that has continually brought
light out of darkness for him and his breed. This principle
of alternation is somehow seated in the nature of things, and
Cadmus' daughters exemplify it, long-haired Semele who
died by lightning to live on Olympus as Dionysus' mother
and Ino who leapt into the sea to obtain immortality among
Nereus' wavy girls. "And for mortals no fixed point of
death is known, nor even whether we shall bring to an end
with undiminished good one day in peace, a sun's child. But
currents forever changing advance on men with happiness
and with pain." (vv. 31-34) Yet a bias toward the good
is in the drift as it applies to Theron and his family. This
notion of a fate guiding a family could be seen as nothing
more than Pindar's validation of actual past success, a way
of approving what luck and the world have already approved. But to him it is much more than that; it is the mysterious hand of the gods revealing itself in the history of
those whom they have chosen to favor. The family claimed
descent from Thersander, grandson of Oedipus and son of
Polyneices, and the alternations of fortune notorious in them

seem to Pindar the key to all that has followed down to the present.

So far the poem could have concerned any victor. Vicissitude is the obverse of success, and the lives of heroes exemplify both. That the Orphic passages now follow without jar is a clear sign that Pindar is not writing only to please a patron, but sees in the Orphic scheme a heightening of ideas already his own. The turning point is his notion of riches. "Wealth inlaid with virtues can wait the opportunity in things, keeping within a hunting heart, conspicuous star, first luster to a man." (vv. 52-56) Few passages better express the this-worldly side of Pindar's mind, his love of accomplishment, feeling for achieved form and excellence, and pleasure in wealth because it offers tests. The outlook resembles Aristotle's in the *Ethics,* that wealth serves virtue by giving opportunity, but stands in clear contrast to Aeschylus' sense that wealth corrupts and justice shines in smoke-stained houses. To Aeschylus Helen and Paris have been thus corrupted, and the purple on which Agamemnon walks to his death is the color of his infection. Aeschylus' promptings are moral, Pindar's formal. The one reflects a new society seeking severer standards, the other a settled society which is used to seeing its values distilled into form and is a good judge of form. But wealth, Pindar goes on, is a star and luster to a man, "only if owning it he knows what is to come, that of those who die here outrageous souls at once pay penalties, and for sinful acts committed in this realm of Zeus there is a judge below the earth who tells the reckoning with necessity harsh. But ever in sunlight through nights and days alike the good receive a life that is free from toil, troubling no more the earth with strength of hand nor the sea's wave in an empty livelihood, but having had joy in oaths well kept they live by honorable gods a tearless episode, while the others bear affliction not to be looked at. As many as waiting thrice on either side dare keep the soul en-

tirely from injustice complete the road of Zeus to Kronos'
tower. There around the island of the blest winds, daughters of the ocean, breathe. Golden flowers blaze, some land-
ward from glorious trees, and water nurtures others, with
fronds of which they wreathe their arms and crown their
heads, in Rhadamanthus' upright sway." (vv. 56-75) In
other poems the blaze of immortal gold flashes in an earthly
victory. Here it shines in the future, not in the past. The
static moment of rest and realization after toil which is elsewhere fugitive, though the brightest thing that life can give,
is now permanent. Theron's past alternations of pain and
triumph have dropped out of sight or, rather, have been
caught up in a longer process of vicissitude leading to a still
brighter and more lasting victory.

Several fragments, possibly from dirges, are similar in
tone. In one, which Milton evidently knew, the virtuous occupy their happy release with horses, games, dice, and music
much as the fallen angels distract themselves in Hell. "In
meadows red with roses are their suburbs, shadowy with
frankincense, laden with golden fruit. — — Among them
flowering happiness blooms entire." (fg. 114) The coloring
is very full. The games, the gold, and the fruit contain a
quite physical sense of the wholeness of life. In another
fragment the soul wakes and lives its own life while the body
sleeps. (fg. 116) Here and once elsewhere (fg. 121) the soul
is said to come from the gods. In a fourth fragment Persephone sends back to the world those from whom she has
exacted penalty for wrongs, and from them come kings, athletes, and poets, who are later deemed heroes. (fg. 127)
The doctrine of return to life resembles that of the present
poem, and kings, athletes, and poets are elsewhere Pindar's
types of excellence, men capable, that is, of inspiration. Here
also there is heightening but not violation of his normal doctrine. The difference is that he is ordinarily content to look
to the present world alone. The movement by which honor

and courage by a god's help and a longer gravitation toward
excellence finally emerge into a moment of timeless brightness needs for him no counterpart in another life. In one
mysterious and disputed fragment he seems to say that the
life of the dead is only in the continuing life of the family.
(fg. 83. 8-11) But the meaning is uncertain, and it is enough
that he can talk differently of the after-life depending on his
emphasis. He is consistent only in his faith that something
divine can touch a man through his own hard-won merits and
the gods' benignity. The present poem to Theron closes in
this spirit. After saying that Peleus, Cadmus and Achilles
reached the land of the blessed, he breaks off. "In the quiver
below my elbow are many fast arrows that speak to those
who comprehend. For the mass they need interpreters.
Those who have merely learned resemble harsh and garrulous crows that chatter futilely at Zeus' sovereign bird."
(vv. 84-88) The statement about the arrows may mean that
he knows he is speaking mystic doctrine, but it has a more
obvious meaning also. He had criticized in O. 1 the false
charm by which poets corrupt the truth, and now only states
more openly his feeling of himself as discoverer of the final
laws. The crowd may not understand these; here speaks
his besetting difficulty as he mounted to a more complex symbolism dealing with ultimate things. But as he sees a divine
hand in triumphs, so he feels it in poetry. The scholiast says
that Simonides and Bacchylides are the crows,[36] and the dual
verb lends some slight confirmation. We cannot answer such
questions. It is clear only that as the athlete was to him no
mere exhibitor of feats, so the poet was no simple purveyor
of words. Both were caught up in a process by which the
gods give value to life; they were equally dependent on the
gods. Hence he rejects mere learning as contrasted to
natural gifts. The attitude is the same as that by which he
sees in victory a man's long-implanted gravitation toward excellence. In both cases he wants to see, not accomplishment

alone, but accomplishment as token of a transforming power
beyond itself.

Isthmian 3. To set *I*. 3 and 4 beside *O*. 2 because of
their similar theme is to feel again Pindar's difference at home
and abroad. He is more fully among friends and equals now,
and since legends carried accepted local meanings, had less
reason to feel himself a lonely voice. The two Isthmian poems
are for the Theban family that on one day had lost four men
in battle, evidently at Plataea on the Persian side, but had
now so far recovered that one of its members had won at
successive games in the pankration and with the chariot. The
dates seem soon after Pindar's return from Sicily. *I*. 3 commemorating the second victory is prefaced to the earlier *I*. 4,
and has the unique interest of showing what themes, on re-
considering a poem two or more years old, he felt so dominant as to dictate the character of the new opening. This insight is the more helpful because the main poem, obviously
one of the most deeply felt, is intensely figurative, whereas
except for one moment he rose only to lucidity by the time of
the new lines. The moment is at the end. He had begun
by ascribing all mortal excellence to Zeus in the faith that he
rewards those who shun the insolence of power. Like
Theron, these men claimed descent from the Labdacids, the
family of Oedipus, and had inherited its wealth and love of
horses. He concludes, "Life with circling days brings other
things at other times. Unwounded yet remain the sons of
gods." (v. 19) The heroes having notably suffered, some
scholars have wanted to read in the sons of gods the gods
themselves, but against Pindar's evident meaning here and
usage elsewhere. What he says is that in spite of suffering
the heroes emerged triumphant, even if, like Heracles and
Achilles, only after death. The real surprise is not that the
line refers to heroes, but that it rings out like a great trum-
pet call when he had been speaking of the family only. A
kind of syncopation has taken place. In thinking of the

family's stubborn virtue through reverses and their present long-deferred success, his mind leaps to the heroes. Intermediate steps drop out, and the archetypal figures of the beset but unconquered demigods emerge as the only commentary on these men. No passage more clearly shows Pindar's basic outlook or is a better commentary on the odes.

Isthmian 4. It also shows what he thinks the earlier *I.* 4 was about. This enchanting poem is both tender and powerful, and it moves with a sureness of touch that makes the Sicilian poems slightly glittering by contrast. He obviously admires this settled clan which could point to past warriors, magistrates, and athletes but had remained unpretentious. "They were horsebreeders and pleasing to bronze Ares. But on one day war's savage snowcloud stripped of four men their blessed hearth. Now on a wintry dusk of months the pied earth blooms again as with red roses by the gods' will. The Shaker of the Earth who haunts Onchestus and the sea-bridge by the walls of Corinth, in giving the clan this glorious song, rouses from bed its ancient name for fairfamed acts. It had fallen asleep but wakes with glowing skin, like the radiant Dawn-bringer among the other stars." (vv. 14-26) The familiar imagery of light and darkness is very fresh here. Poseidon, whose power is seen in storm and winter, is also a god of shining seas, and spring, roses, the bright cheeks of waking, and the dawn-star tell the family's and the city's better hopes as the war recedes. But even in the past they had failed of major victories despite attempts. "There exists an inconspicuousness of lot even when men strive, until they reach the steep end." (vv. 33-34) This poem has recently been denied to Pindar on the ground that he recognizes only success.[37] But Hector and Amphiaraus are elsewhere for him brave figures who failed, as is Ajax, whom he now cites. In one sense he is always writing about failure, our incapacity for any but momentary brightness. Happiness is our full awareness of these rare times and courage is a kind of waiting. All the virtues are involved in waiting and thus appear in the doctrine of vicissitude, but they are the step before the last, not the last step, which is transcendence. The thought is in effect as mystic here as in the Orphic doctrine of the poem to Theron. For it is poetry that grasps this transcendence, even though men die misunderstood, as did Ajax. Pindar often says that he writes for warriors and athletes, and the fact that he looks so consistently to the heroes implies this association in his mind of war with games. Yet men did not die at Olympia and Delphi as they did at Salamis or Plataea, and the success of living athletes has a curious counterpart in that of dead warriors. No doubt there is exaggeration in this linking, but the important point is that, though the odes look to festal occasions, they carry an undertone of incompleteness, not only because of the long preparation for success and its actual brevity, but because what he is writing about is an ideal equally above life and death.

Homer, he goes on, lifted the dishonored Ajax to his just fame. "What is well said goes immortal and singing. Over the fruitful earth and beyond the sea passes the flash of brilliant deeds ever unquenched." (vv. 44-46) He prays for a like power and sees in the victor the example of Heracles who, after vast toils, in death won Hebe, Youth, and became, in the line already quoted, "a king of golden halls and Hera's son." (v. 66) The gold of Heracles' transcendence is that which now touches the victor and his family after their labors and sorrows. Its light is essentially unearthly, and poetry, like victory, does not possess but only catches it. Heracles, the Theban hero and closest to Pindar, is much in his mind at the end. In an amusing and usually misunderstood passage he calls the victor "contemptible to look at" in his recent match (v. 54), just as Heracles was small when he faced the giant Antaeus. But since Heracles obviously was small only by comparison, it follows that

Melissus had to face some Goliath of an opponent and was contemptible only on first impression. In any case he won by the arts of the fox as well as of the lion. Pindar likes toughness and seems pleased at this compensation in Melissus for too little of the fox in unsuccessful forebears and even in Ajax, as if to his mind an ounce of the fox, the will to survive, were necessary if one is to emerge from troubles. The local and familiar tone of these lines is echoed at the end when the victor is said to have won in the two-day Theban games in honor of Heracles' children, "for whom at the rays' sinking a climbing blaze flares all night long, kicking the sky with savory smoke. On the second day is the fixed time of yearly games, strength's task, in which as a man, head white with myrtle, he showed two victories and a third as a boy before." (vv. 71-78) The blaze in the night, reminiscent of the night-fire in O. 1, fits the family's long resistance to trouble and obscurity, as the white crown of the second day shows the victor's final emergence. In the background the presiding figure of Heracles, whose emergence was only after death, gives to the whole process the hint of a divine sanction.

One more chief poem turns on this theme of vicissitude, and two others generalize it into a law of nature. O. 7, of 464, from the period of Pindar's highest ease and fame just before the dark years of the Athenian invasion of Boeotia, is for the eventually legendary Diagoras of Rhodes, who, himself a victor at all the four games, became the father of three and grandfather of two Olympic victors.[38] A group commemorating the six stood at Olympia and Diagoras passed into a by-word, "Die, Diagoras. You will not climb to heaven."[39] This poem, which is said to have been inscribed in gold letters in the temple of Athene at Lindos,[40] has been diversely thought coolly professional and the unclouded product of Pindar's sovereign years.[41] If his temptation was to overvalue success and hence to let his religious

symbolism sink into ornament, the former judgment seems
the closer. Achieved splendor tends to replace lyric suggestion, as if it were the curse of mastery to convey fully what
it intends but nothing more. But repose can be underesti-
mated, and he is at his most reposed here. Like *O.* 13 of
the same year for Xenophon of Corinth, the ode is less for
the victor than for his city, as if Pindar now felt himself an
almost official bestower of fame, and like the narrative *P.* 4
of 462 for Arkesilas, tyrant of Cyrene, it has a scope and
brilliance suggestive of the great narrative canvasses of the
high Renaissance. When all is said, it remains more memorable than either of these poems. Even at this moment
of fullest intoxication with his own and his patron's splendor,
he does not lose a saving sense of danger and incompleteness.

Olympian 7. The metaphor, not the simile, was earlier
called Pindar's vehicle. The opening here is a partial exception. "As when with opulent hand a man takes up a cup
splashing with the grape's dew and gives it to his daughter's
youthful bridegroom drinking her from her old home to the
new, the golden pinnacle of his wealth, in pleasure at the
feast and honor to the bond of families, and makes him en-
viable to his present friends for his harmonious bed, so I the
nectar poured, the Muses' gift, sending to athletes, sweet
fruit of my mind, find grace with Olympian and Pythic victors. Happy he whom glad reports invest." (vv. 1-10) It
is evident that the gold, formerly mystical, has only its own
sheen here, and one misses in the confident assertion of his
powers an earlier sense of dependence on the Muses. Wealth
and success seem slightly too assured, and the tone has sunk
to a merely worldly brightness. Yet the theme of the poem
is precisely the lack of assurance in the world. "Around
men's wits mistakes unnumbered hang, and this one cannot
find, what now and in the end a man had best meet." (vv.
24-26) Having passed from the victor to Rhodes, child of
Aphrodite and bride of the Sun, he describes three events

progressively more remote in time, each of which began with seeming mistake but through divine favor ended happily. This is the familiar theme of vicissitude which despite the bravura of the ode and much express optimism is gloomier here because no release from the process is suggested.

The retrograde movement of the ode prompts comment on Pindar's narrative method, the so-called circular composition inherited from oral poetry. It is characteristic of Homer to make his directest effects first, hence to state at the start what is nearest in time and to work backward from there, gradually circling again to the point of beginning. When at the end of the *Iliad* Achilles bids Priam eat, he begins by saying that fair-tressed Niobe took food, then tells her sorrows and at last repeats that even she took food. (*Il.* 24. 602-613) A gifted recent commentator sees in the Odes an advancing movement accompanying such circular designs.[42] Having worked back to the core of a narrative, Pindar reaches fuller implications which introduce a new development, and a first statement which seems to express his full meaning contains, when worked out, a fresh departure. So here, relatively recent events in Rhodian legend lead to remote events and these to the island's very origin, while at each step the dominant motif of the poem becomes more explicit. It may be fanciful to see something illustrative of Pindar's mind in a manner which he shares with such a younger contemporary as Herodotus. Yet his characteristic chain of progression from men to heroes to gods is in fact well matched to a manner of thought which, starting from things near at hand, gradually uncovers their inner meaning, and then returns to the point of departure, the victor, with new and much wider implications.

The three episodes of O. 7 that move progressively backward in time are Tlepolemus' founding of the Dorian colony in Rhodes, the institution there of the cult of Athene at the time of her birth, and the claiming of the island by the

Sun while it was still below the sea. Tlepolemus, the son of
Heracles, killed a kinsman in Argos and was forced to flee,
yet left his descendants their happy lot in Rhodes. When
long earlier Athene sprang from her father's head with a
mighty shout and heaven and earth trembled, the Sun bade
the Rhodians be first to worship her. "But neglect's mist
comes obscurely on and turns the true path of things out of
the mind." (vv. 45-46) The Rhodians forgot to offer sacrifice with fire. At this point the unhappy consequence goes
unmentioned, but since one could not speak of Athene's city
without evoking Athens, Rhodes, the silence implies, remains
second to Athens. Pindar's comparative silence about the
family has also been taken to imply the discomfort of Dorian
oligarchs in the Delian Confederacy,[43] and the poem seems
to mark a stage in his cooling toward Athens. Yet, to return, despite the imperfect sacrifice, good again came of error. Zeus showered the island with gold, evidently still felt
in Rhodes' high fortune, and Athene gave the island its
legendary fame in sculpture and the crafts. Finally, when
the gods aboriginally drew lots for their possessions on earth,
the Sun being absent was neglected, but though Zeus would
have had a new draw, the Sun had seen the island beneath
the waves and chose it as his own. What is to be read from
this series of benign error? The poem ends dubiously, "in
one mite of time winds veer fitfully in changing ways." If
this is perhaps no more than a conventional warning, it is far
from the triumphant peal at the end of *I. 3,* "unwounded yet
remain the sons of gods," far also from the faith of *O. 2*
that there is escape from vicissitude. Pindar seems weary,
even with success. Though mistake has kept issuing in good,
continuity and process remain steadily in the background,
permitting high but not the highest hopes. It is true that
vicissitude and victory are always very evenly matched in his
mind. Yet in his more confident moments, something in victory seems to obliterate vicissitude, giving sight, however

temporarily, of things absolutely excellent and beyond change. This is the mystical gold, which is replaced here by the common gold of wealth and high fortune. However brilliant the poem and however lightened by the sense of the gods' repeated beneficence, it thus hardly escapes a wearisome awareness of mere process, and the winds at the end blow chillingly out of an indefinite future.

Nemean 6. Finally, the theme of vicissitude is generalized in two odes already mentioned, *N.* 6 and *N.* 11, both of uncertain date, the former probably from the middle or early 460's, the latter probably contemporary with *P.* 8 of 446, the last dated poem. The famous opening of *N.* 6 on the relationship of gods to men was quoted earlier. "One is the origin of men and gods, and from a single mother we both draw breath. Yet potency utterly distinct divides us, so that the one is nothing, but the brazen sky remains a seat secure forever. Yet we are a little like the immortals in great mind or form, though we know neither by day nor through our nights to what goal fate has written that we run." (vv. 1-6) The meaning of the first two lines, though long disputed, is established by the parallel of the corresponding lines of the early *P.* 10, where a first bold statement linking Sparta and Thessaly is explained, as here, by a second statement describing common descent. The difficulty springs at bottom from the ambiguity of the word *genos.* If, as might on first sight appear, it means 'breed' or 'race,' Pindar must be credited with the unimaginable declaration that the race of men and gods is one. Parallels either to the statement or to the sentence structure are lacking. If, on the other hand, *genos* means 'origin,' as it does for example in *O.* 6. 25, he will appear to have known the line of the *Works and Days* (108) on the common descent of gods and men from Earth, and the present passage will be a searching of that deeply moving idea. This is in fact its character.

The tentativeness, hence the oscillation, of the lines has been noted. To assert men's kinship with gods risks overstatement because gods endure and men fade. The bronze of heaven states the gods' bright but forbidding repose; men's race through days and nights to their unseen goal contains their restlessness and their ignorance.⁴⁴ The strange affinity, which thus exists yet can hardly be expressed, is revealed in men's mind or form. "Great mind" evidently means both vision and courage, as for example in Pelops' youthful vision in O. 1 of a great enterprise to be pursued and his courage to prefer it to a nameless length of years. Similarly Pindar exhorts himself both to the illumination which the Muses give and to the will to grasp it. "May I be inventive to mount fittingly in the Muses' car, and may courage and capacious power attend me," he prays in O. 9. (80-83) "Form," physis, the other ground of resemblance, seems simply physical form. In Homer beauty and courage accompany each other, though he will sometimes candidly report exceptions to the rule, as in the remark that the great Odysseus was unimpressive at first sight or the curious statement in the Catalogue of Ships that Nireus of Syme was the handsomest man at Troy except Achilles, but feeble and accompanied by few followers, a kind of minor Paris.⁴⁵ Solon speaks of the strength "which men have as virtue's sign,"⁴⁶ and Pindar often couples a victor's beauty with his deeds. "He was beautiful to see, and in act shaming not his form, victorious in wrestling, proclaimed his fatherland Aegina of the long oars." (O. 8. 19-20) The present passage states more clearly than any other Pindar's common ground with the Greek athletic sculptors, in the assumption of something godlike in physical form, not wholly in the form itself since it is lightened by spirit and mind, but not in those alone since they are at home in form. As for the passage as a whole, it well explains what we have called the tacit and incomplete

metaphor underlying the odes. There is something godlike
in men; hence the relevance of their high acts to the demigods
and even to the gods. Yet the difference betwen gods and
men almost negates the resemblance; hence the impropriety
of pressing the comparison fully home or of completing the
metaphor. The odes, like this passage, turn basically on the
guarded yet aspiring statement, "nevertheless we are a little
like the immortals in great mind or form."

Though man's resemblance to the gods thus finally shows
itself in mind or form, it originates in kinship to the common
mother, Earth. In Hesiod's *Theogony*, Heaven and Earth
initially bear the primal deities of sky, sea, and land, who in
turn bring forth the gods of the formed and present cosmos.
Through his father Kronos, youngest son of Heaven and
Earth, Zeus and the Olympians share this common descent.
The created universe thus springs from the mingling of
spirit, Heaven, and matter, Earth, which once stood apart
and distinct, and nature is deployed between the once divided
extremes. The Olympians' dominant strain is evidently
from their progenitor, Heaven; men's from the progenitress,
Earth. But though at the summit of the scale of being, the
Olympians yet inherit enough from the ancient mother that
something of them continues to live and show itself in her
life. This immanence of the gods in nature is the undertone
of the poem, and through it the theme of vicissitudes takes
on the force of natural law. The effect of the law is double.
It binds man's life to the sleep and darkness of Earth, yet
lifts it to periodic bloom and brilliance. The gods are felt
in both processes, and vicissitude becomes both submission
and emergence.

"And now Alcidamas gives token of this kinship in visible likeness to the fruitful fields, which alternating yield
now from their plains abundant life for men, then again resting catch their strength." (vv. 8-11) This vision of alternating yield and fallow, hence of some deep kinship of men

to earth, comes to Pindar from observation of the victor's
family, only alternate generations of which had bred victors.
The young Alcidamas emulates his grandfather, as had the
latter his. As Pindar's imagination goes back to past generations of victors and from them to the Aeacid heroes of
Aegina, the sense of periodicity remains, and past crowns
and past songs take on the character of natural yield. These
men gave theme to the plows of the Pierides; at Delphi they
won the sprigs of Leto and shone with song at evening by
Castalia; at Nemea the lion's haunt crowned them beneath
the primal darkling hills of Phlius. Strength and poetry, act
and realization, thus spring from an eternal fecundity, and
if a divine law is felt in men's submission to the earth's
cycles, it is felt also in their blossoming.

Nemean 11. It is at this point that the connection appears with *N*. 11, the poem usually taken as of Pindar's extreme age. There also he sees the strength of ancestors in
the young victor. "Ancient excellence renews its power by
alternation in the ages of men. Black furrows yield their
harvest discontinuously, nor in all circuits of the years will
trees bear fragrant blossom with like wealth, but changing-
ly." (vv. 37-42) But as noted in the last chapter, the tone
is darker in this late poem, and he doubts now that the flowering can be foreseen. "No certain sign from Zeus attends
mankind. We nevertheless set foot on proud acts, desiring
multitudinous ends. Our constitutions are prisoner to shameless hope. But the rivers of foreknowledge lie remote. Seek
limit in gaining. In unattainable loves are the sharper madnesses." (vv. 43-49) This uncertainty of the flowering
states the dark side of process and the bond to earth. "Let
him recall he dresses mortal limbs, and last of all will don a
dress of earth," he tells the victor earlier in the poem. (vv.
15-16) The silent fallows in a family's history portend a
still quieter fallow to come. The poem thus resembles the
Rhodian poem, *O*. 7, in expressing our inability to stand

clear of change and succession. The earlier *N.* 6, on the other hand, like *O.* 2 to Theron and the wonderful Theban poems, *I.* 3 and *I.* 4, sees a transcendence which also reflects our relationship to the gods and which carries emergence into pure being. As the gods spring from both Earth and Heaven, so, though in very different proportions, do men, and the dark and bright shades in the theme of vicissitude express the ambiguous kinship.

ii HARMONY

If to Pindar the specific facts surrounding any victory tend to drop away (as they do not for Bacchylides) and in their place imagination lifts the transitory event to a plane of absoluteness, it is because he can feel that victory implies poetry and poetry vision. This assumption betrays the communal origins of Greek choral verse; more than that, it reveals the need of a society, as yet largely untouched by rationalism, for mythological statement of its standards. The time was coming when philosophers would assume this interpretative social task, with gains but at the cost of fraying the fine tie between act and import, the thing done and the thing implied. The poetry of an age of faith like Pindar's does not so much 'give to airy nothings a local habitation and a name' as, contrariwise, transport local habitations and names to the ideal range of airy nothings. The odes have a formal likeness to such a painting as El Greco's "Burial of Count Orgaz," which by showing in the lower part the Count's miraculous burial in the presence of his contemporaries and, in the upper part, his reception in paradise, places him in the setting of his society and the society in that of its faith. Yet if inherited social practice underlies the odes, Pindar's intensity drew this inheritance toward his private vision. At no point is the fact clearer than in the odes about to be discussed, those loosely connected by what we have called the theme of harmony. They fall into two main classes: those which in the serene moment of celebration catch sound of a higher order, partly moral, partly of music and poetry, partly religious, and those troubled odes which miss this order. In the latter Pindar's loneliness is quite clear, and one sees to what privacy of symbolism he had come, however communal in origin his poetic role was and however passionately he wished to see himself in this role. The parallel to El Greco, different as he is from Pindar, suggests how productive of a strongly individual style this complex union of private vision with accepted forms can be.

Olympian 14. The short poem *O*. 14, for a young victor of the near-by Boeotian town of Orchomenus, has a quality of limpid effortlessness unmatched in the odes. Though the early date usually ascribed to it has lately been questioned,[47] it carries the tone of at-homeness in the familiar which has seemed characteristic of the years before the war and the journey to Sicily. The fact that the Charites, Graces, whom it addresses are at once cult figures in Orchomenus and inward figures of Pindar's imagination, closely associated with his view of poetry, may help explain the intimacy of the poem. "Guardians of the fair-horsed seat which shares the streams of the Cephissus, O royal and storied Charites of bright Orchomenus, watchers of the Minyae bred of old, hear me since I pray. Through you all joyous things and sweet are won for mortals, if a man be wise, if a man be fair, if a man be glorious. Even the gods hold neither dance nor feast without the holy Charites, but keepers of every act in heaven, enthroned by Pythian Apollo of the golden bow, they hymn the quenchless glory of the Olympian sire. — O lady Aglaia and Euphrosyne who take delight in song, children of the mightiest god, attend now, and Thalia, lover of melody, seeing this festal band at fortune's moment stepping light. In Lydian strain and meditated verse I come singing Asopichus, because through thee the Minyan land is called

Olympic victor. To Persephone's black-walled house go,
Echo, now bringing the sounding message to his father, that
seeing Cleodamus you may tell how among Pisa's famous
dells his son crowned his young hair with the wings of brilliant triumph."

In the first strophe, the three Charites are joint presiding
presences; in the second, they descend to touch the particular
occasion and moment and, in so doing, take on separate iden-
tities. They are reposed at first, then, so to speak, join the
festal dance. Their presence is harmonious order, and Pindar first feels this order in the pleasant setting of the ancient
city by the meadows of the Cephissus. The harmony then
passes inward and is felt in the long Minyan past, but in the
present also as shown in wisdom (poetry), personal beauty
or the beauty of act ('if a man be wise, if a man be fair, if a
man be glorious'). At last it is fully seen as a divine principle, forever present in the beauty of the gods' pure being.
When the Charites are called 'guardians of all acts in
heaven,' the words suggest Aristotle's definition of pleasure,
as a tone of happiness accompanying right function.[48] But
these goddesses are more than an attendant tone; they are
the completion and actuality itself of right and happy things,
and come nearer being principles of achieved and expressed
form. Thus they accompany Apollo's singing as the fact of
its perfection, are present in the gods' entirely beautiful life,
and their celebration of Zeus's power is the actuality of his
lucid order.

This idea of harmony as the special trait and possession
of the Olympians is of course not unique to Pindar. No idea
is more classic in its emphasis on repose as opposed to striving, attainment as opposed to search, rest through vision of
the intelligible as opposed to excitement through sense of the
unknown, preference of the limited (in Plato's terminology)
to the chaotic and unlimited.[49] Needless to say, these latter
states are not foreign to Greek; they notably underlie the

Promethean mood of struggle from which tragedy sprang. Nor, despite the present poem, does Pindar keep the vision of repose much more steadily than does Aeschylus. Just as the vitality of late archaic sculpture strains against a sense of limit, so, as argued earlier, does the intense vigor of both men's styles. The ordering synoptic mind is always being disturbed in them by the assaults of impressions. Yet the vision of repose, impossible though it was for them to keep, is their strongest common bond. If we had the lost plays of the Promethean trilogy, in which Prometheus and Zeus, striving and limit, were brought into final harmony, the fact would be clearer, but the merging of the dark possessive Furies in the Olympian light of freedom and mercy at the close of the *Eumenides* shows sufficiently how Aeschylus' mind, however involved in process, sought finally to transcend it. Pindar comes nearer doing so. The moments of transcendence which we have just considered in the poems on vicissitude are a way of expressing order and harmony. The difference of the present poem and those now to be considered is that they are more fully given to the festal moment of celebration. Xenophanes' poem on the banquet,[50] in which he seeks a grace of speech and act consonant with reason, shares Pindar's desire for a time of pause when former urgency is at rest and the imagination's higher shapes rise clear. This is the moment when music crowns athletics, and since to him athletics includes war and, more widely, testing action of any kind, music in turn embraces all goals of action, almost in the sense of Aristotle's final cause. It is, in effect, contemplation. The Charites of the present poem are close to Apollo and hence to poets, but they are in the natural beauty of Orchomenus also, as well as in its past and in all present grace of person or act. When he says of the Grace, Thalia, in the second strophe, "through thee the Minyan land is called Olympic victor" (vv. 19-20), he feels that everything best in natural surroundings, tradition, and train-

ing has brought the boy to his victory, and it is the beneficent
harmony of all these that he wishes to catch. Being akin to
such influences, poetry can draw them into itself and see them
for a moment as part of the greater Olympian peace. It can
even in the exquisite last lines send beyond the grave its apperception of this timeless order.

Pythian 1. If this limpid poem, like the Theban odes
I. 3 and 4, shows Pindar in the world which he knew and
loved best, it is otherwise with the famous opening of *P.* 1,
the coruscating ode in honor of Hieron's chariot victory at
Delphi in 470, some years after the poet's return from Sicily.
Victory again rouses associations of music and these again
a vision of the celestial order, but a virtuosity second to none
in the odes now replaces the earlier mood of gay and tender
grace. He starts with the lyre, which leads to thoughts of
music's enchantment, which in turn puts wrath to sleep (the
eagle, sign of Zeus as power) and rouses song (sign of Zeus
as harmony) on Olympus. "Golden lyre, Apollo's and the
violet-tressed Muses' joint possession, whom the step heeds,
joy's overture, and whose commands singers obey when
throbbing you create the rising chords of preludes that invite
the dance. And the warrior bolt of the eternal fire you
quench. Sleeps then on Zeus's staff the eagle, sheathing on
either side his pinions swift, the king of birds. Upon his
beaked head you strew dark-visaged cloud, his eyelids' sweet
confinement, and slumbering he lifts his liquid back, by your
tides bound. And even savage Ares leaving far his spear's
harsh edge softens his heart a-dozing, and your shafts enchant the souls of deities through the art of Leto's son and
the deep-bosomed Muses." (vv. 1-12)

It is interesting that Pindar cannot dispel images of violence when he thinks of Hieron. As the story of the cannibal banquet rises to his mind to be rejected in *O.* 1, so here,
though the fires of the thunderbolt are quenched by music,
and the eagle and Ares sleep, their violence seems at first

only hypnotized, not dead, as if music held no sure ascendency. This lurking doubt about the security of order in everything having to do with the tyrant runs through the poem. Pindar prays that Hieron may remember his military triumphs with joy and calm of soul, but knows that he is ill and likens him to the suffering Philoctetes. Again, he prays that Hieron's newly-founded city of Aetna may keep peace and Doric order, yet he both implies disorder and fears war with the Carthaginians and Etruscans whom Hieron had defeated at Cymae in 474. "I beseech thee grant, son of Kronos, that tame at home the Phoenician and Tyrrhenian war cry stay, that saw with groans its pomp of sail at Cymae; so did they suffer shattered by the lord of Syracuse, who struck their youth into the sea from their swift-faring ships, and drew Greece up from heavy slavery." (vv. 71-75) What Salamis is to Athens and Plataea to Sparta, he says, Gelon's and Hieron's victory over the Carthaginians at Himera is to Syracuse. Yet even this splendid praise does not still a sense of unrest. As in the ode to Theron, Pindar stops short because, he says, people murmur at the great; nevertheless he bids Hieron persist in glory and not give up such celebrations as this. "What citizens hear of others' happiness burdens their secret soul. Yet — since envy passes pity — spurn not magnificence. Steer the people with a tiller just. On an unequivocating block beat out your speech. If never so slight a flashing spark fly up, it is held great because it comes from you. You are the treasurer of men's destinies, and witnesses exact attest your either course." (vv. 84-88) The danger of suppressed violence lurks behind this cryptic advice, and the impression remains of a tense equipoise between serenity and harshness, both in the forces that beat on the king and in the king himself. The poem closes with a contrast between Croesus' benign reputation and the dark name of the tyrant Phalaris. Pindar's nominal point is how differently they were commemorated in history, but this difference of reputation only states outwardly the inner and spiritual difference between harmony and violence which is the theme of the poem.

To return then to the lyre and eagle of the start, the lyre was at first simply the music of the choral dance. But presently it became the universal and divine music which is the beauty of the world and the repose of the soul. Yet he is not so sure at the beginning as he was in O. 14 that the gods represent only this harmony. The savage eagle that watches on Zeus's sceptre is, when awake, the living power of his thunderbolt. In the marvelous lines on the eagle's sleep a vision of the world as possible harmony rises, and strife drops away from the gods. Here, perhaps at its clearest, is Aeschylus' and Pindar's great common theme. Hesiod's *Theogony* had prefigured the rise of Zeus's serene sway out of the conflict and disorder of the generation of the Titans, and the *Prometheia* and *Oresteia* trace the winning of a similar peace out of suffering. Pindar is less directly interested in suffering, though the allusion to Philoctetes here and statements in other poems about endurance of pain and danger show that to him too harmony emerges out of struggle. He is characteristically more concerned with the state of peace itself than with its acquisition. In the odes the contest is over, and celebration brings the moment of vision which is the goal and reward of effort. In the present poem, as we have seen, this vision is at first not quite secure. Yet after the opening lines he rises to a great affirmation that harmony is in fact the mark of the gods, reflected in all orderly and beautiful things and menaced only by the brutal residue of the Titanic past. Zeus then becomes wholly identified with harmony, and the fires sent up from Aetna by Typhos, the imprisoned enemy of the gods, become the violence that cannot yield to calm. "But all things that Zeus detests flee over land and the restless sea at the sound of the Pierides' singing, he too who lies in Tartarus harsh, the gods' foe, Typhos the hundred-headed. A many-named cave in Cilicia nurtured him long ago; now Sicily and Cymae's sea-fenced banks oppress his shaggy chest, and a heavenly pillar holds him, icy Aetna, the keen snow's yearlong nurse. From whose recesses pour pure fonts of unapproachable fire, as rivers coil by day ablaze their stream of smoke, and nightly the red flame carries and rolls cliffs with a crash to the sea's flat. That ancient serpent spouts Hephaestus' terrible springs, portent awesome to see, awesome for dwellers near to hear. Such is the creature bound beneath the dark-leaved peaks and plain of Aetna, and the raking bed he lies on stabs his back. O Zeus, who keepest this mountain, brow of the fertile land, may it be ours to please thee." (vv. 13-29) The fear and reverence of the last lines express Pindar's disturbed contemplation of violence. But if Zeus had once used force to restrain the unruly harshness of nature, it is now buried alongside this harshness and no longer a part of him. The soul can and must put away its agitation; this is the plea to Hieron. Civilization is capacity to hear the intelligible order in the world, and the music of the lyre reflects a harmony in Zeus himself.

Nemean 9. In a number of odes the idea of harmony extends more generally from music to life and conduct. It has of course these associations in the poem to Hieron but they are clearer elsewhere. In *N.* 9, one of two poems to Chromius, the Syracusan viceroy in the newly founded town of Aetna and long a lieutenant of both Gelon and Hieron, the man's tried fidelity in war and council is conceived as flowering at last in quietude, *hesychia*. To Thucydides[51] the word means a settled and conservative outlook characteristic of the Spartans and opposite to the restless Attic temper, and Pindar's use is similar, if less political, more suggestive of settled personal habits and tastes. In the background of the ode is the dark sense of an impending last struggle with Carthage, and this darkness imparts itself to the account of

the deaths of the noble Amphiaraus at Thebes and of Hector
at Troy. But Chromius, whose honor and courage have
resembled theirs, has been luckier than they. "If with his
many goods a man gain honorable fame, no farther promon-
tory may the foot of mortal touch. Quietude loves the banquet, and the green of triumph grows fresh and new with
the calm of song." (vv. 46-49) Chromius has come more
whole-heartedly and gracefully than Hieron to this state of
peace, and though war and danger may still await him, they
do not touch his spirit.

   Pythian 4. The two odes to Arkesilas, tyrant of Cyrene,
P. 4 and 5, products of Pindar's summer mood in the 460's,
are similar. His feeling for Apollo, always clear, is especially present in these poems, the god having not only directed Battus, the founder of Cyrene, to Africa eight generations ago and repeated his favor in the present victory, but
being the god of music and of all measure and repose. The
lines from *P.* 5 to Apollo were quoted earlier, "he who from
heavy sickness offers men and women cure, who brought the
lyre, and gives the Muse to whom he wills, inducing warless
harmony in their hearts, and holds his secret mantic seat."
(vv. 63-69) These ideas of prophecy, music, and healing
flow together in *P.* 4 to give this longest and most elaborate
of the odes its special character. Medea's prophecy of a return to Africa by descendants of the Argonauts is mystically
fulfilled many generations after when Apollo welcomes the
stammering Battus at Delphi and directs him abroad. Jason
as leader of the Argonauts has an identifying gentleness and
even chivalry of spirit which mark him as the healer. Pindar
connected his name with ἰάομαι, to heal, and he tells Arkesilas, for whom Jason is a prototype, "you are time's opportune physician, and Paean honors in you a saving light.
A gentle hand must touch and tend the wound's affliction.
Even the weak can easily shake a state, but to set it in place
again is bitter struggle, unless of a sudden a god become the

leaders' guide." (vv. 270-274)   But if healing is in both
Jason and Arkesilas, its manifestation is a spirit molded by
music.   When Jason first appears in Magnesia to reclaim his
birthright from the insulting Pelias, he refuses to answer insult in like terms.   "I claim to keep Chiron's instruction.
From his cave I come, from Charicles and Philyra, where
these holy centaur women brought me up.   And through my
twenty years no evil act or word spoke I to them." (vv. 102-
105)   The *Precepts of Chiron*[52] was a work attributed to
Hesiod which enjoined respect for Zeus and parents (commands reflected in *P*. 6), but which was taught by the lyre
and carried associations of music.   The name Philyra surely
evoked this meaning to Pindar.   When then Jason meets his
old father and kinsman, "he received them with gentle words
and entertainment shared, while in hospitality fit he drew out
bliss entire through five whole days and nights plucking joy's
holy flower." (vv. 127-131)   Here again, if on a somewhat
massive scale, is the festal moment of pure being almost like
the gods', such as he felt in the boy Asophichus' festival at
Orchomenus or the old Chromius' banquet at Aetna.   But it
has more express overtones here of a harmony not only of
music but of conduct and word.   This emphasis (characteristically in this poem of the 460's, close in date to the Rhodian ode, *O*. 7) is more of the world, less visionary and
lyric, and has the golden mood of a placid landscape.   The
ode was ordered for Arkesilas by an exile from Cyrene, one
Damophilus, and if Jason's quality as a healer looks to the
king, his balance and restraint apply to the petitioner also.
Pindar expresses the latter's wish to find happiness with music and quiet of mind near Apollo's spring at home, and in
urging mercy toward him, reverts to the language of *P*. 1 by
saying that Zeus with time released the Titans.   The accents
both of the poem to Hieron and of that to Chromius return:
the higher order which is Zeus's benign triumph, and the
quietude which is the soul's similar release from struggle.

The prominence of Apollo in this poem and in its companion, *P. 5*, matches the mellower vision which feels less sharply now the struggle of Zeus against his enemies, harmony against discord, but sees, perhaps too placidly, the happy working of healing and order through good men.

Pythian 8. This summer mood of confidence in the world was broken by the Athenian conquest of Boeotia and Aegina in the last years of his life. The apocalyptic close of *P.* 8 of 446, the latest dated poem, was quoted earlier to show his change of outlook, and we shall return to it. Here the opening of the poem may serve as a final statement of the theme of harmony and of its attendant motif of repose. In these abrupt, allusive, and deeply felt lines, Quietude, Hesychia, has become an animate presence, herself embodying the inner character of harmony. "Loving-hearted Quietude, o child of Justice and strengthener of cities, you who hold the final keys of councils and of wars, receive for Aristomenes this rite of honor for his Pythic crown. You understand with perfect tact alike the gift and the acceptance of gentle things. But when a man lays in his heart cold rancor, you harshly face the enemy's assault and scuttle his insolence. Porphyrion did not know you when he taunted you unprovoked. The gain alone is glad that comes from the house of a willing giver. Violence trips the vaunter in the end. Cilician Typhos, the hundred-headed, escaped this not, nor the monarch of the giants, but they fell before the thunderbolt and Apollo's shafts, who welcomed with kindly heart from Cirrha home Xenarchus' son crowned with Parnassian green and with the Dorian song." (vv. 1-20)

It was said earlier that such symbolic and mythological thought as Pindar's moves simultaneously in the inner realm of state of mind and the outer realm of act, and the statement is well illustrated by this brilliant and moving passage. The kindliness of Quietude is a natural inheritance from her mother Justice, and it is through equity grown into graceful and generous habit that she makes cities great. The keys of councils and wars that she holds are her evenness of mind and freedom from obsessive and assertive moods. Her civic judgments are right because she can value such moments of private happiness as this festival for Aristomenes. "You understand with perfect tact alike the gift and the acceptance of gentle things." (vv. 6-7) In this statement Pindar is thinking not so much of the goddess as of a state of mind that can give with joy and receive with grace because it is at ease with itself and with the minds of friends. Her wrath, if ignorant of a final charity, comes near righteous anger. Her enemies are the violent and self-assertive, men who cannot feel a cheerful mutuality of giving and hence destroy the idea of community. Pindar presently reverts to the language of the poems to Hieron and Arkesilas, and Typhos and the giant Porphyrion are destroyers of an order which they cannot understand. At the date of this poem they obviously signify Athens, not by a simple equation but by exemplifying the will to conquest by which Athens had been led to destroy what he feels the benign older regimen of Greece. He no longer recognizes the city which he knew as a young man and of whose performance at Salamis he wrote the famous dithyramb. "That gain alone is glad that comes from the house of a willing giver" (v. 14) expresses perhaps naively an ideal of international action identical with private courtesy, and the breach between national and personal morality which Thucydides was to feel does not occur to him. When at the end it is Apollo who, with Zeus, destroys Porphyrion and the same god welcomes the victor home, it is clear that music and poetry continue for Pindar the sign of a more general harmony of act and impulse. This last poem lends weight to the early vision of the Charites as divine principles which he had had in the almost Arcadian O. 14. The feeling is graver now and much more aware of the possible dangers to har-

mony, but more conscious also of the range of spirit which
harmony can include.

But his confidence in harmony sometimes failed. The
word is being used in a slightly different sense to mean harmony between Pindar and his audience, though to him the
meanings coalesced. He could not feel an order in the
world which showed itself in the beauty of act and became
fully manifest in music as an ordering and divine principle,
yet at the same time feel no such bond between himself and
his patrons. His discomfort at such moments is partly only
his chagrin at not being appreciated as he expected to be, but
it reflects also a sense that the very assumptions of his art are
challenged. Outlooks were changing, and with time a victorious athlete would no longer be regarded with Pindar's
eyes as the flower and ideal of a community, but simply as a
practitioner of one, and not a very high, specialism. Similarly, a poet would come to be looked on as a practitioner in
words, like the Pindarist in the *Birds* (905-959) who wants
to supply an ode for the cloud-city. Beneath both changes
would be an individualism which separated men from their
communities or at least told them that knowledge of one's
unique and separate self was the prerequisite to entering a
higher and less tangible community of the mind. Tragedy
was obviously a step in this new direction since it showed a
disorder in the world and a loneliness in aspiration. Even
though most of Aeschylus' heroes rediscover a community
and Sophocles' early and late plays (all, that is, except the
Trachiniae and *Oedipus King*) bring a similar repatriation
of some kind, the old, half Eden-like rightness of the world
had vanished and men were more aware of being alone. It
is this rightness in the world that Pindar wants to see: hence
it is this loneliness that disturbs him. Yet, as was argued
earlier, the sixth century had already opened the path toward individualism, in monodic poetry, for example, or the
signed vases of potters, and Pindar's very epinikion applied

to notable men the choral forms once used toward gods
alone. His heightened imagination and imperious style carried, whether he wished it or not, the marks of visionary inwardness. Thus the chagrin of the odes about to be discussed seems at bottom directed less against his patrons than
against himself, as if he were being forced, like Oedipus, to
see what he both wanted and did not want to see, namely, the
loneliness of his imagination. The late poems that accompany the defeat of Boeotia and Aegina draw part of their
power from his final realization that strength springs from
within men rather than from a fixed social order, and by
compensation these same poems find sources of renewal for
the community. Conversely, the tendency to bland expan-
siveness in the Rhodian *O.* 7 and the long *P.* 4 to Arkesilas
suggest the painful fact that lyric vision of the beauty of life
and the unity of things does not easily survive years and success, at least in its pristine freshness.

Pythian 3. Two final poems to Hieron, *P.* 3 and 2, illustrate this breach of Pindar with his world, though the former less in itself than by anticipation of the latter. The
cannibal banquet in *O.* 1 and the resistance of Typhos to the
celestial music in *P.* 1 make clear that he from the first felt
something acrid in the tyranny at Syracuse, and the coruscation of these odes partly reflects his nerving of himself
against the unfamiliar. Certainly he could not easily apply
to the tyrant's court those ancient communal associations of
myth and rite which victory roused in him at home. *P.* 3
does not commemorate a specific victory but is a poem of
consolation to Hieron on his illness mentioned in *P.* 1 and a
reminder to him of both the peace and the glory which
poetry gives. It is the gentlest of the poems to Hieron, and
its tender hope that he may share and take comfort from
Pindar's view of poetry prepares the way for the disappointment of *P.* 2. Its date is unclear, evidently after Pindar's
return from Sicily and probably but not surely before *P.* 1 of

470. It has to do with the possible and the impossible.
Hence it recalls, though more softly, the theme of O. 1,
Pelops' position as a courageous man between his father
Tantalus' one-time felicity on Olympus and later entire exclusion. Pindar would be a healer like Asclepius or the
centaur Chiron who reared him, but his healing would be the
courage which poetry gives. In keeping with this wish is the
opening mood of green and fresh remoteness with which he
describes the girl Coronis, who was wed by Apollo long ago
in Thessaly. "But she yearned for things impossible, sickness which many have. There is an idle-witted breed of
mortals which scorns the thing at hand and searches the remote, hunting the wind with incompleted hopes." (vv. 19-23)
She yielded vacuously to a stranger though she had already
had union with Apollo, and like her was her son Asclepius,
whom the god saved when she and her whole village were
destroyed in punishment. He had the Apolline gift of healing but, like his mother, lacked the Apolline sense of limit,
and Zeus destroyed him in turn for accepting money to bring
back a man from the dead. "We must ask from the gods
with mortal hearts what fits us, knowing the near path, of
what destiny we are. Dear heart, crave not immortal life,
but drain the practicable device." (vv. 59-62) The device
is courage, like Pelops' in O. 1 but of a quieter and more defensive kind as fits the sick king. Pindar holds up to him a
bleaker truth than that with which Achilles consoled Priam
in the fable of the jars of Zeus, that the gods give us two
evils for every good, "which fools cannot decently bear, but
the brave can, turning the fair side out." (vv. 82-83) But
this good, thus outweighed in quantity by evil, outweighs
it in worth and permanence, and Pindar sees again the vision
of Peleus and Cadmus, happiest of mortals, who, though
tried, yet had the supreme joy of marrying goddesses and
seeing the calm Olympians on golden chairs at their wed-
dings. What is this happiness which Peleus and Cadmus

won, and with something like which Hieron may triumph
over illness? It is in part the god-given fact of fame but
in part also consciousness of an inner light matching the outward luster. "I will be small in small things and great in
great, and I will tend in my heart my guiding god, serving
him with the means at my command." (vv. 107-109) Pindar exhorts to the healing which he can give, the medicine
of fame, but the tender and personal tone promises chiefly
an inner healing. Asclepius and his mother Coronis, though
touched by the god, betrayed their fortune through desire for
an unattainable perfection of power or happiness, but Peleus
and Cadmus were wiser in cherishing through later troubles
the inner knowledge of their once-perfect joy. They are the
true models, not so much in their glory as in their luminous
and persistent gratitude for high fortune, and it is this tenacious joy that Pindar wishes the king.

Pythian 2. P. 3 seeks more transparently than any
other ode to draw reality into Pindar's imaginative net. He
would throw the skein of his verse around the king's life as
if by so doing he could hold it. The complexity of his disappointment in *P. 2* is the measure of his hope. To the
degree that he is made to realize that he cannot in fact transform the king and yet would not break with the real world
as the subject of his verse, he feels that he alone is to blame
for his self-deception, hence that he must remain loyal and
grateful to Hieron. But as he also reflects that Hieron had
not valued his generosity of feeling or had been influenced
against him by jealous men, he is angry at him or at them
rather than at himself. Mixed with both moods is a religious awareness that the gods deal unpredictably with men,
but even this comfort is clouded by the sense of his enemies'
indecent satisfaction. The occasion of this flood of emotion,
C. M. Bowra brilliantly saw,[53] was probably Hieron's choice
of Bacchylides over himself to celebrate his last and greatest
victory, with a chariot at Olympia in 468. Bacchylides' odes

5 and 4 had been composed for the same victories respectively as *O*. 1 and *P*. 1, but, despite the extreme beauty of *Ba*. 4,
evidently as minor and secondary commissions. Bowra
argued that Pindar's disappointment was now the greater
both because he had himself in *O*. 1 expressed the hope of
celebrating some day such a final success by Hieron and because Bacchylides' actual poem for the occasion, the weak
Ba. 3, notably borrows from Pindar.⁵⁴ If the two crows in
O. 2 which chatter futilely against Zeus's sovereign bird are
in fact the uncle and nephew, Simonides and Bacchylides,
Pindar's animosity is of eight years' standing. In Bacchylides'
lucid and gentle style, with its clear succession of narrative
and aphorism, any such symbolic complexity as Pindar's is
quite lacking, and it is clear that he had felt, as Pindar had
not, the force of the rational Ionic spirit which reduced
poetry from its earlier interpretative pretensions to a largely decorative role. The heavy weight of meaning which
Pindar's mythic figures carry reveals a mind which speaks
and feels through such figures, whereas to Bacchylides narrative is simply narrative and carries no such symbolic burden.
Accordingly beneath all overt reasons for chagrin there exists in Pindar's disappointment the sense that what is involved is his way of seeing reality through myth. If Hieron
had failed to grasp or value what he had said of men's relationship to the gods through the figure of Pelops, or of harmony through the lyre and the rebellious Typhos, or of the
impossible and the possible through the contrast of Coronis
and Asclepius to Peleus and Cadmus, Pindar could well question all the social assumptions of his art. At least, his disturbance here and in *N*. 7 and 4, the two odes that show
similar distress, touches his art because he is forced to recognize that visions which he thought social and communi-
cable were in part private and lonely.

He begins by praising the formidable military strength
of Syracuse, calling the city, as he had Athens, "god-in-

spired," *daimonios*. Through the familiar train of thought
that prowess commands praise, he then reaches the ideas of
poetry and of gratitude, and it is with this last that he
wrestles. Citizens and allies have cause for gratitude to the
great king. "As he whirls on his winged wheel, they say,
Ixion by edict of heaven thus warns mankind: O return again
and again to requite benefactors with payment glad." (vv.
21-24) In *O.* 1 Tantalus had been ungrateful to the gods,
but Pindar had rather seen in him a certain mortal vagrancy
and shallowness of mood which could not endure the bright
Olympian calm. Ixion's story begins like his with acceptance
on Olympus but ends much more violently with his attempt
to seduce Hera. "Once in many-recessed chambers he attempted Zeus's wife. But in measure of himself must a man
find limit in things. The errant union threw him into ruin
complete when he came to bed; for he lay with a cloud, the
madman, intent on his sweet delusion. In look she resembled the highest of goddesses, Kronos' daughter, but Zeus's
hands set her, this pretty bane, as the man's trap. So he
made his own four-spoked knot as his destruction, and falling
in ineluctable fetters, got his message for all mankind."
(vv. 33-41) Ixion's traditional punishment was to be
stretched on a rolling wheel, and Pindar sees in him a fearful copy of the love-charm, the iunx, which was a bird similarly bound and whirled. But Ixion's love was not in fact
love, since Hera was beyond him, and in seeing her he saw
only his own intense ambition, hence lay with a cloud. He is
for Pindar a terrifying self-hypnotism which has lost its grip
on reality and constitutes a love-charm directed toward itself.
It is part of the power of this passage that the cloud-woman
proves not to be a dissolving wraith but a creature as alone
as her lover. The next lines describe the offspring of the
union, which was the unnatural and inhuman Kentauros, who
by further union with the mares on Pelion begot the centaurs.
This misshapen progeny is not less descriptive of Ixion's

mood. Pindar is not thinking of such a centaur as Chiron,
whose half-animal form conveys a bond with earth and hence
ancient kindliness and wisdom of the sort that made him a
primal Socrates, fit teacher of Jason and Achilles. The centaurs here are the wild creatures that appear in the metopes
of the Parthenon, and their violence is the offspring of
Ixion's state of mind.

Pindar is even more shocked by this vision than by that
of Typhos in *P*. 1, and as there, his mind goes to Zeus. "God
completes for himself each end as he desires, god, who
catches the winged eagle and passes the dolphin in the sea
and bends the lofty-minded man and proffers others ageless
celebrity. As for me, I must shun the crackling tooth of
slander. From far off I have watched railing Archilochus
defenseless for the most as he battened on his harsh-tongued
enmities. Riches in wisdom with a happy lot is best." (vv.
49-56) The mood of revulsion is almost Dante's. God
alone gives fame and greatness, and to snatch at them is to
end in angry and futile overreaching. Pindar is talking to
himself when he draws back from the satirist Archilochus'
state of mind. He contemplates him with the horrid fasci-
nation with which Dante looks at the furious souls in the
bubbling swamp, or in Euripides' spirit when at the end of
the *Hecuba* he has the queen transformed into a howling
dog. To Archilochus the world had become a place which
a man could only rail at, and he had wallowed in hatred.
In *P*. 3 Pindar had told Hieron that brave men can endure
the evils that outnumber the good of life by turning the fair
side out, and now he needs this advice himself. His alarm
is both that he sees his code of honor in danger (the code
which is implied in the idea of harmony and which in *P*. 4
makes Jason refuse to answer Pelias with insult) and that
by his own standards he knows that he must cling to the
world and to worldly success. He had seen the hand of divinity in Hieron's life, and his whole poetry rested on the

belief that triumph is not meaningless. It is with these thoughts that he turns from Archilochus to reassert that wisdom and happy fortune are in fact the best things in life: which is to say, that there is meaning in the social order, that he must accordingly remain loyal and grateful to Hieron, and that he must not drift with the mood of Ixion that he had evoked.

Yet he had been deeply hurt. One has the impression that he intended to end with the farewell to which he now rallies, praising Hieron for courage and wisdom and for a name second to none in Greek history. But just as what looks like the final epode draws to a close, he spins off in a strange and cryptic epilogue "Learn what kind of man you are and become it. A monkey is pretty to boys, endlessly pretty. But blessed was Rhadamanthus because he gained wisdom's untarnished fruit. No inward pleasure takes his soul in deceptions, such as always haunt mankind from the whisperer's arts." (vv. 72-75) Hieron, he feels, has betrayed his own nature. The command that he learn and try to become the kind of man that he inherently is has a Delphic force. It tells much also of Pindar's view of his poems to the king, which were not to his own mind mere praise but revelations of Hieron's position toward himself, history, and the gods. If he had been fighting his own ingratitude, he now feels that the temptation is behind him and that he can at last address the king with a clear conscience. The monkey of folk tale, Bowra further argued, is incomparably the mimic; hence the boys who like the monkey are people who cannot distinguish authentic from borrowed and misused insight. This interpretation points the passage against Bacchylides and his supporters. But beyond any such reference is the more general meaning that these merely childish people and, much more, those others who take pleasure in intrigue and evil-speaking miss the sense of the permanent which Rhadamanthus had and which it is the task of poetry to con-

vey. Though he is describing men around Hieron, some of
their fault obviously infects the king.

He goes on, "A curse to both that none can fight are
slander's covert spokesmen, intensely like foxes' hearts. And
yet how gets the vixen profit in the end? I, as it were, while
the other gear has its salt labor in the deep, remain the cork
above the seine, unsunken by the brine. The slippery man
can speak no solid sentence among the noble; yet he fawns
and weaves his curving way toward all. I do not share his
confidence. Let me love my friend. As an enemy I'll fly at
my enemy like a wolf, in divers seasons treading devious
paths. In every rule the straight-tongued man advances: by
tyrants, or when the passionate crowd or when the wise survey the state." (vv. 76-88) Some have seen a dialogue in
these hard lines,[55] but they seem reasonably clear as they
stand. Pindar's slanderers are the foxes and also the net,
while he is successively the cork and the wolf. The foxes'
devious efforts get them nowhere; the cork neither shares
the net's dark work in the depths of the sea nor is sub-
merged. While the fox becomes almost a fawning dog in
his attentions to people, the wolf straightforwardly loves his
friends and hates his enemies. To be sure, he is a law unto
himself and will walk in crooked paths when he sees fit. The
line recalls Quietude's anger against her enemies in *P.* 8; she
too can be relentless. Pindar's unconcern for politics as compared with a man's personal standards speaks in the last lines
on tyranny, democracy, and aristocracy. Though he favors
the last, he is interested in the honest mind for itself. The
poem ends in this inward tone. He reverts to previous
thoughts on the gods' unpredictability, who elevate now one
man, now another. "But even this softens not the minds of
the envious." (vv. 89-90) They believe as Ixion had that
they, not the gods, create their own advantage, but fail
through this delusion. He is at last at rest; he will bear his
yoke lightly and not kick at the goad. "Be it mine to live

acceptably with the just." (v. 96) He has returned by a
complex road to the harmony which in happier moments he
had assumed could unite character with music. Though he
has again found meaning in the social order, he has done so
only after a struggle with himself and with it which has
yielded a more interior meaning.

Finally, two poems, *N*. 7 and 4, of uncertain date[56] but
evidently of much this same period of the late 470's and
early 460's, show him in like straits nearer home. Both
odes are for Aeginetans, and his distress is the greater because he might have expected fuller understanding than
Hieron's from men of upbringing like his own. He himself
largely created his troubles, and it was observed earlier that
nothing in the odes throws a sharper light than this incident
on the complicated blend of piety and nationalism which was
Greek hero cult.

Paean 6. The most nearly complete of the papyrus
fragments, *Paean* 6, was composed, he says, as a gift for the
festival of the Theoxenia at Delphi, a ceremony intended to
avert famine in Greece and lacking this year an appropriate
song. "At the water by the bronze gate I heard the voice of
Castalia lorn of men's dancing; therefore I came to redeem
your brethren's plight and for my honor. I obeyed my heart
as a child its mother sage as I drew near Apollo's grove, the
nurse of crowns and feasts." (fg. 40. 7-15) The fact that
the poem ends with praise of Aegina casts some obscurity on
these lines. Was the chorus Aeginetan and did Pindar
simply furnish the paean, and perhaps not as a gift, or did
Aegina occur to him because Aeacus legendarily first averted
famine by the cult of Zeus Hellanios, or, an unlikely pro-
posal, did he add the final passage when the paean proved
offensive? The fragmentary state of the ending prevents an
answer. But what is quite clear, and the most interesting
and impressive thing about the poem, is his intensity of religious illumination. He asks a question about the gods,

which is likewise unclear because of the imperfect papyrus, and answers, "This the gods can impart to poets, but that men discover it is impossible. Yet since you know all, you maiden Muses, and through the father clothed in black cloud and through Mnemosyne have this right, then hear me now." (vv. 51-57) These more than conventional prayers for inspiration are in keeping with the visionary account of the fall of Troy that follows. His motive is praise of Apollo, whom he describes as violently opposing Athene and Hera in an effort to save his beloved city. "But resting on Olympus' golden clouds and peaks Zeus, the watcher of the gods, dared not dissolve the fated. Must then for high-tressed Helen the blaze of shining fire obliterate broad Pergamon." (vv. 92-98) Yet as Apollo had brought Achilles to his death, so he dealt with Achilles' son Neoptolemus, though he could not prevent his sacking Troy. "But he never afterward saw his mother sage nor the horses of the Myrmidons in his father's fields." (vv. 105-107) Apollo had him killed in Delphi in a quarrel over the division of meats. This was the legend, but hardly with the emphasis which Pindar gives it. He is so carried away by his vision of Apollo that he both imputes violence to an Aeginetan hero, one of those to whom except for Heracles he usually feels closest, and forgets his own precept, "leave war and every strife remote from the immortals." (O. 9. 40-41) The paean well illustrates the privacy of his imagination. His call to the Muses for knowledge that mortals alone cannot gain brings a revelation of the power of the angry god that blinds him to all else. Despite his concluding praise of Aegina as the "bright star of Zeus Hellanios" (apt praise for a city that had dedicated golden stars as a thank-offering for Salamis[57]) and despite the marvelous line about Zeus's union with the island nymph, "then hid the golden tresses of the air your native mountain shadowed" (vv. 137-139), Aeginetans felt the slight.

Nemean 7. N. 7 is his attempt to explain himself.

73380

Even the obscure last poem to Hieron has no such complexity of allusion and undertone as this, the most errant of the
odes.   The reason for the obscurity has been repeatedly
groped at: the natural imprecision of symbols, or perhaps
not so much their imprecision at any one moment as their
Protean way of gliding into new meanings.   They are like
vine branches that rerooting take on new life.   He begins
meditatively with the mysterious coming into existence of
beauty and achievement, a theme to which we shall return
in the last section.   "Eleithyia, enthroned beside the deep-
thoughted Moirai, child of mighty Hera, you who bring
children to birth, o hear me.   Without you, seeing neither
light nor the black kindly-time, do we gain your sister Hebe
of the bright limbs.   Yet we draw our breath not all to equal
ends. Difference divides each yoked to his own fate. Through
you in his turn Theagenes' son, elect for prowess, Sogenes is
sung in glory among pentathletes." (vv. 1-8) Pindar feels
the hidden forces that from the dark of birth and through
the light and dark of childhood have brought the boy to his
present brightness, and Eleithyia, the goddess of birth, acts
in unseen accord with the Fates, with Hera, goddess of marriage, and with Hebe, goddess of youth.   But the sunlight of
achievement thus benignly and mysteriously brought is
hedged by the second darkness of death; "even great forti-
tude falls in shadow deep for want of song." (vv. 12-13)
Presently death becomes the storm that will come the day
after tomorrow, which the wise man foresees.   The meaning
is slightly obscure because the wise man, the *sophos,* can also
mean the poet, and some take it in this sense from the first.[58]
But Pindar seems to glide from one meaning to the other as
he goes on.   "Rich and poor voyage past death together.
Odysseus' tale, I think, grew greater than his plight through
sweet-voiced Homer, since on his fancies false and winged
devices a glory sits, and art deceives beguiling us with
words." (vv. 19-23) So far Pindar has traveled a familiar

route, though with singular freshness and serenity: that the
golden moment arises, to vanish except for poetry, which
holds its timelessness. But having evoked Homer as the prototype of poets and through him Odysseus, he comes to the
latter's enemy Ajax, the exemplar of mistreated and misunderstood men. The myth which had begun as illustration of
the poet's power to commemorate now illustrates misunderstanding, and Ajax's position includes Pindar's.

"The greater mass of men is blind of heart. Could it see
the truth, brave Ajax furious from the armor had not driven
the smooth sword through his chest; whom best in war save
only for Achilles the escorts of blowing Zephyrus bore in
vessels swift to Ilus' town to gain blond Menelaus' wife. But
common comes the wave of Hades and falls unforeseen even
on him who foresees. Yet honor lasts for them whose flowering fame god nurtures when they are dead." (vv. 24-32)
The sequence of thought recalls the words to Hieron in O. 1
on the deceptive charm of poetry which finds credence
through the blindness and rancor of man, and as there, the
two elements of false charm and human short-sightedness
serve to elicit the true character of the poet as visionary. He
sees what escapes the crowd, clarifying the true fame that
the gods give. Pindar is now in a position to explain his
seeming slight to Neoptolemus in the paean, which he does
more handsomely than persuasively by saying that the hero
had come to Delphi with the pious intention of dedicating
spoils of Troy but died there through the god's wish that an
Aeacid forever lie near the temple as guardian of heroic
processions and sacrifices. "No witness false attests the
deeds, Aegina, of your and Zeus's offspring. This is my confidence as I state the sovereign road of song that from their
home leads radiant virtue out." (vv. 49-52) The witness
has been variously understood as Neoptolemus, Apollo, and
Pindar,[59] and though it seems to be Pindar, the point is

minor, because he remains in any case the seer and spokesman of the god's purpose.

The poem is only half over, and he returns twice again
to his honorable intentions toward Neoptolemus. He even
compliments the victor's father on his 'courage for fair
things,' which must mean courage to engage Pindar, and asserts his own high reputation among the Epirotes, Neoptolemus' people, and at home. "If there was burden, happiness follows greater. O give me place. If being lifted up
I cried beyond the measure, I am not gruff to pay the victor
grace. Light is it to weave crowns. Strike up. The Muse
sets gold together and ivory pale and the lily flower which
she draws from the wash of the sea." (vv. 75-79) Having
asserted his role as poet and the harmony of life which
should accompany it, he can at last admit a possibility of dam-
age from his exalted state at the time of the paean. The
crown which he weaves in amends is, like the images at the
start of O. 1, one of those perfect and no doubt unconscious
statements of his purpose. The gold has its now-familiar
glint of heroic achievement; the ivory, like white things elsewhere,[60] is shining fame; and after the wave of death which
sounded through the opening of the poem, the lily flower of
coral which the Muse harvests from the sea is poetry's triumph over death. Intuition can hardly be purer. The poem
ends with that tone of regained ease in a familiar world
which we have seen in O. 14 for the young victor of Orchomenus and in the Theban I. 4. The legendary bonds between Aeacus and Heracles, both sons of Zeus, express the
living bonds between their cities, Aegina and Thebes. Hence
Pindar feels special meaning in the fact that the victor's
house lay between two shrines of Heracles, as in a yoke. "If
man make test of man in anything, we'll call a loving and
firm-hearted neighbor a happiness to neighbor worthy all.
If even a god confirm this, then through you, o queller of the
giants, Sogenes prays to keep in fortune and with fond heart

toward his father the rich and holy street of his ancestors.
For by your sacred groves as in a chariot's four-horsed yoke,
his house lies as he leaves on either hand." (vv. 86-94) The
boy's and the family's future lies with Heracles. Pindar as
a Theban votary of the hero expresses in the prayer both his
allegiance to the standards which Heracles embodies and his
sense of him as the prototype of victors. The injured Ajax
of the beginning has become the triumphant Heracles of the
end, and the change is more relevant to Pindar himself than
to the boy. He concludes with a smile, "My heart will never
admit to have torn Neoptolemus with rancorous words. But
to rehearse the same thing three and four times is penury,
like the senseless chant of children, 'Corinth, the son of
Zeus.' "

At first glance the cause of Pindar's difficulty was simply
his injudicious account of Neoptolemus in the paean. But
that account showed in turn the privacy of his inner vision,
and his attempt at self-exoneration was wayward and cryptic.
He spoke intimately only in this mythological language;
hence was in the position of trying to correct misunderstanding while leaving its true cause untouched. This is the characteristic poetic dilemma, that a man cannot know how clear
to others those images will be which to him carry brightest
meaning, but to Pindar, as we have seen, the difficulty was
greater, because social tradition and the setting of the epinikion as well as all personal attachments to community and
cult told him that his role was communal.

Nemean 4. A final poem, *N. 4*, shows him facing this
dilemma, and his victorious solution of it seems to carry a
new stage of self-awareness. This is one of three Aeginetan
poems, including *O. 8* of 460 and *N. 6*, which mention the
Athenian trainer Melesias, and the lighter tone of the reference to him here and in *N. 6* has been used to date these
poems ahead of *O. 8*;[61] which is to say, farther from the out-
break of hostilities between Athens and Aegina. "Joy is the

best physician of finished toils, and songs, wise daughters of
the Muses, touch and exorcise them. Even hot water wets
not the limbs so soft as praises married with the lyre. The
word lives longer than the deed which from the profound
mind the tongue draws through the Graces' chance." (vv.
1-8) The opening lines were quoted earlier to illustrate his
association of praise with water; the final lines are of more
concern here. Words that rise with mysterious grace from
the depths of consciousness live their own life, outlasting
their occasion. He says more serenely and without sense of
a contrasting falseness and deception in poetry what is said
in the previous poem and to Hieron in *O.* 1. The young victor's family, like the family in *N.* 6, had known many victories and many songs, and were his father living, he would
have bent to his lyre playing this ode. Pindar remembers the
boy's happy reception at the games for Iolaus in Thebes, and
the memory again evokes the legendary comradeship of
Heracles and the Aeacid Telamon, at Troy and against the
rock-throwing giant Alcyoneus. "Unproven of war would
he be shown who fails to grasp my words. For the doer is
likeliest to suffer also." (vv. 30-32) The words suffice for
the background of pain, which Pindar understands but passes
over in favor of the moment of triumph. The contrast to
Aeschylus is very clear, as is the fact that victory has again
been caught up for him into his other world of heroic reality.

At this characteristic moment of transvaluation, he
strangely pauses. The gesture has something in common
with the many devices by which he marks new stages of
poems, but goes well beyond those. "Rule and the pressing
hours check me from length of story. Yet by a love-charm
my soul is drawn to touch this new-moon rite. Then, though
the deep sea's surges hold between, resist conspiracy. We
shall be deemed to have come in light superior to our foes.
Another man with jealous eyes revolves in the dark a hollow
wit that falls to earth. What virtue Fate, the lord, has given

me, I know well, creeping time will complete destined. O straightway then, sweet lyre, in Lydian tones weave this song too, beloved of Oenone and Cyprus, where Teucer distantly rules, the son of Telamon. Ajax holds his native Salamis and Achilles his radiant isle in the Euxine sea. Thetis rules in Phthia, and Neoptolemus in the reaches of Epirus, where high aloft the pastured headlands sloping fall from far Dodona to the Ionian sea. And Peleus visited with an enemy's hand Iolcus by the foot of Pelion and gave it to Haemonians in subjection." (vv. 35-56)

The steps of his thought are worth following carefully. The victory, as said, has carried him to his ideal world, but he knows that the canons of the epinikion forbid his drifting indefinitely into this world and away from the occasion at hand. Yet the love-charm that draws him 'to touch this new-moon rite' (namely, the present festival which is being held at the new of the moon) is precisely that he sees it as a time when the present is lifted up into the past and the meaning of both becomes bright. It is clear that criticism rather than any rule of art is the true cause of his hesitation. He may not be in Aegina; at least the line about the sea holding him says so if taken literally. If it is metaphorical like the cork and net in *P.* 2, he is caught in and must resist a sea of misunderstanding. His rival or critic is a man who ventures on no such symbolic flights as his but keeps to the shadow and the ground. What was said in connection with *P.* 2 about Bacchylides' lucid, gnomic, and unsymbolic style could apply to this rival, though there is no reason to connect him with Bacchylides. Quite evidently what is objected to in Pindar is the more than earthly light in which he sees victory; for it is on passing into this light of ideality that he hesitates. Here more than before his whole way of thinking seems challenged, and he stands face to face with a kind of thought which does not, like his, see reality through myth. If the

Athenian conquest of Boeotia and Aegina foreshadows the end of an older way of life, these lines equally foreshadow the end of an older way of thinking. His critic was far nearer the rational world of the sophists than ever Pindar could be. But he rallies, and in his restored confidence is a self-knowledge which leads to the greatest late poems. Milton remembers these lines when in the sonnet on his twenty-third year he states his faith that he will come, "to that same lot, however mean or high, Toward which time leads me and the will of Heaven." The two men's feeling for their task is not unlike. That Pindar in fact now feels new assurance is clear from the next lines. When he bids his lyre weave this song too (namely, as he had composed other songs) in honor of Aegina and Cyprus and all those distant lands where legend placed the Aeacids, he reënters the heroic world which was to him the only true commentary on the present world. He goes on to tell again the story of Peleus' attainment of the sea nymph. "He married one of the high-throned Nereids and saw about him seated in majesty the kings of sky and sea, who wove him gifts of strength to his after-race." (vv. 65-68) This is the ultimate Cadiz of Pindar's song. Peleus had clung to Thetis when she changed into a lioness and into fire, and something of his persistence and his reward remains both to the victor and to Pindar. Triumph over vicissitude is here, as well as the harmony which unites the poet with his community, and both with the divine order embodied in the heroes.

iii ATTAINMENT

Pindar's themes are never wholly distinct but flow in and out of each other like the changing currents which oceanographers find at different levels of the sea. The theme of harmony is allied to that of vicissitude because he does not see time and process as entirely governing life but as casting up moments which stand clear of change, having meaning in themselves. In these moments the divine timelessness breaks into sight and, through harmony, into sound. The change that takes place is qualitative, and though he knows that we receive two evils for every good, the good alone has value, expressing as in *N*. 6 our bond with the gods or as in *P*. 1 or *O*. 14 our apperception of their timeless music. It is because of this deep desire in him for wholeness of illumination that he was compared earlier to Parmenides. The dark of Pelops' life in *O*. 1 before he rose to his heroic act resembles Parmenides' non-being; and his achievement Parmenides' bright and static being. Pindar is in essence a contemplative, and though a thousand responses bound him to present and past, he in the end seeks a reality beyond both. We shall now consider certain poems which have to do with emergence from the one to the other reality. These are beyond others the poems about heroes, and there is no ode that does not in some way state this theme of attainment. We have already seen it in Pelops' courage in *O*. 1 and in the victor's voyage beyond the sea in *N*. 5, and the odes now to be considered resemble these two in turning centrally on this theme.

The love of gods for mortal women is a mythological way of stating how brilliance enters common life, and the two characters of the *Iliad* in whom Homer feels inexplicable power, Helen and Achilles, are half-children of gods. Two poems, *P*. 9 and *O*. 6, differ from others in having to do with such unions, and it is notable of both odes that the woman whom Apollo loves is first associated with silence and remoteness, as if it were from such inaccessibility that brightness comes into being. The women thus evoke privacy, earth, stillness, potentiality; the god its transformation into speech and light. This imagery has appeared already in Poseidon's love for Pelops in *O*. 1 and in the hero's passage from shadowy mortality to bright heroism, but it is fuller in these enchanting poems, which show Pindar at his lightest and happiest. The transformation of secret darkness into known and visible light is obviously relevant to poetry also, and these odes bear complexly on his feeling for his verse. The fact will appear in the explanation to be given below of a highly involved and personal passage which, as L. R. Farnell first saw, places the scene of *P.* 9 at Thebes and shows Pindar defending himself against charges that he lacked patriotism in celebrating Athens' glories in the Persian war.[62]   Later authors several times state that a fine, which the Athenians proceeded to pay, was levied on him at home for his eulogy of Athens, and whatever truth may underlie these stories seems connected with the state of feeling visible here.[63]   *P.* 9 was composed in 474, shortly after his return from Sicily, for a Cyrenaic victor, but why it was sung at Thebes is unknown.

Pythian 9.   It tells the story of the nymph Cyrene, who became the eponymous goddess of the African colony: "She whom the long-haired son of Leto once stole from Pelion's wind-echoing dells, and he carried the huntress girl in a car of gold to where he made her queen of lands, rich in sheep, richest in fruit, to hold blooming the earth's third lovely root. And silver-footed Aphrodite kindly met the Delian guest, touching his divine car with her right hand, and on their happy bed shed love's respect." (vv. 5-12)   He characteristically tells the outline of the story first, then circles back to its details.[64]   But the main contrasts are clear even here: the girl's original remoteness in her northern valley, her later serenity as queen in Africa, and the love which was the change from the one state to the other.   She sprang remotely from Earth and Ocean.   "She did not love the loom's back-pacing paths, nor the pleasures of meals among home-keeping girls, but with bronze javelins and sword assailed and slew the creatures wild, making much tranquil peace for her father's kine, and slight upon her lids she took the sweet bedfellow sleep that descends toward dawn." (vv. 18-25)   In

her kinship with wild places is some inheritance from her ancestors, Earth and Ocean.   When Apollo first sees her by
Chiron's cave, he asks who she is who thus knows "the hidden places of the shadowy hills" and whether he may fitly
marry her.   "The prophetic centaur then, softly laughing
with benignant brow, gave back his thought. 'Secret are the
keys to holy loves which wise Persuasion holds, o Phoebus.
Gods and mortals equally pause at this, to attain openly the
happy bed.' " (vv. 38-41) Pindar seems to be correcting
an older narrative which merely described Apollo's desire,
and the spirit in which he corrects it is clear.   Persuasion
holds secret keys to the soul, and the step which neither god
nor man may honorably take is that which fails to win inward
consent.   Apollo's union with Cyrene therefore tells as much
of her mind as of his.   She who had lived in stern loneliness
and disciplined shadow is now ready to advance into the light
of history.   The change is at once from youth to maturity,
from secret thought to known act, from potentiality to fulfillment.   "The meditations of the young," says a fragment,
"circling with toil discover glory.   Then shine through time
acts lifted up to heaven." (fg. 214) To Pindar the soul's
willing capacity for change is the subject of wonder.   The
god does not come as a mere exterior force, and though he
brings more than the mind had conceived, the mind fulfills
itself in welcoming him.   The centaur goes on, " 'Were you,
who cannot touch deceit, led to dissembling words by a gay
mood, and do you ask whence the girl springs, o lord? You
who know all things' endings and their journeys, how many
leaves earth in the spring puts forth, how many sands by sea
and waves of rivers and tides of winds are rolled, and what
will come and whence.   But if I must contend even with the
wise, then I will tell.   You entered this dell her bridegroom
and will bear her to Zeus's peerless garden beyond the sea,
where to a plain-fringed hill you will lead an island folk and
make her a city's queen.   And Libya now, lady of meadows

broad, will greet in golden halls the fair-named bride.' "
(vv. 42-56) The awe expressed here for Apollo's mysterious knowledge recalls the praise in *P.* 5 of the god of healing,
music, and prophecy. The contrast could hardly be greater
between the austere and silent girl and the brilliant god, smiling in his omniscience, and when she is changed through him
to a great queen, a transformation involving three steps is
complete: silent inwardness, change won through consent,
and emergence into history. If the first stage is preparation
and the third is result, the second is the crucial act of turning,
and it is there that the god is most felt.

The myth ends with Cyrene's glorious state in Africa and
with the birth of her son Aristaeus, the god of bees in the
Georgics, here a guardian of men and flocks. If there was
something of Artemis in Cyrene as a girl, there is now something of Hera in her golden serenity as mother and queen.
The affinity with nature which ran through her girlhood is
perpetuated in her child, who is reared by Earth and the
Seasons. With the possible exception of *O.* 14, there is no
more optimistic vision in the odes than this of the god's transforming beneficence to the mother and child and toward the
happy future over which they preside. At this point Pindar
breaks off, returning to the victor and the present, and the
connection now appears between the myth and his verse.
"Great virtues are always many-storied. To weave brief
tales in the long is hearing for the wise, and the crowning
moment contains the summit of all. Iolaus did not dishonor
it in his time, as seven-gated Thebes beheld. Whom, when
he had wasted Eurystheus' head with his sword's edge, they
buried beneath the earth in Amphitryon's grave, his father's
father, where he lay the Sown-men's guest, having dwelt
among the Cadmeans' white-horsed streets. Alcmena wise,
united with him and Zeus, bore in one birth two mighty sons
supreme in war. Dull is the man who swathes not Heracles
with his speech or fails to celebrate ever the streams of

Dirce, that reared him and Iphicles. I'll sing to them in
payment of a vow and for kindness had. O may the clear-
voiced Charites' clean light never forsake me. Thrice at
Aegina and by Nisus' hill I swear I glorified this city, shunning by act the helplessness of silence. Wherefore, though
a citizen be friend or foe, let him not hide a deed well done
for the common cause, nor spoil the old man of the sea's advice. He bade us praise with all our heart and justice full
even an enemy who does noble acts." (vv. 76-96)

   As in *N*. 7 and 4, the train of thought moves complexly
through figures of heroes, and one sees once more a mind
which apprehends its main realities through such shapes.
Again as in *N*. 4, the transition contains a curbing statement
which draws him from his other realm to the present. Acts
of heroic virtue beget a mass of stories but "to weave brief
tales in the long is hearing for the wise." He had told
Theron in *O*. 2 two years earlier that the arrows of his verse
speak to those who understand but for the mass need interpreters, and this remark is similar. He will adorn only a
small part of a potentially far greater area, but the discrimi-
nating will understand the whole through the part. He goes
on to state his principle of choice, and it is this that both gives
rise to the rest of the complex passage and makes connection
with the myth. "The crowning moment contains the summit
of all." The crucial word, here rendered by 'crowning
moment,' is *kairos,* which means both a point of time offered,
so to speak, from without and an inward readiness to grasp
and act on it. It marks the collision between circumstance
and the perceiving mind, hence tests and reveals the mind.
The odes, he therefore says, contain incidents which are at
the heart of an event, and it is the import of these that men
of understanding perceive. Life is evidently seen as offering
brief but intense clarifications which momentarily reveal the
character of darker adjacent times. The description may be
valid of lyric as contrasted to other kinds of poetry; it well

expresses at least the difference between the single moments through which Pindar sees reality and the trains of conflict and evolution which absorb Aeschylus.

Having marked the importance of the decisive moment, he characteristically sees it in legend. Iolaus, the great Theban hero and son of Heracles' mortal brother Iphicles, had seized such a moment. He was famous, among other reasons, for having protected Heracles' children after the latter's death and for supporting Athens, where they had taken refuge, against attack by Eurystheus, the event which is the subject of Euripides' *Heracleidae*. But instead of mentioning Athens openly, as he evidently hesitates to do, he is led by thoughts of Iphicles and Heracles to statements of devotion to his native city. It was in Thebes that Amphitryon had lived and Alcmena had borne two great sons to him and Zeus. The train of thought recalls the opening of *I*. 7, lines intended to solace the still darker period of Theban history after the defeat of Oenophyta: "In what past local glory, o blessed Thebes, did your heart most take joy? When you brought to the light flowing-haired Dionysus to share the throne of Demeter to whom cymbals clash? Or at Heracles' begetting when you greeted the highest god at midnight snowing gold, as he stood at the door seeking Amphitryon's wife? Or in Teiresias' counsels wise or the shrewd horseman Iolaus?" (vv. 1-9) He best understands the city through these figures that contain the secret of its greatness. Thus he cries out that no man is so dull as to forget Heracles or the springs of Dirce, but that he will sing to him in gratitude for prayer answered. The words could perhaps mean some recent benefit but more naturally express continuing and repeated dependence. This sense of dependence then wells out in the prayer that the light of the Muses may never leave him. The whole complex train of thought, involving the crucial moment, the seizing of it by heroes, and the divine inspiration that guided them, culminates in this prayer for his

own inspiration. It seeks the same kind of self-transcendence
that was in the story of Cyrene, and, as there, the crucial
moment, the *kairos,* implies a double act of mortal readiness
and divine help. When he now at last protests that he had
not concealed his patriotism in recent odes in neighboring
cities, he prepares his defense for having praised Athens.
Even an enemy's noble acts must be acknowledged, and like
Iolaus, he had supported the hostile city because she had been
in the right. The ode closes with the victor's triumphs in
Athens, when women and girls admired his beauty, and with
the amiable story of how an ancestor had won his bride in a
foot-race in the handy manner in which Danaus' forty-eight
daughters had legendarily been won, all in a morning.
Echoes of the original theme die away even here. The victor and his ancestor had their decisive moments, which for
them too were crowned by gayety and success. The erotic
coloring expresses the emergence into full and happy actuality of which Cyrene was the prototype. As for Pindar, his
decisive moment is the light which the Graces bring, and his
readiness for it has its model in Iolaus and Heracles, whose
courage was notably crowned by divine help.

　　Olympian 6. Gay and touching as this poem is, it is
hard not to see a deeper statement of the same theme in *O.* 6,
the superb ode of 472 or 468 for Agesias of Syracuse, a lieutenant of Hieron and member of the Iamid clan which held
hereditary rights of priesthood and prophecy at the altar of
Zeus at Olympia. A scholiast of unknown reliability says
that he lost his life in the revolution following Hieron's death
late in 468,[65] and dark tones in the ode may argue for this
date as against that of four years earlier. Agesias was connected through his mother with the Arcadian town of Stymphalus, and the ode was to be sung there as well as at Syracuse, "from home to home." The contrast of *P.* 9 between
silence and speech, early shadow and emergent light, is even
more present here, and the exquisite passages on the birth of

the child Iamus in the still wilderness have a sense of surrounding and enfolding nature suggestive of Chinese landscape painting. Behind the populous and brilliant Olympia
of the present and behind Agesias' renown there and at Syracuse lie the quiet places of the family's first beginnings, and
its prophetic gifts reflect this tie with Earth. No ode expresses more delicately the mystery of emergence and attainment or holds so subtle a balance between the brightness of
life and its still origins.

Unlike *P.* 9, the ode begins with this brightness, and danger, of the present. The first triad describes the present, the
next two retrace the mysterious past, and the last two return.
"As lifting pillars of gold by a house's fair-walled door, we'll
build a dazzling hall. Far-seen the frontage of a rising work
must stand. If he be Olympic victor and guard of Zeus's
mantic hearth at Pisa and fellow-founder of great Syracuse,
what hymn shall that man flee as he encounters grudgeless
citizens in enchanting songs? The son of Sostratus shall
know that in this dance he treads a step inspired. Danger-
less virtues with men or hollow ships gain no respect. Many
remember something beautiful done." (vv. 1-11) The
famous golden columns of the start state Pindar's principle
(inherited from oral poetry and connected with the circular
style) of beginning brilliantly, but they serve the further purpose of presenting at once the crowded and flashing present.
When he turns to the past in the second triad, he bids
Agesias' charioteer drive out from Olympia through imagi-
nary gates of verse to the family's place of origin by the
Eurotas in Lacedaemon, and these gates lead from shining
buildings, which are the world of today, to the woodland
which is the world of yesterday. Danger and envy are felt
to surround Agesias as they surround Hieron in *P.* 1. Yet a
god's favor is in the fortune of this celebration, and Pindar
compares the victor to Amphiaraus, the exemplar of prophet

and warrior combined.   Then as the chariot leaves Olympia,
the poem enters a remoter world.

The nymph Pitana, the eponymous ancestress of the town
in Lacedaemon, bore a daughter Evadne to the god Poseidon
but in fear of her union sent the dark-haired baby to one
Aepytus in Arcadia to be brought up.   She in time was loved
by Apollo.   "She did not keep through all her time from
Aepytus the offspring of the god, but he went to Pytho pressing with sharp pain in his heart unspoken wrath, to consult
on this intolerable misfortune.   But laying down her purple
and saffron zone and silver pitcher in the dark blue thicket,
she bore a god-hearted boy, and the golden-haired one
brought to her merciful Eleithyia and the Fates.   Issued then
from her womb with happy travail Iamus to the light, but in
distress she left him on the ground.   Two grey-eyed snakes
through the designs of heaven gave him food, with the bees'
blameless venom ministering to him.   When from rocky
Pytho the king came driving, he asked all in the house of the
boy whom Evadne bore, and said he sprang from Phoebus as
his father, to surpass mankind as mortals' great diviner, and
his line would never fail.   So he disclosed, but they swore
neither to have heard nor seen the baby four days born.   He
lay hidden in the rushes, the limitless wilderness, his tender
body steeped with the rays of violets, yellow and purple.
And this his mother took as sign of his immortal name for
time entire." (vv. 36-57)   Pindar derives the name Iamus
from ἴον, the violet. A century later Plato could still debate
in the *Cratylus* whether words spring from and reflect the
nature of an object or are merely conventional, and Homer
and the tragedians as well as Pindar feel ties between a man's
name and his fate.   In this passage he even finds a second
significance in the bees' blameless venom, ἰός, the honey with
which the two snakes feed the baby. These more than
verbal plays merge with the coloring of the scene as methods
of conveying its meaning.   Evadne's and Aepytus' distress,

though milder than Io's in the *Prometheus,* resembles it in
signifying the disturbance made by the gods' acts in mortal
events, and the first impression is of Evadne's helplessness.
Yet she has pride and courage also; the purple and yellow
zone and silver pitcher in the dark blue thicket express her
identity as a human being against the unknown background
of nature, the light contrasting with the dark, the man-made
thing with growing things.   But nature presently appears not
wholly dark.   In bringing the birth-goddesses to Evadne the
golden-haired god irradiates the wilderness, and the grey-
eyed snakes, traditional bearers of secret knowledge, show
kindness from within the earth, matching Apollo's from beyond it.   The feeling resembles that of *N.* 6 where the divine
is felt both in the fallow and sleep of the earth and in its
blossoming.   But by far the chief characteristic of the passage is the persistent contrast between dark and bright: the
purple and the yellow of Evadne's dress, the dark thicket and
the silver pitcher, the woodland and the golden-haired god,
the snakes and the honey, the rays of the purple and yellow
violets shining on the baby.   All these contrasts culminate in
the last, which gives Iamus his name and hence describes
him.   He is the child of two worlds, earth and sky, fully reflecting his parentage.   But, as in *N.* 6, the gods, though
distinct from earth, are not wholly removed from it, and remote as Evadne is from Apollo, he does not come to her as
quite alien.   Mysterious ties exist between them, and the union between the mortal and the god suggests the fire in *O.* 1
that blazes in the night or the fruit-trees in *N.* 11 that bloom
from the black earth.   The earth has its claim on the sky,
and Iamus as resolution of the opposites contains the divine
element in human things.

When Iamus grows up he wants, like Pelops, to fulfill his
destiny.   "Descending to the middle reaches of the Alpheus,
he called the mighty god Poseidon, his forebear, and the
archer watchman of god-founded Delos, asking for his life

the honor of rearing a people, under the sky by night. And
in clear speech his father's voice rang back, answering him,
'Arise, my son, and come this way to a joint land of peoples,
following my voice.' And they reached the sun-trod cliff of
high Kronion, where he gave him a double right of divination." (vv. 57-66) The poem has returned to Olympia
from which Pindar had bidden Agesias' charioteer drive out.
As he goes on to sketch Heracles' founding of the festival,
it has also returned to the known scenes of history, and the
lonely night of Iamus' prayer has yielded to the populous
daylight of his and his descendants' celebrity. The birth of
the baby potentially contained the change, which is now
merely worked out. The transformation again involves three
stages like those in the story of Cyrene. The individual and
society stand at the two extremes, and the god in the center.
In their silent isolation Evadne and Iamus were exposed to
danger and doubt, yet supported by courage and conscious of
subtle bonds with nature. Olympia, as a known and existent
institution, both validates their struggles and itself draws
meaning from them. Apollo inspires and assists the act
which reaches out toward history and, in so doing, imparts
to history a significance from outside it. There is less in this
poem than in *P.* 9 that bears expressly (however much may
bear indirectly) on Pindar's sense of poetry. He concludes
by bidding the chorus-leader carry the ode to Stymphalus, to
which he feels ties through the river Metope, mother of
Thebe, "whose waters fair I drink weaving my many-colored
song for warriors. Bid your companions now, Aeneas, first
sing Hera Parthenia, then make known whether in candor
we escape the ancient jibe, Boeotian swine." (vv. 85-90)
The jibe, which contains the rancor of the present, is singu-
larly out of tune with the waters of Dirce and the legendary
past. It has been observed that Pindar with the years increasingly used contemporary turns of speech[66] — which may
be to say, felt more sharply the gulf between the actual and

the ideal. In any case, he is content that, if Boeotia generally evokes fat and torpid comfort, he expresses his country's true character. If the poem is contemporary with the last ode to Hieron, there is no sign of the bitterness of *P*. 2. He speaks handsomely of the tyrant and wishes Agesias the quiet peace of soul that he wished Chromius in *N*. 9. "Two anchors are well put down from a swift ship on a stormy night." (vv. 100-101) Agesias' two anchors are Stymphalus and Syracuse, and Pindar prays Poseidon to protect both. Iamus too had prayed to Poseidon at night, and though these last words hardly evoke the enchanting beneficence revealed in Iamus, they at least recall his courage. It is interesting that the end of neither of these two poems fully confirms the beginning. As repeatedly said, Pindar's metaphors are always incomplete: the present world has its analogy to the heroic world but he hesitates to press it. Yet the exquisite myth of this poem, and to a less extent of *P*. 9, seems to stand at unusual distance from the present, as if he subconsciously doubted his conscious faith that society fully validates and answers the individual's inner search. A world where Boeotians are called swine is far from that where the child Iamus lay among flowers. This is only to repeat what we have also seen, that Pindar's imagination persistently outflew the occasion at hand, substituting visionary for known reality.

Though *P*. 9 and *O*. 6 stand apart in their treatment of love, several other odes state the theme of attainment in very similar terms. We shall consider these more briefly, reserving two odes, *N*. 1 and *N*. 10, for fuller comment at the end. Emergence and attainment involved three elements, and these poems differ among themselves chiefly as they emphasize the hero's resolution, his merging with history, or the divine impulse which guided him.

Olympian 3. In *O*. 3 and *O*. 10, both of which poems describe the founding of the Olympic games, the heroic act has largely passed into an historic institution. In the former, the public ode for Theron preceding the private and consolatory *O*. 2, Heracles is described as first establishing the games, then as bringing the olive tree from the land of the Hyperboreans to Olympia for shade and crowns. "Already at the hallowing of his father's altars the month-dividing moon lit her full eye before him in the golden-charioted evening, and he fixed the great games' sacred trial and the fifth-yearly festival by Alpheus' holy cliffs. But the land by Kronian Pelops' dells offered no pleasant trees, and naked of them the sacred place seemed servant to the sun's fierce rays." (vv. 19-24) It was noted earlier that the opening figures of *O*. 1, water, gold, and the sun, recur in this poem, but without the last. "If water is best and of possessions gold is most revered, Theron from home now journeying to the bourne touches the pillars of Heracles." (vv. 42-44) We have seen that water carries the softness of poetry and gold the flash of heroism. The intolerable radiance of the mid-day sun was the sign in *O*. 1 of Zeus's dazzling power, and it is precisely from this harsh light that Heracles would protect Olympia by planting olives. As an earthly institution the games are shielded from the glare of full divinity. Heracles' two acts, the gentle act of creating shade and crowns and the stern act of instituting games, correspond to the water and gold of the final lines, and the scene of the first celebration in the summer moonlight expresses this tempered legacy.

Olympian 10. *O*. 10, composed soon after for a boy victor from Western Locri, paints the same scene. "The lovely light of the fair-visaged moon kindled the evening, as the whole space rang with songs of joyous festivals in the mode of victors' hymns. True to which first beginnings even now, in namesake honor of proud victory, we'll sing the thunder and fire-handed bolt of Zeus, the thunder's wakener." (vv. 73-81) The myth describes Heracles' establishment of the traditional contests, the first victors in which Pindar enumerates. The event is to be imagined as just preceding the planting of the olives described in *O. 3*. A sense of time and continuity runs through the poem. When Heracles founded the contests, "the Fates stood close beside the first-born rite, and Time the sole vindicator of clear truth." (vv. 52-55) He also named the hill of Kronos above the precinct, "which formerly, while Oenomaus ruled, was drenched nameless with many snows." (vv. 50-51) As the woodland of *O. 6* evoked the dim past from which Iamus emerged into history, so the snow on the nameless hill stands for the unknown ages before Heracles came, since when Time and the Fates have perpetuated his act. Similarly Pindar, who feels himself late in sending the poem, in time vindicates himself. "The waited time from far approaching shamed my heavy debt. Yet usury can redeem the sharp reproach. Observe then how the flowing stream will wash the rolling stone along and how we'll pay the joint account for friendship's sake." (vv. 7-12) Poetry is a stream, as it was the rain in the short companion poem *O. 11*, and it washes away the pebble of indebtedness in a way honorable to Pindar and fitting to the city which he calls the home of honor. At the end, still thinking of time, he compares his poem to a late-born child who perpetuates his father's name. In all these cases there is memory and continuation. To be sure, the lines on Zeus's thunderbolt express a blazing power that nullifies institutions, but through Heracles something of Zeus is adapted to the world. In this poem also the scene of celebration in the moonlight conveys a shaded effulgence which, unlike the sunlight of *O. 1*, expresses not so much transcendence of history as continuity within it.

Olympian 9. *O. 9* and *O. 13* see a like continuity in the victor's city but with more emphasis on the divine impulse which gave it rise. The former, an elaborate poem of the 460's for a victor from Opuntian Locri, carries in its vivid rhythms Pindar's warmth toward the city which he calls the

home of Themis and her saving daughter Eunomia (the
Athenians dissolved the Locrian aristocracy after Oenophyta
in 457)[67] and his friendship for the victor and a kinsman
whose joint crowning he once attended at the Isthmus. It
is among the lucidest of the odes, constating an inspiration in
poet and athlete which perpetuates the heroic acts of the
Locrian past. "Lighting this beloved state with passionate
songs, faster than mettled horse or winged ship I'll send my
message, if with a power bestowed by fate I keep a garden
of the Muses set apart. It is they who give delight, and
through divinity men become brave or wise." (vv. 21-29)
This sense that one must wait on a divine power draws him,
exactly in the manner of *P*. 9, to the example of Heracles,
and he asks how the great hero could have fought with gods,
as some myths held. "O lips, reject this statement. To
vilify gods is bitter wisdom, and senseless boast is folly's
obbligato. Babble not such. Leave war and every strife
remote from the immortals." (vv. 35-41) Dependence on
the gods is for good only, and echoes of the divine peace of
P. 1 and *O*. 14 are in these lines. But the emphasis is different; he is not now principally saying that the gods are
harmony and order, but that all mortal achievement comes
from them and must be in their serene image. The myth describes how Locri was repeopled after the flood by Deuca-
lion and Pyrrha with stones that became men, and how Zeus
later begat and brought Opus there, as Iamus was begotten
and brought to Olympia by Apollo. It was from Locri that
Patroclus went to Troy to gain his great name and Achilles'
friendship. In all these ancient events the hand of the gods
is visible and it is still the only guiding force. "Best is all
that comes by nature," he says at the end, "though many
with rote-learned virtues rush to grasp fame. Acts without
god are not the worse for silence. There are roads which
reach farther than other roads and one preoccupation will
not nourish us all. Wisdoms are steep." (vv. 100-107) The

contrast between native and merely studied virtues goes back
to *O.* 2 and resembles the statement of confidence in his own
art in *N.* 4. He recognizes different paths to virtue but sees
in all of them, if they are in fact such paths, a continuing divine influence like that which was in the planting of the city.

Olympian 13. *O.* 13, by contrast, states its similar view
by one of those brief clarifying incidents of which it was said
in *P.* 9, "the crowning moment contains the summit of all."
Of the same date, 464, as *O.* 7 to Diagoras of Rhodes, it resembles it in virtuosity and tone of worldly splendor, as well
as in celebrating a man almost Diagoras' equal, Xenophon of
Corinth, twice victor at Olympia in that year and winner of
innumerable prizes. Pindar wrote for him presumably at
this time what is surely the most astounding of the poems, a
skolion preserved in fragments to accompany Xenophon's
dedication of fifty hetairai at the temple of Aphrodite on the
Acrocorinth (fg. 107). It addresses them as "hospitable
girls, handmaidens of Persuasion," pleasantly adding, "with
necessity all is fair." The third strophe slightly apologizes
for the poem, which in fact puts rather nicely the question
at what point an heroic style like his degenerates into ornament and from there into absurdity. The risk of overstatement of course haunts all the odes and has been noted of
some, chiefly of *O.* 7 and the long *P.* 4 to Arkesilas, of this
same bland period. Perhaps it is not so much this period of
his success which tricked him into slight vacuity, as his incapacity to feel any longer the excitement in famous and
strange patrons that he felt toward Hieron and Theron.
Poems for familiar cities, like the nearly contemporary *O.* 9
which we have just considered, speak with his authentic
tones. But it is one of the most impressive things about Pindar that just when he begins to cloy and the suspicion enters
that the glitter is not gold, it becomes gold. So in the present poem. He first sees in Corinth an old and rich civilization. "Many an ancient art the flowered Hours have

prompted in your citizens' hearts. To the inventor the whole work belongs. Whence came Dionysus' rites of the ox-driven dithyramb? Who to the harness set the checking bridle, or the twin king of birds on the temples of gods? Blossoms there the sweet-breathing Muse, there Ares in the young men's deadly spears." (vv. 16-23) Herodotus notes the development of the dithyramb in Corinth, and Thucydides describes the city's naval, if not her military, prominence in early times.[68] The Corinthian origin of the pediment seems less clear. After rehearsing a long list of Xenophon's triumphs, he turns to Corinth's legendary heroes, Sisyphus, Medea, Glaucus, and Bellerophon, and with the last the poem suddenly comes to life: "who craving to catch Pegasus, the snake-formed Gorgon's foal, by fountains labored until the maiden Pallas brought him a golden-fronted bridle. At once from dream was waking truth, and she spoke to him, 'Sleep you, Aeolid king? Come take this horse-charm and with sacrifice of a white bull show it to your sire, the Tamer.' With darkling aegis in the shadow the Maiden as he slept seemed to speak so, and he leapt on his feet erect and grasped the marvelous thing that lay beside him." (vv. 63-72) He consults the prophet, duly sacrifices to Poseidon, and builds an altar to Athene Hippias. "The power of the gods easily gives the attainment which lay beyond oath or hope. Bellerophon reached out and held the winged horse, slipping the soft enchantment on his cheek." (vv. 83-85) He mounts in the cold air and fights the Amazons and the Chimaera, but Pindar stops short of his fall when he attempted Olympus, saying only that Pegasus remains in Zeus's ancient stables. Familiar themes return in this fine passage: the dark night of the hero's uncertainty, the presence of the transforming goddess, the ensuing daylight and open sky, and the import of all this for history. Even the wealth and arts of Corinth, like those of Rhodes, reveal the gods' acts, and though the poem is oppressed by a mortal weight of affluence and success,

Pindar himself recovers Bellerophon's route to a clearer air.

Finally, two admirable poems, *N*. 1 and *N*. 10, state the theme of heroic attainment at its fullest. They can serve as companion pieces to the poems on love with which we began. As recipients of the god, Cyrene and Evadne were not colorless; they had their own grace and courage, and there was a bond with earth in the darkness against which they are seen. Yet the transforming god was the chief figure and, though the heroines in some sense deserve him, it is he who irradiates their lives. In the present poems, by contrast, the hero's own responsibility is at the center, not as divorced from the divine will, much less as in conflict with it, but as somehow standing in its own right, stubborn and masculine. Such heroic responsibility is the companion element to divine grace in the theme of attainment. If the gods come, they do so at times of their, not our, choosing, and meanwhile a man is alone with his courage. Pindar inclines to see the brilliant moment of inspiration and fulfillment, as the tragedians, especially Sophocles, incline to see the dark anterior process of uncertain act. Even Pindar of course repeatedly shows awareness of the earlier period: in the theme of vicissitude, in the reverses of the family in *I*. 4, in Hieron's illness, in the successively tested lives in *O*. 2, in the deaths of Ajax, Hector, and Amphiaraus, in the night-searches of Pelops, Iamus, and Bellerophon, in the doctrine of toil preceding victory. "Unproven of war would he be shown who fails to grasp my words. For the doer is likeliest to suffer also." (*N*. 4.30-32) The present poems differ from most others in placing at the center what is usually at the side, and in *N*. 10 Pindar is closest to Sophocles. Can one feel with equal force the transforming beauty and goodness of nature or the mind and the dark uncertainty of effort? Pindar on the whole could not. Yet the states are complementary, and he would be less than he is if he were not aware of struggle almost to the degree that he wants to see attainment.

Nemean 1. *N.* 1, composed during the visit to Sicily for Chromius, Hieron's brother-in-law and vice-regent at Aetna, precedes the more festal *N.* 9 which was considered among the poems on harmony. The joyful quiet even of that poem stood against the background of impending war, and the present ode shows this fighting man in the tide of his career. Heracles is the central figure. If he sometimes rises to Pindar's mind from thoughts of patriotism or as a more general figure for divinely given strength, he is fully himself here, showing even in infancy the tough will to survival which made him the support of men in hardship and danger and which or something like which Pindar felt in Chromius. "Beginnings from gods are my foundation for this man's heaven-implanted strengths." (vv. 8-9) The foundation is both that of the poem seen architecturally and of the mighty cities and warlike peoples of Sicily, which are the subject of the first triad. The odes to Hieron and Theron drew Pindar into the special atmosphere of their station as tyrants; he is free from such attraction here and able to see the power of Sicily for itself. "Chanting my fair song I stood at the court-door of this hospitable man, where a fit banquet waits adorned and the hall lacks no experience of guests from far. To him have fallen noble friends, bearers of water against the revilers' smoke. Arts differ, but in straight paths walking a man must fight by his inborn gifts. Strength performs in the deed, thought in the plans of them whose native power foresees the future." (vv. 19-28) The arrangement of the figures at the banquet corresponds to that in the coming myth. Chromius, the man of inborn courage, walks the straight path and fulfills himself in act. The next lines praise further his large hospitality and the wealth which he shares with others; "for common go the hopes of laboring mortals." (vv. 32-33) All men, that is, want to fight clear of troubles, and Chromius' generosity has something of Heracles' cheerful and supporting massiveness.

Pindar, by contrast, though he too walks the straight path and has this bond with Chromius, is less the man of act than of foresight. The description of foresight recalls the lines in the nearly contemporary *O.* 1 to Hieron on the poet's function as detector of the hidden, and the water which Chromius' friends bring against the revilers' smoke suggests the water of poetry in the other poem. As for the revilers, they look forward to the snakes in the myth.

"With my whole heart I hold by Heracles for virtues' mighty heights as I tell an old account, how when from his mother's womb to radiant day the son of Zeus came with his twin from travail, not unobserved by gold-throned Hera lay he in saffron swaddling clothes. Quickly the queen of the gods in anger sent two snakes, which at the open gate passing into the wide back room would have coiled around the babies their darting jaws. Then he raised his head erect and first met battle, seizing the snakes by the necks with his matchless hands, and the noose that throttled them breathed the life from their horrid shapes. Speechless fear dumbfounded the women, present to comfort Alcmena's child-bed, and she, as she was, from bed and robeless sprang on her feet to meet the violent brutes. Soon came the Cadmean princes crowding in with weapons bronze, and Amphitryon pierced with sudden pain, swinging his naked sword. One's own presses each alike, but at other's loss the heart is soon untroubled. He stood suffused with wonder painful and glad. For he saw in his son courage and strength beyond our breed, and the immortals had reversed the messengers' tidings." (vv. 33-59) Amphitryon consults the prophet Teiresias who foresees and relates Heracles' destiny: "how many fortunes he would meet, how many lawless beasts he would kill on land and sea." (vv. 61-63) He describes his destroying some great malefactor, Cycnus or Antaeus, and his support of the gods against the giants at Phlegrae. The poem ends with predictions of immortality: "And he in peace continuous for all time, as his great labors' high reward having won serenity in blessed halls, possessing flowery Hebe as his bride and feasted in marriage beside Kronian Zeus, will laud that lofty realm." (vv. 69-72)

As narrative the passage moves fast to its revelation. The better critics have noted that Pindar paradoxically does not use his highly colored style to tell a story for itself.[69] Details are omitted here, for example how the message mentioned at the end reaches Amphitryon, and the minor figures are turned sharply toward the central figure. Thus Alcmena's anguish as she leaps from bed toward the children catches the miraculous character of the event, and Amphitryon's stupefaction prepares for the prophecy to come. It is incorrect to conceive of Pindar as using his skill in a humanistic spirit for verisimilitude, even heroic verisimilitude. The high colors are for the bright light of divinity. It is true, as just said, that a reciprocity exists between the stamina and courage of human nature and its divine irradiation, and that the former element is stronger here than in most odes. Yet the picture of Heracles as an infant rests this element of human excellence quite simply in noble instinct, something deeper than the conscious or the planned, and at their root. In this deep realm of native response to life is a man's *phua,* his nature, Pindar's criterion. It is revealed in many forms, and as there is something of Heracles in Chromius, so there is something of the observer Amphitryon and the prophet Teiresias in Pindar. Insofar as a man's *phua* is indeed his own and shows itself in wise or brave acts, it is a mark of human virtue. But as such traits are seen to contain elements of absolute worth, they both causally and, so to speak, existentially reveal the gods, who are the origin and being of excellence.

Nemean 10. The Sophoclean *N.* 10 states still more powerfully this element of native and human virtue. Probably of the middle 460's and the one extant poem for an

Argive, it also rises to a myth which, occupying the end without comment by Pindar, contains his vision of the victor and the occasion. The position of the myths at the end of these two poems illustrates more clearly than before his double means of seeing an occasion, what one could call the explicit and the implicit means. By explicit is meant all his express comments on inspiration or native gifts, all connections with cult, all mythological links with the past or with personifications: in short, all the schematic lines by which he fixes the present in his greater design. The implicit means, which is the myth, is by contrast an in-living into some part of this scheme; it needs no comment, constating existence rather than relationship. It contains the very actuality of the state of virtue to which the explicit means lead up or make allusion. This difference is well exemplified in the present poem which begins, like the opening of *I.* 7 quoted earlier, with a kind of catalogue of myths. Should he praise Argos, Hera's city, because of Perseus or because of its connection with Egypt through Io and Epaphus or for Hypermnestra, Diomedes, Amphiaraus, Adrastus or Lynceus, or for its women visited by Zeus, Danae, and Alcmena? Any of these events could conceivably have become the myth. As it is, they serve in the poem to set the city and the occasion in a certain light; they do not convey virtue, felt as something lived, but are so far only a link with it. "Weak are my lips to tell how great a share of virtues the sacred grove of Argos holds." (vv. 19-20) He sees the whole city as comprising a precinct of Hera, and the catalogue of myths creates this wider light. The victor, a Tirynthian who had moved to Argos (because, Farnell perceived, both Tiryns and Mycenae were abandoned in these years)[70] hopes for an Olympic victory to crown his minor triumphs. "Zeus father, his lips are dumb of what he yearns in heart. In thee is action's every end. He asks this grace offering courage and a spirit trained in toil." (vv. 29-30) In the nearly contemporary *O.* 8 of 460

Zeus is invoked as answering men's piety, and the unrivaled
N. 8, to which we shall turn in the last section, sees human
excellence as lodged in nature, sharing its divine life. The
present ode expresses a like assurance. An epiphany of the
Dioscuri, Castor and Polydeuces, Pindar goes on, once took
place to an ancestor of the victor, and he feels it natural that
their athletic prowess descend in the breed. Such appear-
ances by heroes are occasionally mentioned, and in *P.* 8 Pindar says that on his way to Delphi he himself once met the
hero Alcmaeon, whose shrine stood near his house in
Thebes. A sense of this mystical penetration of nature by
the divine now opens before him, and in the last line before
the myth he rises to the affirmation, "In truth the progeny of
the gods is loyal." (v. 54) It recalls the similar affirmation
of *I.* 3, "Unwounded yet remain the sons of gods," but is
more interior, less expressive of triumph than of inner support. The cheerful sense in *N.* 1 of the capacious vigor of
the infant Heracles has become faith in the Dioscuri's guiding nearness. Zeus laments in the *Iliad* that he must aban-
don Hector and Sarpedon to death, men who had shown
most honor to him, and he seeks amends by giving Hector
glory and bidding Sleep and Death bear Sarpedon home to
Lycia.[71] Homer's sense of tragic necessity is only partly
solaced by glory, Sophocles' slightly more so in the burial of
Ajax and the vindication of Antigone. Pindar's vision too
can go beyond death; the Muses sang at Achilles' pyre. But
with him, except in the dark *P.* 8 and *N.* 11, assurance tends
to outweigh tragedy, and the myth in this poem echoes his
statement of a divine constancy.

Castor and Polydeuces resembled the twins Iphicles and
Heracles in being, the one mortal, the other immortal. In
the lost *Cypria*[72] and the fragmentary first poem of Alcman
the story was told of their fight with two primeval enemies
in Lacedaemon, Idas and Lynceus, the latter so sharp-sighted
that he could look through trees and stones. From the top

of Taygetus he here sees the Dioscuri seated in a hollow oak,
and he and Idas presently catching the mortal Castor alone
give him a death-blow. Polydeuces, who comes to his help,
is struck by a great grave-stone, but he pierces Lynceus and
Zeus hurls his thunder at Idas. "They were burned together in that lonely place. Hard warfare for mortals is it
to meet the mightier ones." (v. 72) Polydeuces now sees
Castor dying. "The Tyndarid turned quickly back to his
mighty brother and found him not yet dead, racking his
breath in gasps. Groaning and with hot tears he cried,
'Kronian Father, where will be an end of mourning? Bring
me to death, O king, with him. Honor forsakes the man
deprived of friends, and few the comrades in our need that
shoulder weariness.' So spoke he and Zeus came to him face
to face, replying 'You are my son. This man his hero sire to
your mother later got as mortal seed. I give you nevertheless this choice. If clear of death and hated age you choose
to hold Olympus by me with Athene and black-speared Ares,
that is your lot. But if you defend your brother and would
share in all identically with him, half then breathe your life
beneath the earth, half in the golden domiciles of the sky.'
To these words the hero's heart gave no slow verdict, but he
waked the eye and then the voice of bronze-belted Castor."
(vv. 73-90)

The exact detail of the story — the brothers seated in
the hollow oak, the grave-stone which Lynceus seizes in his
last battle — fits its tone of urgency. The choice which Zeus
offers Polydeuces contains the forbidding side of the gods.
Their timeless realm is open only to themselves and their
offspring, and Polydeuces' love for his brother conflicts as a
tie to earth with that untroubled state. The austerity of the
brazen sky of *P.* 10 and *N.* 6 and of Zeus's dazzling midday
in *O.* 1 is in these lines. Yet Zeus's offer, though carrying a
price, expresses another side of the gods, which is their ac-
cessibility. So in *N.* 1 and *I.* 4 Heracles attains Olympus,

and in *O*. 2 Thetis wins Zeus's consent to bring Achilles to
the island of the blest, where Cadmus and Peleus also are.
This duality is at the heart of these poems on attainment.
The women Cyrene and Evadne with whom we began are
figures deeply identified with the earth; more clearly than
Heracles in *N*. 1, Polydeuces here honors this tie, even in the
act of releasing Castor from the earth's full control. Except
in the great opening of *N*. 6, "yet we are a little like the
immortals in great mind or form," it is not said how this
duality, ambiguous even in demigods, applies to men. The
chain of connection in the odes which leads from men to
heroes to gods is in effect the only answer. Pindar's concern
for the moment, moreover, places the question less in the
future than in the present. So considered, Cyrene and
Evadne become not so much our bond with earth as the silence and waiting of the spirit which are transformed through
some willingly accepted power into speech and act, and Polydeuces' love for Castor becomes the heroic will which both
accepts and transforms reality. The gods are in the present
as well as beyond it, and the odes express a like duality, of
the particular seen as containing more than itself.

iv Essence

This final section will attempt three related subjects: the
late poems, the appeals to gods and semi-abstract presences
which are notable in these poems, though not confined to
them, and some fragments of the religious poetry. *P*. 8 of
446 has only a brief heroic episode, *N*. 11 has none, and
though the other late poems are in his usual manner, it is
hard not to feel that at this date heroic stories were too full
of the hot breath of life any longer to catch his mood entirely. But questions of date are secondary. We have repeatedly seen a side of his mind which sought to pass not
merely from the present into legend but from legend into

the bright and static sphere of being itself. The Graces of
O. 14, the lyre and drowsing eagle of P. 1, the marriage of
Peleus and Cadmus to goddesses in N. 5, P. 3, and N. 4,
Heracles' attainment of Olympus in I. 4 and N. 1, all verge
toward this final realm. If more of the religious poetry had
come down to us we should better understand this side of his
mind. The twelfth-century commentator Eustathius contrasts the Odes to the religious poetry as "closer to man, of
short myths, and not largely obscure, by comparison at least
with the rest."[73] He seems to be repeating ancient opinion,
since he knew no more than we of the lost thirteen books,
less in fact, since he lacked our papyrus fragments. But the
statement is likely enough. When unchecked by duties to
specific patrons Pindar could have drifted much farther into
the more-than-worldly regions which he enters gladly and
leaves reluctantly even in the odes. The distinction made
earlier between myth, legend, and folk tale is relevant here.
Most heroic incidents of the odes partake of myth and folk
tale but, as involved in local history and speaking the glory
of the past, are in basis legendary. Hence the so-called
myths of the odes are, strictly speaking, not largely myths.
Pindar did not of course make these distinctions, and the
whole region of story was to him the region of truth, where
history, nature, theology, and the human mind stood indivis-
ibly revealed. Yet at times he would pass farther out of
history than at other times, and Eustathius' comment suggests that he did so especially in the religious poems. It is
with these final and, in the strict sense, mythic apperceptions
that this last section will chiefly deal. We shall begin with a
few fragments of the religious poems in order to catch what
Eustathius states, their removal from the relatively tangible
world of the odes; then return via like passages in the odes
to the poems of the last period.

   O. 14 and P. 1 concerned the Olympian harmony which
is echoed in nature, music, and serenity of mind. A frag-

ment of a hymn on the marriage of Zeus and Themis states
this order more mythologically. "On golden horses from
the springs of Ocean the Fates in the beginning brought
heavenly counseling Themis by a radiant road to Olympus'
august stairs to be the primal wife of saving Zeus. She bore
the unfailing Hours, golden-veiled, bright of fruit." (fg.
10) The Horae are Eunomia, Dike, and Eirene — Order,
Justice, Peace. As natural forces, they are the Seasons; as
social forces, they are a prospering order in human life
analogous to the order in nature. Thus in O. 13 it is they
who have given Corinth her ancient arts, and Opuntian Locri
in O. 9 is the home of Themis and Eunomia, much as Orchomenus in O. 14 is the home of the Graces. Hesiod's declining ages, the gold, the silver, the bronze, the age of heroes,
and the iron age in which he lives, express a loss similar to
the loss of Eden, and Prometheus' theft of fire marks a
breach between nature and man. But not even Aeschylus,
much less Pindar, sees this breach as unalterable. At the
triumphant close of the *Eumenides,* natural fertility and human justice merge with each other, and Athens is in entire
accord with the earth. This sense of a possible equipoise
between man and nature was caught from classical antiquity
by the Renaissance painters, and the present fragment has
something of Raphael's poise and Titian's wide light.
Themis, like her daughters, is both natural and moral order,
and her union with Zeus is, so to speak, her union with actuality, the marriage of order and power. The golden horses
which bring her, the shining road which she travels, the
solemn stairs to which she comes, are all preludes to her en-
thronement, and the golden-veiled and fruitful Hours are
Zeus's fitting offspring by her. The imagery closely resembles that of Parmenides' journey beyond space to the bright
gates of being.[74] Pindar's mythical statements are not allegorical, if, as earlier, allegory be defined as the conscious
clothing of concepts in animate form. He did not apprehend

life by concepts but by presences. As we have seen them hitherto, most of these presences have been those of heroes, figures bridging the interspace between mortal change and the divine changelessness. As Eustathius says, they are more recognizable and closer to experience. With the present mythic figures the interspace has disappeared, so that life is felt as wholly one, free of contradictions, controlled by beautiful and mighty powers. The change is toward a completer state of contemplation. But this rapt mood, if purer here, is not absent from the odes, and the themes of harmony in *O*. 14 and *P*. 1 and of seasonal flowering in *N*. 6 reach up to a like unity.

If the Olympians are peace and order, they are also vitality and delight. To judge by the following fragment of a dithyramb, Pindar would not have grasped Nietzsche's sharp differentiation of Apolline order from Dionysiac excitement but would have felt both present in all divinity. In a somewhat different spirit Dante can see the souls in Paradise as simultaneously serene and intensely ardent. "Formerly crept the chant of the dithyramb stretched like a rope and the *s* came false from the lips; now portals fresh stand open for our holy circling choruses. Sing then, you who know the Bromian rite which even by Zeus's sceptre heavenly gods hold in their dwellings. The whirl of the tambourines begins by the austere Mother great; castanets beat and the torch with yellow pine ablaze. Then wake the Naiads' piercing moans, frenzy, battle-cry, tumult with neck thrown back. The almighty thunder breathing fire stirs and Enyalius' spear; Pallas's fighting aegis rings with the cry of myriad snakes. Swiftly moves lone Artemis, she who yokes the wild lions' breed for Bromius' Bacchic rites. He is soothed by dancing herds even of the beasts. The Muse has roused me, chosen herald of verses wise, invoking fruitfulness for Greece, land of fair dance, and chariot-driving Thebes, where once, the tale is, Cadmus through wisdom

high got sage Harmonia as his bride and heard the voice of
Zeus and left a glorious breed for men." (fg. 61) The disputed opening apparently contrasts the present circular dance
of the dithyrambic chorus to former straggling processions,
and Pindar's literary Greek to a local pronunciation in which
he disliked the s's. His pride in his art, here and at the end,
recalls his confident rejection in *O. 6* of the old insult,
Boeotian swine, and the dignity with which he presents *Paean*
6 to the Delphians. In the revel on Olympus the statelier
gods are in the background; to that extent Nietszche's distinction is just. Ares' spear and the fiery thunderbolt, which
in *P.* 1 are calmed by music, here quiver with life, sharing
the emotion of the Great Mother, the Naiads, and Artemis'
wild creatures. Yet even these violent powers are vivid
rather than savage. Pindar does not feel the conflict, intensely disturbing to Euripides, between the gods who express the sheer energy of nature and those others who are
intellect and control. The dithyramb as a Dionysiac form
of course looked to the former, but there is no sense of the
dislocation which in the *Bacchae* pulls emotion and reason
apart, nothing of Plato's fear of emotion. The world as
profusion and vitality is in accord with the world as order.
Pindar's style shows much the same reconciliation, and it is
characteristic of him not to conceive an option between a
purely intelligible order and a purely chaotic vitality.

Another dithyramb, as a spring song, may convey the
spirit of this accord more clearly. The Olympians accompany Dionysus to the altar of the twelve gods in the Athenian market place and share his festival. "Hither to our
dancing-place, O Olympians, and give us sounding grace, O
gods, you who in holy Athens haunt the city's thronged and
fragrant center and the glorious brightly-colored market
place, to take your share of violet-woven crowns and songs
gathered in springtime. Behold me sent with radiance of
songs by Zeus a second time for Bromius, whom mortals call

the Mighty Shouter. I come to sing the son of highest sires
by Theban women. Bright signs deceive the seer not when
spreads the chamber of the rose-robed Hours and fragrant
spring draws on the nectar growing. Then, then sweet knots
of violets strew the earth, and roses deck the hair, and singing voices blend with flutes, and choruses seek Semele circlet-
crowned." (fg. 63)   Nature and man are in perfect sympathy, and the joy of Dionysus which the previous dithyramb
ascribes to wild powers here expresses itself by roses worn
in the hair. The Hours, who in the hymn are the calm
daughters of Zeus and Themis, now lead in Dionysus' glad
season. No poem better shows the intense impressionability
to joy which is at the heart of Pindar's style. Though the
poem is undated, it falls naturally in the period of the famous
dithyramb on Athens' performance in the war and reflects
the early attachment to Athens which he defends at Thebes
in *P.* 9.[75]   A fragment of a poem to Pan, the first line of
which is from an Attic skolion, shows the same attachment
and the same feeling for wild nature. (fg. 85)   In the consolatory poem to Hieron, *P.* 3, he says that he makes vows
for him at a shrine of Pan and the Great Mother, where his
daughters sing close by his house. Much of this feeling for
wild nature was in the figures of Cyrene and Evadne in *P.* 9
and *O.* 6, and though the lucid Apollo remains closest to
him, he is no more irreconcilable with the wilder gods,
Dionysus, Pan, and the Great Mother, than he is out of
place in Cyrene's and Evadne's lonely wilderness. Only in
the lines on Typhos in *P.* 1 does Pindar contemplate a sav-
agery of nature incompatible with the Olympians, and he
thinks it now subdued. But these dithyrambs show, if the
fact needed showing, that the Olympian order is far from
tame. The heroes who in the odes burst mortal limits reveal the divine vitality, and Pindar's world flashes with a
profusion which is also intelligible.

The paeans, except the previously considered *Paean* 6,

are more domestic, as is the charming fragment of a parthenion. Two paeans speak as personifications of cities.
Abdera tells of her youth, the wartime sufferings of her
mother's mother, Athens, and the toil of generations that
wrested her Thracian lands from savages (fg. 36). Ceos
(Pindar writes for Bacchylides' city, presumably during the
latter's unexplained exile[76]) describes the austere poverty of
her island life which is yet brightened by athletic victories
and Dionysus' gift of wine. "I am horseless and ignorant
of cattle-tending but Melampus would not leave his fatherland to rule in Argos." (fg. 38.24-26) The words recall
Odysseus' love of rocky Ithaca. Another early king, Ceos
goes on, feared the anger of Zeus and Poseidon if he chose a
seventh part of Crete's hundred cities in preference to his
city, hearth, and kindred. "Forget, o heart, the cypress, forget the reaches of Ida. I have but a little land, . . . but own
no share in pain and conflict." (vv. 46-47) These poems
are much closer to common reality than are the hymn and
dithyrambs. The previous pages have somewhat neglected
Pindar's feeling for his victors as friends and members of
known communities. The main bent of his mind was visionary, and he seeks the glint of the absolute in the changing.
Yet it was partly his intense attraction to the changing which
led him to see divinity in it. In this respect he resembles
Sappho more than any other Greek poet; for both, the divine brightness moves, not on some remote battlefield nor
even in the pretense of the theatre, but among known scenes
of life. The present paeans state this charm and sacredness
of the actual even more strongly than do the odes. A paean
for Thebes, on an eclipse which has been identified with that
of April 30, 463,[77] states clearly this impinging of the divine
on the familiar present. "O radiance of the sun, wide
searcher, mother of eyes, why did you conceive this theft by
day of the supreme star? Why did you render purposeless
for men their strength and the path of wisdom, speeding on

your shadowed track?" (fg. 44.1-5) He speculates whether the sign means war, famine, revolution, or deluge. "But I lament nothing that I shall suffer with all." (v. 21) The poem has been taken to show how little influenced he was by Ionic physics. A contemptuous statement is quoted from him allegedly against philosophers: "They pluck wisdom's incomplete fruit." (fg. 197) This is to say again that he saw life as in the hands of animate presences. The spirit who brings the eclipse is other than the sun; she may be connected with Theia, the Bright One, who is invoked in *I*. 5 as the essence of all bright things, a passage to which we shall return. But she is not a merely physical power. As the light which makes strength and thought possible, she suggests Plato's celebrated comparison in the *Republic* of the sun to the idea of the good.[78] Such personifications are steadily relevant to general experience. The cities Abdera and Ceos express their special tone and past, and the goddess of sunlight has reference to vision, mind, and even the loyalty which makes Pindar content to accept disasters shared by others.

A fragment of a parthenion may serve as a last example of the religious poetry. Two books of maiden-songs existed, all apparently for Thebes, the ceremony[79] being elsewhere attested only at Sparta, where Alcman composed in the same form. In the spring an olive-pole, called a *kopo,* was decked with myrtle branches and carried by a man attended by a boy, the daphnephoros, and followed by girls also carrying myrtle. A girl or the girls sing; Pindar's singular could apply like Alcman's to the whole group.[80] Several people are mentioned, though their relationship is slightly unclear. Agesikles is evidently the daphnephoros, and since his parents are praised, they should be among those named. Aioladas thus seems to be the grandfather and Pagondas the father, perhaps the same as the Theban commander at Delium in 424 (if so, a reason to date the parthenion late in

Pindar's life[81]).   Andaisistrata is less certainly the boy's
mother.   The son of Damaina carries the *kopo* and is followed by his daughter, perhaps the chief singer (unless one
think of all the girls as singing).   If the ceremony is public,
it nevertheless centers about the family of the daphnephoros
and the song rehearses past glories almost in the manner of
an epinikion.   "For Loxias in kindness comes to shed on
Thebes immortal blessing.   Girt in my robe with haste, a
shining spray of laurel in my soft hand, I'll hymn Aioladas'
and his son Pagondas' house, my virgin head abloom with
crowns.   Singing to the reedy flute I'll mimic the siren cry
which quiets Zephyrus' gusty breath or shuddering Boreas
when he hastes in winter's strength and lifts with his advance
the running sea . . . I remember decking many a bygone joy
with verse; Zeus almighty knows the rest.   A girl's thoughts
must I think and speak, forgetting no due song for man or
woman among whose sprigs I stand.   I join the dance, true
witness to Agesikles and to his noble parents, of old and now
renowned for kindnesses to neighboring states and far-known
triumphs of their coursing horses.   Whence on the beach of
bright Onchestus and by Itonea's fabled shrine they decked
their hair with crowns . . . Ill-minded hate of these men's
steady quest later perversely bred harsh feuds, and yet they
loved the right's trustworthy paths.   Son of Damaina, lead
off now with prosperous step.   Your daughter first in line
will gaily follow, her sandals close upon the fair-leaved
laurel.   Andaisistrata trained her in many arts . . ." (fg.
84.3-55)   Even more clearly than in *I.* 4 or *O.* 14 Pindar is
at home among friends.   The rhetorician Dionysius of Hali-
carnassus excepted the maiden-songs from the manner of the
rest of the poetry but felt even in them a certain "grave nobility keeping the antique bloom."[82]   The lines on the siren
song stilling the winds and on the family's victories might
be from more formal poems, but the girl's self-description,
her reminder to herself to talk as girls should, and the com-

mand to the leader to begin, all have the freshness of girlhood and unspoiled provinciality. "Ah, happy, happy
boughs! that cannot shed/Your leaves, nor ever bid the
spring adieu." If this is a late poem, it shows a pleasure in
the young like Sophocles' in his Neoptolemus or Homer's in
Telemachus and Nausicaa (if one shares Longinus' view of
the *Odyssey* as an old man's poem[83]). The argument has
been mentioned that, as he grew older, Pindar tended to
mark off two spheres more distinctly: that of common life
for which he increasingly used current turns of speech, and
the gods' sphere toward which he became increasingly abstract. In any case, his love of the particular and the present
is the obverse of his feeling for the absolute. The two elements create the brilliant tension of his style, in the religious
poems as well as in the odes. If the hymn to Zeus and
Themis catches the supernal brightness, the maiden-song
shows this light diffracting into the variegation of events.
The procession in this poem recalls by contrast Dicaeopolis'
procession into the fields in the *Acharnians* (245-279).
Aristophanes' sense of country life has the pungency of
herbs, Pindar's the freshness of flowers and leaves. But this
freshness keeps its flash because it has something of the gods,
and it is Apollo who in the first verses of the song sheds his
grace on Thebes.

We have thus seen two related sets of contrasts in the religious poems: between the gods as repose and as vitality,
and between the divine order and mortal variegation. The
latter antithesis bears more obviously on the odes, which
are in effect a means of connecting the scattered events of life
with immortal being. But the former contrast is not to be
forgotten as we now return to the odes. It is vigor which
relates men to heroes and heroes to gods — not, to be sure,
a mere opulence of outpoured strength, but strength intensi-
fied into form. This union is an essential mark of the classic.
The Greek lucidity would be thin without the Greek power.

Their interplay forces intellect to grasp the outflung profusion of life, yet refines profusion into higher shapes clothed
with the mind's calm. As several times said, it was Sophocles, not Pindar and Aeschylus, who best effected this classic
union. Yet they seek it, and if they never quite tamed their
vivid impressionability into clear form, the tension is the
more impressive because it sought form. At least, their
immense vitality is the measure of their attempt to win order
from it.

   Isthmian 6. To turn now to the divine presences in the
Odes, the sense of this irradiating divine vitality marks the
early series of three odes for the family of the Aeginetan
Lampon with which we began. *N. 5* for the older son
Pytheas was called a poem of movement beyond the sea,
which is a sea of inspiration and glory. The victor finds triumph abroad, Pindar's ode takes ship from Aegina, and
Peleus after travels and labors gained the sea nymph Thetis
and heard Apollo's divine music at his wedding. The second
ode, *I. 6*, for the younger brother Phylacidas already looks
to a third which shall celebrate an Olympic victory. Pindar
imagines the three libations of a banquet, the last of which
will be to Zeus, the god of Olympia. The mood of the poem
is of pause before toil to come, and the heroic banquet at
Aegina at which Heracles summons Telamon to Troy and
names the still-unborn Ajax becomes descriptive of all such
testing hopes. "No city is so barbarous or perverse as not to
hear the fame of the hero Peleus, blessed bridegroom of the
gods, or of Ajax, Telamon's son, or of his father. Whom
for Laomedon's faults to bronze-battled war Alcmena's son
took with Tirynthians in ships to Troy, distress of heroes.
And with him Heracles seized the Pergamon, slew nations of
the Meropes, at Phlegrae met Alcyoneus, that hill-like herdsman, and spared not in his hands the deep-clanging bow. But
when he called the Aeacid to the journey, he found the
heroes dining, and as Amphitryon's son, the mighty spears-

man, in his lion-skin stood, great Telamon summoned him to
begin the sweet libation, proffering a goblet rough with gold.
He raised his matchless arms to the sky and spoke, 'If thou
hast ever kindly heard my vows, o father Zeus, now with
ineffable prayers I ask, bring forth from Eriboea to this
man a hardy son, to be my destined friend. Give him a
frame unbreakable as this beast's skin that enfolds me, first
of my labors, killed at Nemea, and let his courage match it.'
Even as he spoke god sent the king of birds, an eagle huge,
and sweet joy touching him within, he cried as if a prophet,
'Yours, Telamon, will be the son you seek. From the bird
thus shown us name him mighty Ajax, most terrible of the
ranks in Ares' work.' " (vv. 24-54)   The whole scene looks
to the future.   The friendship between Heracles and Telamon which is to be continued in Ajax will be the friendship
between Thebes and Aegina.   The eagle which gives Ajax
his name, as the violet gave Iamus his, is the sweep of Ajax's
courage beyond the earth and forward into history.   The
rough gold of the goblet does not signify, as gold more often
does, the perfect moment of attainment, though there is
happiness in this half-perfect moment of rest and waiting.
It carries rather the nobility of courage already attested,
hence faith in the gods' support in tests to come.   Heracles'
prayer is crowned by Zeus's answer, but the answer brings
the naming of the hero who was known beyond others for
toil and would die at Troy.   In N. 7 Ajax and Heracles are
companion figures, both men of labor, the one misjudged and
overcome, the other victorious.   This poem is more optimistic.   Awareness of the tests that lie ahead is not pressed to
the moment of Ajax's death; he is about to be born, and his
glory awaits him.   In this spirit, Lampon, the father of the
two victors, is praised at both the beginning and the end for
his stubborn hopes on behalf of his sons, for his doctrine of
labor, and for his hospitality.   "If joying in expense and toil
a man create god-founded virtues, and heaven also beget him

lovely repute, then he casts anchor at the verge of bliss, a man whom the gods honor. In such a mind the son of Cleonicus vows he'll meet and welcome death and graying age." (vv. 10-16) Telamon's welcome of Heracles is such an acceptance of the gods' offer of fame and virtue at the price of courage, and the joy of the heroic banquet speaks the contemporary joy which Pindar celebrates. But the happiness of triumphs already had serves chiefly as token of faith toward triumphs to come, both the boy's at future games and the father's as he approaches the final adversaries.

The Olympic victory did not in fact take place. Instead Pindar rises in *I.* 5, the third poem, to exalted praise of Aegina's performance at Salamis, and the family's glory merges with the island's. The problem of dating the three poems has been mentioned. The natural assumption is that the first two preceded the great events of 480-79 which breathe in the third.[84] Otherwise Pindar's silence on the wars in the first two poems (and Bacchylides' also, whose admirable thirteenth ode celebrates the same victory as *N.* 5) remains very odd. Moreover, on one interpretation, *I.* 5 just precedes Plataea. Yet echoes of phrase in later poems have been used to date all three odes after the wars and the present poem nearly a decade after.[85] The point in question is the speed of Pindar's response to the war. On the second view one would have to say that its import did not burst on him with nearly instantaneous glory, as the first view would have it, but grew slowly in his mind through and after his Sicilian journey. *I.* 8 states his vast but sombre relief that the stone of Tantalus has been lifted from Greece, and the myth intensifies the tone of sadness: Zeus's and Poseidon's quarrel over Thetis is healed, but the price is her marriage to a mortal and the death of her radiant son in war. Such sorrow seems a Theban's natural first response to the war, and he perhaps needed time to rally from it. The famous dithyramb for Athens apparently falls at about 474, the date of his self-exoneration at Thebes in *P.* 9. The mind's time is uncertainly related to historical time. At least the two are not the same, and if it remains a good deal easier to see the recent flash of Salamis in the present ode, the flash is not less real if it has lingered.

Isthmian 5. The mystic invocation of *I.* 5 was quoted in connection with the gold at the opening of *O.* 1. "Mother of the sun, Theia of many names, through thee mankind deems gold of mighty strength beyond all else. Yes, and ships upon the sea contending and horses at chariots through an honor, Queen, from thee grow things of wonder in swift-whirling races." (vv. 1-6) As a deity of sunlight in the fragment on the eclipse moves visible events and the minds of men, so Theia here is a primal brightness behind gold, ships, chariots and what they denote of men. Named in the *Theogony* (371-374) among the aboriginal children of Earth and Heaven and as mother of the Sun, Moon, and Dawn, Theia is evidently not a known and worshipped deity like the Olympians. The term, 'many-named,' carries Pindar's sense of her as an undetermined power, operative in the fitful brilliance which he sees in the world. *N.* 5 had somewhat romantically felt this brilliance as beyond the sea; the less visionary *I.* 6 had, so to speak, domesticated it to courage and effort. Now its blazing power entirely possesses him. In the glint of gold, of oars flashing in the sun, and of racing wheels he feels the working of a force which is simultaneously the exaltation of great acts and the glory that rests on them. No passage expresses more openly the excitement, half felt as in things, half as in the mind, which lies just below the surface of all the odes. Different as is the description of Salamis in the *Persae* (353-432), Aeschylus' feeling of sunlight and courage catches the same flash of strength, victory, and the sea.

The familiar triadic sequence of gods, heroes, and men carries this brilliance into history and to the present. Praise

is asked for the victor on the grounds that it was similarly
given the heroes. "They are glorified with lyres and the
full-stopped cry of flutes this myriad time and, honored for
Zeus, have cast a theme to poets." (vv. 27-29)   The sequence is quite clear.   Zeus's hand is in the heroes, and the
brightness revealed in them is the essential search of poets.
Diomedes and Meleager are thus revered as heroes among
the Aetolians, Iolaus at Thebes, Perseus at Argos, Castor
and Polydeuces at Sparta, and the Aeacids at Aegina.   The
passage states with utmost clarity the bond of the odes with
the hero cults of the states for which they were written, hence
their religious inspiration.   The divine flash that has shone
in the Aeginetan heroes now lights the present city.   "For
them the lips declare Aegina fatherland, far-shining isle. She
has been walled of old, a tower for courage high to climb.
My ready tongue has many a shaft to sound for them. And
Salamis, Ajax' town, can now attest that it was lifted high
by sailors, in the consuming rain of Zeus, the hailing death of
countless men. Yet quench all boast in stillness. Zeus
awards this and that, Zeus of all things sovereign." (vv.
43-53)   Advocates of the early date see in these last words
a warning that the Persians are still in Greece and a final
test awaits;[86] hence place the ode in the early summer of 479
after Salamis but before Plataea.   But exciting as this view
is, the question of date is minor.   The mystic invocation to
Theia comes as near as any passage to stating the source of
Pindar's inspiration.   As a kinship with the gods is felt in
N. 6 in men's great mind or form, so the brilliance that here
touches life is a mark of the divine.   That Theia is not a
common divinity of cult shows how mysterious to Pindar
this irradiation is.   This is the light which blazes in the
heroic nightfire of O. 1, shines in the gold of Peleus' and
Heracles' final attainment, and in some way touches all victory.   Pindar's constant coupling of poets with heroes and
victors means that he sees poetry as both recording and itself

catching this joy and this brilliance. The odes have to do, so to speak, with a shaft of sunlight that on a cloudy day transfigures a small space and all the objects in it. The light does not emanate from the objects but, being invested with it, they flash with its glory. Their own form then contributes, nature being a child of the sunlight and possessing in herself a kindred vigor. The resultant harmony between the light and the objects is Pindar's world, in which the divine being both suffuses from without and finds response from within the mortal acts and objects that it strikes. In this poem the deeds done at Salamis have kinship with those done at Troy, and both with Theia's pure radiance.

To repeat, Theia is much more than an abstraction; she is a spirit of brightness related but anterior to the gods, hence descriptive of their being. Many similar, if often minor, presences move through the poems. Victory takes men in her arms (*N.* 5. 42) and Grace sheds beauty on them as she does on all things (*O.* 1. 30; *O.* 6. 76). Alala, Battlecry, daughter of War, receives men's act of sacrifice (fg. 66). Angelia, Message, daughter of Hermes, carries news to the dead, as does Echo (*O.* 8. 82; *O.* 14. 21). Parphasis, Excuse, is the daughter of Epimetheus, Afterthought (*P.* 5. 28); Koros, Satiety, is the daughter of Hybris (*O.* 13. 10). Fate is a king (*N.* 4. 42); Time is the father of all things (*O.* 2. 17), who alone attests Truth, herself a daughter of Zeus and the origin of Virtue (*O.* 10. 55; *O.* 10. 4; fg. 194). Custom is also a great king, Hope a kind nurse of age (fgs. 152, 202), figures who interested Plato. In the poems for Opuntian Locri and for Corinth we have met Eunomia, Order, as one of the Hours and sister of Justice and Peace (*O.* 9. 16; *O.* 13, 6). Atrekeia, Exactitude, similarly presides over the Western Locrians (*O.* 10. 13), and we have likewise met Hesychia, Quietude, presiding over Thebes (*P.* 8. 1; fg. 99b. 3). Cities are themselves presences: Abdera and Ceos describe their own pasts, and Thebes,

Aegina, and Stymphalus are related through the river
Asopus. Pindar's songs can board ship or have silvered
faces. The list could easily be extended, and a problem of
editors is to decide where to capitalize abstractions as being
animate. It is not easy to enter into a mind which thus apprehends reality. Such figures of course appear in other
poets from Homer on, and the *Theogony* is a great catalogue
or family tree of divinities varying from fully animate gods
to half-abstractions. When Plato followed the Ionian physi-
cists in deleting the animistic character from ideas, he nevertheless continued to ascribe existence to the ideas. It was by
laying hold on them that a man obtained excellence; they did
not exist merely in his mind but had a being of their own.
This quality of independent being is still more clearly the essential character of Pindar's abstract presences. Through it
they become living forces in the world, sharing the color and
animation of nature. A complex gradation like that of the
Theogony accordingly exists for him also, from forces at the
verge of abstraction to those fully seen as gods. In the
odes this array of powers is complemented by the array of
heroes, and a great spectrum of being thus stretches from a
man's transient individuality, through wider categories of
event and feeling, to pure being itself. Though some of
these forces have greater reality for Pindar than others and
touch deeper ranges of life, it seems fair to say that none are
allegorical. As said, he does not see the world initially
through ideas and then proceed to clothe them with animistic colors, but a sense of life imparts itself from the first to
what he sees and thinks, and his mind flashes with being.

Olympian 12. *O*. 12, probably of 470, illustrates this
cast of thought. It is addressed to Tycha, Fortune, and
celebrates one Ergoteles, an exile from Crete who had re-
couped disaster by citizenship in the north Sicilian town of
Himera and by Olympic victory. There may be allusion to
the political upheavals which accompanied the expulsion of

Theron's son Thrasydaeus. "I entreat thee, child of Zeus
the Freer, guard strong Himera, o saving Tycha. By thee
swift ships are steered at sea, and gusty wars on land and
planning councils. The hopes of men often roll high, then
low again, cleaving delusions windy. No mortal man has yet
attained firm surety from god of any coming act, and blind
are our perceptions of the future. Much falls to men against
their plan, reversing joy; yet upon bitter squalls in a little
time they trade defeat for deepest good. Philanor's son, the
glory of your speed, like a home-fighting cock by his own
hearth, had shed its leaves unknown, had man-opposing strife
not stripped you of your Cnossian home. Now at Olympia
crowned, Ergoteles, and twice at Pytho and the Isthmus, you
glorify the Nymphs' hot baths, on your own acres dwelling."

The ode should perhaps have been discussed under
vicissitude, though it lacks the motif of an indwelling fate
that guides a man or family. Tycha is first seen as a daughter of Zeus the Freer; Himera's new liberty seems in the
statement, as well as the victor's release from misfortune.
Presently Tycha becomes a steersman at sea and in the sea
of events, and a man's life becomes a ship breasting the
changing waves. The roll of the sea, the charming shift to
the local fighting cock which Ergoteles might have been if he
had stayed in Cnossus, the fine repose of his present state at
Himera, even the city's famous hot springs which suggest the
safety and warmth of land after the open sea, all save the
poem from being merely neat. Yet it is hard to feel that
Tycha is so real to Pindar as Theia in *I. 5* or Hesychia in
P. 8. Bacchylides habitually invokes such abstract figures:
Fame, Clio, Glory, Victory, and the day of Olympic triumph,
bright daughter of Time and Night, whom fifty moons have
at last brought. These are evidently largely decorative, and
he seems genuinely touched only by recognizable scenes of
natural beauty or human act. Pindar's more animistic mind

is much more complex.   Reality for him does not inhabit
only the visible world.   Tycha here is at once the inner experience of fortune and the guide through an outer sea.   Indeed, considered as both good and bad fortune, she is herself the sea, which is also the gusty course of battle or decision and the dangerous succession of time.   If she seems less
deeply felt than Theia, it may be because his mind glances
off quickly to the circumstances which are part of her being.
Her chancy, sealike nature contrasts nicely to that of the
Nymphs in the last line, fresh but less mysterious spirits of
the land.   The phrase, 'gusty wars,' well illustrates the movement of his mind.   He would not have thought of wars as
gusty, had he not thought of the sea; nor of the sea, had he
not associated it with Tycha.   Her animate figure does not
preclude scenes from experience, nor these scenes her figure,
but they stand in a kind of electric reciprocity, each affecting
the other.

To turn finally to the late poems, most of them have
come up already in one way or another.   Though we have
hesitated to rely much on date, the evidence being often frail
and revisions by no means out of the question, these odes
have in common a weight and clarity of feeling which suggest the inwardness of age.   Other explanations of this tone
are perhaps conceivable, and the value of these superb poems
is in themselves, not in their biographical suggestion.   Yet
advancing years and the collapse of an order which had
looked stable and to which none had been more committed
than he give a setting to this mood.   The Athenians invested
Aegina in 458, and in the next summer fought the combined
Spartans and Boeotians on equal terms at Tanagra, then a
few weeks later defeated the Boeotians alone at Oenophyta,
going on to occupy much of the country, though apparently
not Thebes.[87]   Pindar's poetic life was described earlier as a
progression from outward to inward, from youthful admiration of a brilliance seen as tangibly present in the lives of the

great and fortunate, to a final sense of meaning imparted to life from inner experience only. The majority of the poems, of a middle period from roughly 479 to 460, fall between these extremes, and in them Pindar clings to a world which, as a visionary, he already overleaps. In these last poems, his confidence in the world is much frailer, not that he admires less the settled oligarchic order that he had known, but that he sees its virtues now as less in the realm of politics than of the mind. The myths of these poems are briefer and sadder, as if the buoyant achievements of heroes were no longer so relevant. Personal statements and visions of higher powers tend to replace heroic narrative, and he sees the present as more directly in the hands of gods.

Nemean 8. The unsurpassed *N*. 8, for an Aeginetan victor, is usually taken as from about 459, either just before or soon after the reduction of Aegina,[88] but an attempt has recently been made to date it the last of the odes, after *P*. 8 of 446, on the ground that its tone of sympathy fits the period when Boeotia but not Aegina had been liberated.[89] The change involves lowering the date in the early 440's usually given Sophocles' *Ajax*, which is clearly affected by the ode and seems in many ways a reply to it.[90] Pindar had twice before treated the death of Ajax: with a certain optimism in *I*. 4, in which poetry is seen as reviving the fame of the misused hero; less confidently in *N*. 7, where the misunderstanding shown Ajax betokens that shown Pindar and is the mark of men's blindness. The emphasis of both these odes is chiefly on later fame and the redeeming power of poetry (of which he is less sure in the second poem), though there is feeling also for Ajax's stubborn virtues. Here the previously minor theme becomes the major: the silent Ajax is contrasted in moral stature to the wordy and negotiating Odysseus. Being directed toward the contemporary world, the comparison evidently extends to oligarchy and democracy; and it is to this broader contrast that Sophocles' *Ajax* is a reply. At the end of the play the interests of three figures stand allied: the man of courage, Ajax, the man of mind, Odysseus, and the bowman, Teucer, all in opposition to the authoritarian Atreidae, pointedly called Spartans.[91]   Ajax, as an aristocratic fighter and eponymous hero of an Athenian tribe, has the virtues of the well-to-do classes who fought as hoplites; the bowman Teucer, who is reproached by the Atreidae for his manner of fighting and for his illegitimate birth, represents the humbly-armed classes who, as Thucydides describes, were to show their power at Pylos; Odysseus, who is portrayed with unique sympathy in the play, has an intelligence which can both venerate the will of the gods and grasp the worth of adversaries. The three figures together express very nearly the democratic ideal of the Funeral Oration, of a polity in which rich and poor may fully coöperate through merit and in which mind does not preclude reverence. The Ajax of the play seems to look to Cimon, who claimed descent from the hero and whose early glories likewise ended in misfortune and obscure death. Moreover, the political issue of the play, which is that of the absolute authority claimed by the Atreidae at Troy, is the issue which led to Cimon's discomfiture at Ithome. On these political grounds, as well as on those of style, the play seems most intelligible at a date near that of Cimon's death in the early 440's. Hence there is reason for not abandoning the early 450's for N. 8. A sense that new standards and new men are dominant in the world, and that old decencies are dying, in any case gives the poem its deeply affecting power. Sophocles evidently felt this power, in that he was prompted to vindicate Odysseus and to show that another political order can equally heed the ancient decencies, if in new ways.

An unequalled gentleness runs through the opening, indeed through the whole poem. Though he will presently see the world's injustice in Ajax, he thinks at first of happier times before injustice was honored, and is drawn to a pro-

foundly moving meditation on youth. "O holy youth, herald
of Aphrodite's deathless loves, you who on boys' and maid-
ens' eyelids rest, you lift up with compulsion's gentle hands
one child, another with other hands. It is beautiful when, unerring to each test, a man finds power to grasp the better
loves." (vv. 1-5)   The lines suggest two other invocations
already quoted.   Hesychia in *P.* 8 has this same power of
unerring choice: "You understand with perfect tact alike the
gift and the acceptance of gentle things." (vv. 6-7)   As Pindar contemplates the young victor, he sees the cloud of er-
rors, the worse loves, which he might have chosen, and feels
the marvel of an instinct that at each stage can choose rightly.   It is impossible to overpraise this feeling for youth as
the time when choices, being made in ignorance and inexpe-
rience, spring from instinct only.   Hence he sees Youth as a
presiding power who works through love, not only placing it
on the eyelids of the young in the sense of making them beautiful, but implanting it in their eyes, in the sense of drawing
them to what they love.   The goddess will lift one youth
with compulsion's gentle hands, another with other, which is
to say, adverse hands. Compulsion, *ananke,* is taken by the
scholiast and some modern scholars to mean the irresistible
power of passion,[92] but this emphasis seems narrow.   Pindar
is thinking of the deep force of a person's inborn nature
which will make one choose well, another badly.   Homer has
much this view of Telemachus' youth, when he has Athene at
each step give the boy power to act as he should.   She is the
unfolding beauty of a right growing-up. Neoptolemus in the
Philoctetes similarly acts from his native self, and Plato
speaks of a god-given impulse which can somehow guide
young men through surrounding deceptions.[93]   The hint of
meditativeness in the eyes of certain athletic statues seems a
listening for this voice.   The infant Heracles in *N.* 1 im-
mediately shows his nature in resisting the snakes, and the

'great mind' which in *N*. 6 is called our bond with the immortals is a similar response of courage.

The other passage which resembles these lines is the
opening of *N*. 7. "Eleithyia, enthroned beside the deep-
thoughted Moirai, child of mighty Hera, you who bring children to birth, oh hear me. Without you, seeing neither light
nor the dark kindly-time, do we gain your sister Hebe of the
bright limbs. Yet we draw our breath not all to equal ends.
Difference divides each yoked to his own fate. Through you
in his turn Theagenes' son, elect for prowess, Sogenes is sung
in glory among pentathletes." (vv. 1-8). Here too is the
sense of a mysterious unfolding. The Moirai, Fates, whose
cult as divinities of childbirth is attested,[94] have a continuing
power also. In that they first exert this power with Eleithyia,
the distinctive goddess of childbirth, herself the daughter of
Hera, the goddess of marriage, children are seen as answering powers beyond themselves as they enter life and make
their way through days and nights toward bright-limbed
Youth. Obscure individual differences are expressed in the
line about our drawing breath to unequal ends, and the Fates
are called deep-thoughted. The young victor wears in his
moment of attainment the beauty of a process perfectly fulfilled. He is seen as a creation of nature, almost as a perfect
tree is seen (Nausicaa in the *Odyssey* is compared to a tree),
but with greater wonder as befitting his more complex and
radiant life. In him the whole progress of growth is embodied, and Eleithyia at the moment of his birth somehow
held in her hands all that was to come. The present lines of
N. 8 are less concerned with the process than with the goal.
The beauty of the boy's achievement contains all his past
choices, and Youth, not Eleithyia, is the presiding spirit. But
whether seen as an unfolding or in its presentness, the life of
the young victor is lapped in divine forces. His individual
merits reveal immanent powers, and he is seen less as himself
than as an act of nature. These two invocations, together

with that of *N*. 6, may be the fullest existing commentaries
on Greek athletic sculpture.

This vision of Youth presently extends to the island's
youth. "To Zeus's and Aegina's bed ministered such keepers
of the Cyprian's gifts. Oenone's son grew up a king, peerless in hand and mind, whom many prayed to see. The
flower of neighboring heroes uncompelled consented of their
choice to keep his judgments, they who in craggy Athens
ruled the host, and Pelopids in Sparta." (vv. 6-12) The
happy forces which nurtured the young victor merge in these
lines with the divine acts which brought Aeacus into being.
The Athenians' and Spartans' willing respect for him evokes
a sense of pristine days, when the likeness of the gods in the
heroes was unobscured and honor and justice reigned. Their
loss brings a hardening middle age of the world and of politics. He continues, in the spirit of *O*. 8, by saying that only
divinely given wealth is stable. As the victor's triumph revealed forces beyond itself, so Aegina's long-standing position wears the strength and rightness of nature. "I stand
with step alert, breathing before I speak. Tales have been
variously told, but to discern the new and put it to the touch-
stone's test is utter peril. Talk is the envious man's sweet
food. Envy attacks the good, fights not the base. It tore
even Telamon's son, casting him on his sword. In the grim
acrimony silence checks the tongueless man, though brave,
and the chief prize rewards the shifty liar. The Danaans
wooed Odysseus with privy votes, and missing the golden
armor, Ajax wrestled with death. And yet unequal were
the wounds they dealt the foes' hot flesh, pressed by man-
fending spears beside new-slain Achilles and through disastrous days of other suffering. So lived deception even in old
times, the consort of false speech, guile-spinner, ill-famed,
malignant. She violates the glorious and decks obscure men
with a cracked renown." (vv. 19-34) His hesitation at the
start is curious. He knows a mass of familiar stories but

seeks something new, though aware of inevitable criticism. Yet once embarked on the story of Ajax, he evidently conceives envy and ill will as not directed against himself but against Aegina and the ancient way of life which he admires in his island patrons. The language of the beginning seems best explained as expressing his identification with them. The legendary stories comprised to him a great gallery of illustrative incident. He seeks the one event which will contain the essence of the present, and the award at Troy of the dead Achilles' armor to the supple Odysseus rather than to the stalwart and silent Ajax becomes the example of the world's blindness. What, if any, present betrayal is intended escapes us; he evidently means the more general change whereby Athens was soon to overpower or had already overpowered Aegina. Part of his sense of novelty in the story must be the deep gloom with which he tells it. On the whole his heroic incidents had been glorious and brilliant; even the story of Ajax as told in *I*. 4 and *N*. 7 contains the redemption of later fame. But to be apposite now was to accept unrelieved darkness. It is interesting that he approaches the tragedians not only in subject but in language, and the heaping-up of descriptive phrases, "consort of false speech, guilespinner, ill-famed, malignant," is the most Aeschylean line in Pindar. This vision of Ajax's death and of the chicane which caused it is the darker because it is contrasted to a fresh rightness of instinct which was once widespread in the world and is still visible in the young.

But having reached this despair of the world, he rises again to affirmation of it. "May my nature never be such, o father Zeus, but let me hold to open paths of life, that dying I may leave my children no ill-spoken fame. Some pray for gold, others for land unbounded, I to shroud my limbs in earth, proved pleasing to my fellow-citizens, a man who praised the praiseworthy, on the corrupt shed blame. Virtue grows like a vine in green dews lifted in the wise and just to the liquid sky. There are manifold uses of friends, in pains the chief, but joy too seeks to give pledge of itself before their eyes." (vv. 35-44). These lines were quoted earlier as witnessing the new light which shines in the late poems. It is not, as in earlier odes, the known and visible brilliance of the external world, but a light which reënters the world from inner experience. Hence it was called akin to the illumination which emerges from tragedy. Yet it is not an unnatural light. Virtue grows in the wise and just as the vine in the dew, in the course of a natural process. The opening lines on youth described such an unfolding in the young; these closing lines carry it forward to the old. The fine statement on friendship defines poetry as he now sees it. Friendship shares sorrow but it also seeks to share joy, and it is this joy which springing from consciousness of known good wells out in the ode. It first issued, with something like Wordsworth's feeling, from an apperception of the unfailing freshness of youth, and is sustained despite darker supervening knowledge by a sense of the same freshness, now tested and carried into age. The ode is the expression of this joy rather than of any outward luster or act of brilliance. He ends by saying that poetry can enchant sorrow. The reference is in part to the death of the victor's father, but in part also to this victory seen against its political background. "Songs of praise existed long ago, before Adrastus' strife with the Cadmeans." (vv. 50-51) He had said that deception too lived long ago, but as poetry amended it then, so it does now, despite the shadow or actuality of war in this last line.

Isthmian 7. Two Theban odes, *I.* 7 and *P.* 11, have been placed after the defeat of Oenophyta, the former more certainly than the latter. At first glance *I.* 7 resembles the earlier ode on the defeat at Plataea, *I.* 4, but the sense of rebirth which gives that ode its special beauty in the images of the dawn star, roses after winter, and the bright cheeks of

waking is absent now. In its place is an interior resistance,
as of a mind clinging to what it still can keep, of the sort that
we have just seen in *N.* 8. Part of the opening lines, which
rehearse the past glories of Thebes much as the opening of
N. 10 rehearses those of Argos, were quoted earlier to show
how he felt Thebes through its heroes, but here again one
sees how the tone of myths had changed for him. The account of Ajax in *N.* 8 illustrated not the glory and brilliance
of the world, but its evil, and this catalogue of former splen-
dors closes with the statement that they are no longer felt.
He follows the manner of *N.* 10 but for a new and sadder
purpose. "In what past local glory, o blessed Thebes, did
your heart most take joy? When you brought to the light
flowing-haired Dionysus to share the throne of Demeter to
whom cymbals clash? Or at Heracles' begetting when you
greeted the highest god at midnight snowing gold, when he
stood at the door seeking Amphitryon's wife? Or in
Teiresias' counsels wise or the shrewd horseman Iolaus or in
the Sown-men's tireless spears? Or when from the stern
shout of war you sent Adrastus home to horse-feeding Argos
of countless friends bereft? Or that you set on upright foot
the Lacedaemonians' Dorian hold, and Aegids, your offspring, took Amyclae by Pythic voice? But ancient favor
sleeps and men forget." (vv. 1-17) Any of these traditions
could have phrased the confidence of happier times, and the
ode rises to no such end as that of *N.* 10, which recaptures
in the story of Castor and Polydeuces the greatness of
Argive legends similarly sketched at the start. As the description of Athens' and Sparta's ancient respect for Aeacus
evokes in *N.* 8 a changed present, so does the account here
of Thebes' part in founding Sparta. The scholiast seems
correct in reading in these lines the feeling of Thebans that
they had been deserted at Oenophyta.[95] The word *charis*
has a number of meanings radiating from the idea of grace.
It is both a favor given or received and the accompanying

kindness or resultant gratitude. It is also grace in the sense of beauty. The statement that ancient *charis* sleeps and men forget thus means a lapse both of old beauty and of an old relationship of friendship and honor, and as in *N.* 8, the contrast to other times makes the present darker.

"But ancient favor sleeps and men forget whatever fails of poetry's high flower, uncaptured in clear streams of verse." (vv. 16-19) The added phrases introduce the second triad, somewhat reviving in the joy of the present festival the beauty that seemed lost. This is one of the many devices which bring an ode back to the victor and the occasion, carrying into the present Pindar's sense of the mission of poetry to give glory. Usually a glint of the absolute accompanies such a return from legend, as it does here, but in a new sense. The victor is praised for beauty and strength and for not discrediting an uncle whose name he bore, "whom bronze-shielded Ares blent with death. Yet honor is requital to the brave. Let a man know who in this storm fends from his land the hail of blood and hurls the ruin back on the enemy's lines, that in his time and city he lifts honor high, living or dying. Diodotus' son, you honored valiant Meleager, honored Amphiaraus and Hector, breathing out your flowery prime in the front line's press, where the bravest bore war's bitterness with final hopes." (vv. 25-36) The glint of the demigods which now irradiates the present is their willingness to die. We have several times seen Pindar linking athletics to war, but hyperbolically. Such overstatements allowed him to keep the best of two worlds, both the nobility of the heroes and the success of the present. This is precisely the optimism of most of the odes. But what was formerly overstatement is now reality, and in this change is the movement of these last poems to something like the vision of the tragedians. The outer brilliance of wealth and success being swept away, he is forced back to final grounds of likeness to the heroes. Not that courage was not always

implied as the foundation of glory, for example, in Pelops
or Heracles and consequently in Hieron or Chromius. But
the will to achievement usually issued in triumph, and whereas Heracles' triumph was on Olympus, Chromius' was in his
palace at Aetna. The darkness of the present poem illuminates by contrast Pindar's almost youthful belief in life, his
love of the summer sunlight of achieved success. But now
success is an inward possession only, and there is a suggestion of Sophocles in the stripping of life to its last grounds
of security.

The ode ends in this inward mood. "I bore unspeakable
sorrow. But now on storms the Shaker of the Earth brings
open day. I'll bind my hair with crowns and sing. May the
immortals' envy not disturb that daily joy I cherish as I fare
quietly toward age and the destined span.[96] Though all alike
shall die, our fates are unlike. If a man peer far on, he yet
falls short to reach the gods' bronze-paved abode. Winged
Pegasus threw Bellerophon, his master, who thought to gain
the stalls of heaven and Zeus's throng. Bitterest ending
waits on unjust joy. O Loxias, abloom with golden hair,
grant us at Pytho too a flowering chaplet in thy games." (vv.
37-51) The lines on clear weather after storm resemble
those of *N*. 8 on friendship. Both justify a remaining joy of
life which is at once both more and less substantial than formerly. Being subject to accident and unconfirmed by the
course of events, it is more tenuous and fugitive, a sunlit interval, not as once a smiling landscape. But as reflecting the
mind's deep and positive affirmation of the good of life, it is
stronger than in earlier poems. In his doctrine of harmony
Pindar had urged on Hieron and others a similar peace, but
the doctrine has more weight now that it is made his own. In
the Corinthian poem, *O*. 13, Bellerophon like Pelops and
Iamus finds divine help in his mortal night to attain the daylight of achievement, but his effort to force his way to Olympus, carefully avoided in *O*. 13, is now a mark of arrogance.

Pindar formerly found violence chiefly in the pre-Olympian Titans or Typhos or in the earth-spirits who oppose Heracles or the Dioscuri. The figures of Odysseus in *N.* 8 and of Bellerophon here attach the sense of evil and discord to the heroes, prototypes of the present; hence bring it to the present. Bellerophon's violence evidently refers to Athens. He is the Athenians' will to rule, as Odysseus in *N.* 8 was their insensibility to old standards. But Pindar is quite certain that they will repeat Bellerophon's fall; "bitterest ending waits on unjust joy." The final prayer to the golden-haired god for a Pythic victory recaptures the brightness of the clear day after storm which Poseidon had given and of the legends at the start. Professionally Pindar is committed to the successes of youth, and he sees these still with a freshness like that which gives charm to the maiden-song. Yet this freshness shines, so to speak, from the other side of sorrow and defeat; hence transcends, though it still includes, the freshness of youth.

Pythian 11. The obscure but vivid and memorable *P.* 11 has been dated at both the years conflictingly given in the scholia, 474 and 454, but is very much more intelligible at the latter.[97] The present victor presumably won at the games, for success in which Pindar has just prayed the golden-haired god on behalf of the victor in *I.* 7. There may be difficulty in that the ode lacks the melancholy of the preceding two. Yet much else unites it with them: a sense in the myth of conflict and bitterness among the heroes, thoughts of death and the excellence of a good name, even what seems an effort to correct the quietism and tone of resignation which mark, or at Thebes must have seemed to mark, *I.* 7. The ode concerns women more than any others except *P.* 9 and *O.* 6. Cyrene and Evadne were earlier seen as the silence and waiting of the mind which the coming of the god transforms into achievement, and much of this feeling is here. The ode has to do with right and wrong success. He rejects the high-

handed ways of tyrants, stating his devotion to the general
good, and the account of Clytaemnestra's murder of Agamemnon, which is the myth, complexly bears on the same
question. The ode begins by summoning the daughters of
Cadmus and the other Theban heroines in the evening to the
shrine of Apollo Ismenius and of his bride Melia, where the
victor will dedicate his crown. Semele, Ino, and Alcmena
are familiar from other odes as having kept through adver-
sity the gods' highest blessing, and the end of the paean on
the eclipse celebrates Apollo's ambrosial union with the
Oceanid Melia.[98] In the civic setting in which they are now
seen these figures carry divine sanction of the deepest ties
of the Theban land and past. But the Pythic victory presently evokes mention of Pylades, who is described as a Delphian, and of Orestes, "whom, when his father fell, his
nurse Arsinoa stole from Clytaemnestra's savage hands out
of sad betrayal, while with gray steel the pitiless woman
sent Dardanid Cassandra, Priam's daughter, with Agamemnon's ghost to the deep-shadowed bank of Acheron. Did
Iphigeneia, slaughtered at Euripus far from home, sting her
to this mighty-handed anger? Or won now to another bed,
was she moved by night's endearments? That is the harsh-
est trespass in young wives, unremedied to conceal from
others' tongues. The talk of citizens is sharp, and riches
win resentment matching them, while he who lowly breathes
mutters unseen. So died the son of Atreus, and was the
prophetic maiden's death, at famed Amyclae when he came
at last, for Helen having loosed the luxury of the burnt Trojans' halls. But he, the helpless child, reached Strophius,
his old ally who dwelt below Parnassus. In spite of all with
Ares' later help he killed his mother and laid Aegisthus in
his blood." (vv. 17-37)

The first and clearest impression is of Clytaemnestra's
contrast to the serene heroines invoked at the start. In her
the world has lost its closeness to the gods and state of un-

spoiled strength. The contrast is not unlike that in *N*. 8
between the early reverence shown Aeacus and the later deception by which Odysseus won Achilles' armor. Though
he calls her pitiless, he is fascinated by Clytaemnestra, and
his speculation on her motives has been taken to show that
he knew Aeschylus' *Agamemnon*, produced in 457.[99] The
two men's Clytaemnestras are in fact very like both in their
intransigeance and in the ambiguity of their motive in Iphigeneia and in Aegisthus. It is not easy to imagine Pindar's
visiting Athens in these unhappy years, and how far plays
circulated in manuscript is unknown; yet he could hardly
have missed hearing of the play, and a mere account of it
might conceivably explain the resemblance. What is in any
case clear is that Clytaemnestra's act has meaning to Pindar
because, like Odysseus' chicane in *N*. 8, it describes an al-
tered world, and, like Bellerophon's flight in *I*. 7, it foretells punishment. Weight has been given the fact that
Orestes when first mentioned is called a Laconian, and the
scene of the murder is Amyclae, not Mycenae.[100] When in
the last lines of the poem Pindar joins the Theban hero
Iolaus with the Spartan heroes Castor and Polydeuces, the
undertone of Sparta in the ode is unmistakeable. Several
themes, all converging on the present, thus contend in the
ode, and it is chiefly the number of these, hence their confusion of emphasis, that makes difficulty. To try to bring
them together, the victory attests Apollo's favor, and the
heroines who gather at his shrine enhance the sense of the
god's saving closeness to Thebes. Orestes enters the poem
through connection with Delphi. Insofar as he is a Spartan,
he carries renewed faith, lost in *I*. 7, in Thebes' ancient ally.
But insofar as in youth he was the surviving hope of justice
and later became its actuality, he transcends his character as
a Spartan and becomes in his youth, strength, and connection
with the god a more general figure for salvation. Clytaemnestra attests that corruption through wealth and passion

that has destroyed the happy order embodied in the ancient heroines. The state of harmony with the gods and the past which was present in the opening is broken in the account of her, and Pindar can only speculate what motives have made this savage breach. These motives, he feels, are rooted in wealth; it is her high position that has made possible her crime. He wrestles obscurely with the problem here, and it is to wealth that he presently returns.

To pause briefly on Pindar's view of women, what is striking is its serenity. The figure of a mother recurs in the invocations of several odes: "My mother, gold-shielded Thebes" (*I*. 1), "O queenly Muse, my mother, I beseech you" (*N*. 3), "Mother of gold-crowned games, Olympia" (*O*. 8). The sun is called mother of eyes in the paean on the eclipse, and in furnishing the paean for the Delphians, he obeys his heart as a child its mother.[101] In *P*. 8 the boys who have failed at the games shrink home by back streets to their mothers. This imagery certainly expresses a profound security, partly social, as of settled families in which women held acknowledged power. The interpretation given earlier to Cyrene and Evadne reflects this secure background, in that the deep and quiet bond with earth that they signify has no conflict with the coming of the god, which is brilliance and attainment. It may be the sharpest single cleft between Pindar and Aeschylus that the latter feels no such deep harmony between the sexes. Conflict between them is a minor theme even in the *Persae,* a major theme in all the other plays. Needless to say, we shall return to it. Only when justice is finally restored in the *Eumenides* is there reconciliation between the female security of earth and the innovating boldness of male mind and will. Pindar's outlook is much closer to Homer's. Helen to both is a worthy cause of heroism, and if Penelope is absent from the odes and fragments, the sense is rarely absent of settled families over which unknown Penelopes presided. This common attitude

no doubt goes back to the assumption that the family is connected with the land. The place of women was clear and
important in country families; the parthenion for the family
of Pagondas gives a picture of one such group. But when,
as in Athens, a mercantile society was in process of replacing
an agricultural society, the change worked adversely for
women, and conflicts within the society took on tones of conflict between the sexes. To return to the present poem, the
Theban heroines express Pindar's view of a society deeply
founded on its women. A reason for seeing Aeschylus' influence in the figure of Clytaemnestra is that, as in the *Agamemnon,* she carries the conflicts of another age and way of
life. She is of course a legendary figure who transcends the
setting of any single period. Yet if this poem is as rightly
dated at 454 as it seems to be, she must carry for Pindar
suggestions of Athens in her destruction of old and founded
relationships. She is for him very much what she is for
Aeschylus, a person caught, as is her husband, in the dangerous currents of wealth and power, hence one who has lost
the profound security and rootedness of the older heroines.

But if the complexity of his story confuses us, it evidently
confused him. "Friends, did I wander down a shifting cross-
road, proceeding straight till then, or did a gust deflect me
from my course like a skiff at sea? If you compacted, Muse,
to show for a price your silvered voice, then riot in other
ways and times, but sing for Thrasydaeus now or for his
father Pythonicus." (vv. 38-44) The lines may be taken
as amiably as they are written. They are a cheerful way of
returning to the occasion at hand, and his frankness in talking about pay has the bantering tone of the passage in *I.* 4
(54) when he calls the victor contemptible to look at. Both
are for Thebans and he is obviously among friends. Yet his
sense of having gone astray seems real enough, and his
curiosity about Clytaemnestra's motives had prevented the
contrast between the opening and her story from quite com-

ing off. After praising the family's glories, he in any case returns to the theme which was tangledly expressed in the myth, of the corruptions incident to great power and wealth. "From god may I love glories, seeking things possible to my life. Since of estates I find the middle station flowering with wider bliss, I blame the tyrant's role, and seek the excellence that profits all. The jealous stand away. If a man gain this peak and dwell in peace escaped from wanton pride, he finds a fairer boundary of dark death, to his loved breed the first of treasures leaving, the grace of a good name. It is this which lifts the son of Iphicles, Iolaus, high in song, and Castor brave and you, King Polydeuces, sons of gods, one day beneath Therapne's courts, the next upon Olympus dwelling." (vv. 50-64) Advocates of an early date have seen a reference to Hieron in this statement on tyranny.[102] But he nowhere else speaks of him in this way, which on general grounds seems most unfitting and unlikely, not least at the moment of his return from Sicily. Moreover, his express concern for death and a good name, very close in tone to passages in *N.* 8 and *I.* 7, is left unexplained. The recent view which sees the lines on tyranny as directed against Athens is much more probable.[103] Athenian aspirations are several times called tyrannical by Thucydides' speakers. The Greek mind readily generalized the private in the civic. Thus in the *Republic* the man of unchecked passions becomes the tyrant, and in the famous chorus of the *Oedipus King* (873-896) just after Jocasta has doubted the oracle, loss of reverence and restraint soon wears the colors of tyranny. The chorus is certainly not there referring to Oedipus; they are simply describing a state of mind, very much in Pindar's manner here. But the truth is that he is not largely thinking of the tyrant, who is invoked to set off by contrast the life which Pindar admires. This is the life of the settled Theban families, squires, magistrates, soldiers, horsebreeders, and athletes, of the kind that appear in the other Theban odes and in the parthenion. The self which he addresses in the first person is often a half-transplanted self which includes the victor. In speaking of the prizes for which all may vie and which benefit all (both meanings are present), he thinks of the victor as well as of himself. With the victor stands his father, and the two together represent a whole class of Thebans, a narrow class by Athenian standards, yet one which to Pindar signifies Thebes. The horseman Iolaus, nephew and charioteer of Heracles, expresses these men's code, which is embodied also in the stubborn loyalty of the Spartan heroes Castor and Polydeuces. These heroes of the end complete the heroines of the beginning, as achievement completes the family and bravery the earth. Clytaemnestra, like tyranny, is the corruption of this founded order, and Orestes, like the victor, carries from Delphi the promise of its restoration. The tone of confidence in Thebes which breathes through the poem may be in part an apology for the inwardness and quietism of *I.* 7. In any case he feels his old faith in his city and, even more, in the code of loyalty which is its meaning. Together with Iolaus and the Dioscuri, Orestes carries a divine favor which is courage and victory.

Pythian 8. Much has been said already of the last and in many ways the greatest of the odes, *P.* 8, as well as of *N.* 11, the poem usually taken with it, which was discussed among the odes on vicissitude. The several strands of the present section meet in *P.* 8. The invocation to Hesychia contains as fully as any passage that sense of divine presences, mysterious, half concealed in events, yet operative behind the visible play of life and nature, of the sort that we have seen in the hymn to Themis, the dithyrambs for Thebes and Athens, and the invocations to Theia, Eleithyia, and Youth. The comparative brevity and sorrow of the myth show a losing confidence in any fixed political order and an inward turning from the brilliance of the world formerly signified in the victorious heroes. The heroes expressed much more than this in the odes of Pindar's confident years; yet as prototypes of triumph they sanctioned worldly triumph also. His account here of meeting the hero Alcmaeon on the road to Delphi has a personal tone which is in keeping with his prayer for a life of harmony with Apollo. The advice to the young victor not to risk repeated competition echoes the sense of uncertainty at the close of *N. 11*; "The rivers of foreknowledge lie far off. Seek measure in gaining. In unattainable loves are the sharper madnesses." Here too is a turning from the world. But at the same time he is closer to small events, and in his concern for the boy's four beaten rivals he notices minor family happenings almost as he does in the parthenion. The apocalyptic close catches again the transfiguring brilliance which he felt at Salamis in *I. 5* and in the nightfire of heroism in *O. 1*. Both the vitality and the sense of a higher meaning and order which were noted of the religious poetry are in these tremendous lines, and if the brilliance which they describe is felt as more transitory, it is closer to the tragic light which overshines defeat.

The decimation of the Athenian occupying forces at Coronea in 447 in effect restored Boeotian independence. The Peloponnesians pressed their advantage by invading Attica in the summer of 446, but what might have been a turning-point in the history of the fifth century passed without event when the king, Pleistoanax, later exiled for his decision, mysteriously withdrew his forces.[104] Whether as a result of this act or because the decision in fact represented the wish of a faction in Sparta to seek terms with Athens, early in 445 the two states reached in the so-called Thirty Years' Peace what was virtually an agreement to divide Greece between them. The clause that secured this end was that which left intact the leagues respectively dominated by the two states, and as a result of this clause Aegina, now a member of the Delian Confederacy, remained under

Attic control. *P.* 8, which celebrates after an unknown interval a victory won in the late summer of 446, is for an Aeginetan. It is written with consciousness of Thebes' freedom and with some seeming hope for Aegina's also. Yet the invasion which might have liberated her had not been pressed, and Pindar is far from confident. The prayer for the island with which he closes perhaps amounts to a confession of hopelessness. If so, it makes still more fugitive the transitory radiance which rests on the victor also.

The invocation to Hesychia, Quietude, was quoted among the poems on harmony. "Loving-hearted Quietude, o child of Justice and strengthener of cities, you who hold the keys of councils and of wars, receive for Aristomenes this rite of honor for his Pythic crown. You understand with perfect tact alike the gift and the acceptance of gentle things. But when a man lays in his heart cold rancor, you harshly face the enemy's assaults and scuttle his insolence. Porphyrion did not know you when he taunted you unprovoked. That gain alone is glad that comes from the house of a willing giver. Violence trips the vaunter in the end. Cilician Typhos, the hundred-headed, escaped this not, nor the monarch of the giants, but they fell before the thunderbolt and Apollo's shafts, who welcomed with kindly heart from Cirrha home Xenarchus' son crowned with Parnassian grass and with the Dorian song." (vv. 1-20) If Theia of *I.* 5 was not a known goddess of cult but a figure mystically seen as the origin and giver of radiance, Quietude is still more fully such a visionary power. But it is quite secondary whether or not the divine presences in the poems are those of known gods. In their different ways all hold in their hands the controlling forces behind men and events. The mind that can see the world through such figures has moved far from a simple animism which populates nature with the shapes of human wishes and fears. It could not refine these shapes much further without itself passing over into introspection and thereby realizing them as its own creations. With that a new step toward rational analysis would have been taken, as it had in fact been already taken by the Ionian philosophers. It is because Bacchylides' sophisticated mind had in their spirit lost the power to envisage such higher shapes as real that his odes, for all their charm and sensitiveness, are vastly more limited than Pindar's. Reality for Bacchylides is in a world of human action and natural scene, beyond which for Pindar stretch farther ranges of being. To consider such a figure as Hesychia in this poem is to see why such an art as his could not go much farther and why the dramatists inevitably took on. For by placing living figures on the stage they implicitly said that men were now at the center and must accept their own thoughts and acts. Pindar has at bottom no such assumption. It is not that Hesychia here or the divine presences in other poems lack connection with human motive. We have repeatedly seen how what is said of them is conceived as flowing out among men, as what is said of men flows back into them. Hesychia is at once a goddess and a way of life. It is rather that she and the other divine figures so loom above any given present as to enfold and surround it with forces beyond itself. This is tantamount to saying something other than what the tragedians said: that the weight of things is with the forces that create us, and we are in their hands. Exact statement in such matters is not easy; neither did the tragedians lack sense of these forces, nor did Pindar see them as dwarfing men. The difference is one of emphasis, yet that emphasis is crucial. Pindar is beyond others the symbolist among Greek poets both because he sees such divine or heroic figures and because the world is to him a place which is most truly characterized by them. That is to say, the world and all things in it sparkle with life; men share in and can perceive this great interplay of being; they have responsibility to themselves, but this responsibility when most fulfilled lifts

them out of themselves to share in brighter and higher
ranges of being. It is these latter which are most characteristic of the world, and a man does not possess them, they
rather possess him, giving him a place in an order flashing
from top to bottom with something godlike, crowned by the
gods' pure being. As contrasted with the tragedians, Pindar's emphasis is on the gods rather than on men, and his
symbolism even in the heroes, much more in such figures as
Hesychia, has to do with apprehending by thought and act
(which is to say, in poets and athletes) the joyous divine vitality, which is at the same time the divine order and repose.

To return to the invocation, it is unnecessary to discuss
it in detail again, but parts of it may be clearer in the present
setting of the late poems. The Theban heroines of *P.* 11,
though less described than Hesychia, are not unlike her.
Both express the rootedness of the life and outlook that Pindar knows, and Hesychia's very trait of repose, which is contrasted in Thucydides and Euripides to Athens' innovating
restlessness,[105] has overtones of the land and the past. She
is in the spirit also of the virtue which in *N.* 8 grows in the
wise and just toward the sky like dew-nourished vines, and
she could be said to continue and perfect the unfolding which
Youth begins in that poem. "It is beautiful when unerring
to each test a man finds power to grasp the better loves,"
he wrote of Youth in *N.* 8. Hesychia in the same way understands unerringly how to give and to receive, as she
knows the courage necessary for war and the steadiness for
counsel. She is a poise of mind which does not seek to wrest
things from others but will defend, because she can value,
friendship and the meanings which speak through the tried
forms of life. The giant Porphyrion, by contrast, suggests
Bellerophon's ambition and fall in *I.* 7, and if his violence
differs from Odysseus' scheming of *N.* 8, they are at equal
remove from Hesychia's peace. It is Apollo who beside
Zeus subdues Porphyrion, music and order beside power and

majesty, and Orestes returns from Delphi in *P*. 11 in much
this redeeming spirit.   A group of related ideas thus runs
through all these late odes, though with different lights and
colors as they are seen through changing shapes.   The rooted
way of life which Hesychia shares with the Theban heroines
of *P*. 11 may be the deepest of these ideas.   It carries the
associations with women which were dwelt on earlier and
which express Pindar's lack of quarrel with earth and nature.
If Ajax in *N*. 8 shared too fully the silent strength of earth,
he was at least not violent toward it like Porphyrion and did
not seek to manipulate it like Odysseus.   These vices of violence and manipulation were to Pindar the Athenian vices.
Thucydides has the Corinthians say of Athens: "Further,
they spend their bodies for the state as if these were not
rightfully their own, yet cherish their minds as their most
private treasure, to act for her." (I 70.6)   The Corinthians
are describing a combination in Athens of individual enlightenment and corporate dynamism, which corresponds fairly
closely to Odysseus and Porphyrion.   But to Pindar earth
issues rather in an Apolline harmony of music and mind, removed alike from self-assertion and from violence.

Other Aeginetan odes contain the legends of Aeacus and
his descendants, but he abruptly forsakes these here for the
victor and the present.   The turn is curious, because, instead
of dwelling on the present, he soon broaches the enigmatic
story of how at the time of the second expedition against
Thebes the prophet Amphiaraus, dead and speaking from
the earth, watched with joy the courage of the sons of those
who had failed in the first expedition.   "By heritage gleams
from sires to sons a noble mind." (vv. 44-45)   Only Adrastus had survived the first expedition, and only his son Alcmaeon will now die in the second.   Amphiaraus watches
Alcmaeon with special joy, and his praise of him is clearly
relevant to the present victor.   But the prophecy as a whole
is difficult.   If the key to it is the success of the second expe-

dition, it expresses Pindar's continuing hope for Aegina, involved with pain and death though any such attempt at liberation would be. Alcmaeon in any case remains the prototype of the young victor. Pindar describes the visionary encounter with the hero which he had on the road to Delphi, possibly for the present games, and says that his shrine stood near his own house at home. Thoughts of him invoke Apollo, whose oracular powers Alcmaeon shared, and the sense of the god's brilliant precinct at Delphi and of his beneficence to the victor invokes a prayer for a life of harmony with him. "Lord, with eager heart I pray that I may see in harmony with thee in all toward which I walk.[106] Justice attends this sweet-voiced revel, but for your future days, Xenarchus, I pray the gods' ungrudging faith. If a man gain success without long toil, he seems to many a wizard among fools decking his life with arts shrewdly contrived. But this rests not with men; god confers, now tossing one man high, catching another." (vv. 67-77) As the invocation to Youth in *N*. 8 leads on to thoughts of age and a life of honor, so the young Alcmaeon and the radiant Apollo prompt longer meditations here. The prophet Amphiaraus watching Alcmaeon is in effect Pindar watching the young victor. Amphiaraus and Pindar share a foreboding of the gods' intervention, which the prophet sees in the coming death of the young warrior, Pindar in the labors and changes which will follow victory. If the myth expresses his hope for the liberation of Aegina, his chief hope, as in the other late poems, is in a life of reverence. The clever man who manipulates events to his advantage recalls the Odysseus of *N*. 8, but he lacks the last word and it is the gods who decide. In neglecting the great Aeacid legends, Pindar seems partly moved by having treated them repeatedly in the past, partly by their association with more confident and victorious years. The fine picture of the young Alcmaeon catches the quality of the young victor, but it looks uncertainly to

the future, both Aegina's and all men's. The prayer for
harmony with Apollo, like the statement in *N.* 8 that joy
seeks to share itself with friends, carries into these uncertainties a hope for the young god's continuing guidance, and
Pindar's mystic encounter with Alcmaeon contains exactly
this protective influence of fresh youth over advancing age.

The apocalypse of the end opens suddenly on these bur-
dened lines. In the spirit of *N.* 11 quoted earlier he bids
the victor not trust his luck too far. All that was previously
said of future uncertainties and that lay behind Amphiaraus'
prophecy of Alcmaeon's death lingers in this advice, and
carries forward into his sympathy for the boy's beaten rivals.
They are the darkness of the future already seen as present.
"No such blithe homecoming fell to them at Pytho nor laughter sweet shed happiness as they sought their mothers, but
they shrink down alleys alone from enemies, gnawed by failure." (vv. 83-87) These lines have been taken to reflect
badly on Greek athletics, but that is hardly the point. They
do reflect a passionate desire to win and, as such, the passionate wish to believe in the world. Such a wish is in the
terrifying last line of *N.* 11, "in unattainable loves are the
sharper madnesses." In that sense they are a commentary
on the flash of success in the earlier poems. But now Pindar
sees such formerly beloved and trusted prospects of an almost godlike happiness as illusory. "He who has won some
beautiful new thing in his great luxuriance soars in hope on
the wings of his strength, his heart beyond wealth. In a
little time men's happiness waxes. So also it drops to the
ground by some checking purpose shaken." (vv. 88-94)
The sudden blossoming of happiness recalls for a moment
the Arcadian mood of *O.* 14, the festal Graces of Orchomenus smiling on the glad procession. Certainly one could
not write epinikia without an unforgotten sense of the rap-
turous excitement of the young. The lines on Youth in *N.* 8
express this sympathy most purely; here the death of Alc-

maeon already prefigures the brevity of such golden moods. They inevitably issue in the odes from thoughts of youth; yet go deeper and come to signify all freshness, joy, and creativity. The epinikion continues a possible form for Pindar because of this wider meaning of joy and triumph. The mood can fall to the ground, 'by some checking purpose shaken.' The nature of this adverse will in things seems left unspecified because it applies to all joys, not only the victor's.

He in any case passes quickly to men generally. "Ephemerids. What is one? What is he not? A mortal is a shadow's dream. But when the Zeus-given radiance comes, a blazing glory rests on men and a honeyed life. Dear mother Aegina, in freedom's course lead on this city through Zeus and ruling Aeacus and Peleus and brave Telamon and through Achilles." (vv. 95-100) The heroes return at the end as Zeus-descended figures who manifest in history the pure being of the gods. This is the chain of participation with which we started, the heroes occupying the middle space between men and gods, attesting their connection. Here they are to Pindar the continuing life of Aegina, and omitted in the relative gloom of the beginning, evoke at the end something of his old sense of the island's strength and glory. As for men, their life is both dimmest shadow and brightest light, both transience and being. In the odes *O.* 3 and *O.* 10 on the founding of the Olympic games, scenes of celebration in the tempered moonlight expressed a third possibility, so to speak, of luminous continuance between the present extremes of darkness and light. But those odes are the exception, and much the present contrast existed between Pelops' or Iamus' mortal night and inspired day, or between Evadne's or Cyrene's silence before the coming of the god and radiance after it. Yet the present lines state Pindar's guiding view more intensely than before. The light which they describe was compared a little earlier to his vision in *I.* 5 of Theia as the giver of brilliance, both that

which is visible in gold or flashing oar or wheel and the inner
brilliance of courage and attainment, and also to the gold at
the opening of O. 1 which flashes like fire out of the night and
which was interpreted as heroism. His repeated use of gold
to signify states of pure being is very close to this imagery
of light. But there is a new finality of statement now, as of
a ruling idea recognized at last without encumbrance. This
view of reality is different, as said, from that which inspired
the tragedians. It gives more to the gods, less to men;
values being rather than becoming; seeks the static and the
timeless. Victory to Pindar is itself only a figure for this
state of being, which is a mark of the divine in the world.
Hence victory and poetry, different as they are, are equally
dependent on the gods, whose hand is increasingly seen in
the late poems in friendship and inner harmony also. To
use the word static of this state of being is to slight its vitality. It is simultaneously alive, lucent, joyous, and at rest.
These attributes, felt of the gods in the religious poetry, are
more complexly stated in the variegation of the odes. But
the common trait of the odes is the effort to grasp the bright
chain that binds men to gods or, better, the radiance that
descends from gods to men, touching events with the divine
completeness.

PART TWO

ATTIC TRAGEDY

GREEK tragedy owed incomparably less to its early origins, discussed as they have been since Aristotle, than to the civic climate in which it took shape. The tie between a society and an art form is nowhere closer than in the Athens of Aeschylus. The dithyramb from which tragedy was evolved, though widespread, failed elsewhere to produce such a form, even at Corinth where, Herodotus says (I 23), heroic legends were set to dithyrambic choruses. When Thespis first added an actor to the chorus and under Peisistratus introduced his primitive plays in Athens, the step may in retrospect seem decisive but would hardly have proved so, had not the tyranny fallen and the democracy followed. It is true that a democratic strain ran through the early tyrannies, which were in effect agencies of transition from a landed to a trading society, and Peisistratus' patronage of Thespis, in looking to the popular god Dionysus, looked to a popular art form. But this form was rudimentary when the democracy came into being in 510, and its growth closely accompanied the democracy's. Why this should be so must be apparent from what has been said of Pindar. The Odes assume a single social standard. When the young victor, bound to his age mates by ties of cult, family, and training, emerged in triumph in his city, all the standards of his age and class and (since it was the ruling class) of his state seemed illuminated in him. These in turn evoked the civic legends, which elevated nominally into the past, but actually beyond present and past, the vision of this momentarily visible ideal. It is characteristic of Pindar that, though his form betrays these origins, in his hands it far outran them. He could simply have been the eulogist of aristocracies; he in fact sought pure harmony and pure being. But Aeschylus' position toward his city was radically new. The overthrow of the tyrants set politics free in Athens, and the mood of dispute which followed is clear both from the history of these years and from the invention of so drastic a device as ostracism. If the Odes show one reigning outlook, tragedy shows the struggle between outlooks. In the democratic society one man's right did not preclude another's, and if they were at odds, only time, conflict, and the discovery of some higher ground of agreement could bring a solution. It is inconceivable that tragedy, the vehicle of conflict, could have originated in circumstances which were not marked by conflict. The British Tudors have been compared to the Greek tyrants, and the seizure of the monastery lands after 1536 set on foot a process of social change analogous to that which led in the Attic democracy. Such ferments gave life to Thespis' nascent art form which, lacking the impulse, would have reached no such lofty end.

This changed outlook which found voice in tragedy produced a series of further shifts. If assumptions of political fixity are to be read beneath Pindar's sense of static being, Aeschylus' assumption of conflict reflects a new view of time. Conflict produces change, and the sense of life as a known cycle yields to belief in novelty. The wind of great events which blew through Aeschylus' years inspired hope in an indefinitely extensible progress. This point was touched on in the first chapter when it was said that, though Hesiod's *Theogony* describes an evolution in heaven from the rough sway of the Titans to the Olympians' bright rule, the *Works and Days* conceives no such progress on earth. Hesiod like Homer sees life as fixed in recurrent categories, and the set epithets of the oral style express an identifiable, hence a foreseen future. Aeschylus first conceived for men the progress which the *Theogony* proclamed among gods. Only Xenophanes rivals his faith in society's improvement. The point now being made is that this sense of time and progress is a necessary corollary to the sense of conflict from which tragedy sprang. It is conceivable that, had the democracy not been created or gone on to its triumphs, Thespis' beginnings could have developed into a tragedy of merely personal deeds against great opponents. As such, it could have caught the spirit of the *Iliad* and even of the Odes, in showing the timeless glory that invests heroism. But this conceivable form of tragedy, if not remote from that of Sophocles, has little or no connection with that of Aeschylus. The struggle which marked democracy was to him not purposeless but, standing in a sequence of time, betokened evolution. Hence arose the characteristic Aeschylean trilogy, which is the vehicle at once of time and of progress. The trilogy as a form is more revolutionary than tragedy as a form. Aristotle found in the *Iliad* and *Odyssey* the prototypes of tragedy,[107] and our hypothetical development from Thespis could simply have asserted heroism. But when this heroism stands in a trilogy, it becomes more than itself: it both denotes a character and is a stage in a progression leading to a farther and higher state of being. Aeschylus was too modest when he described his plays as slices from Homer's banquet.[108] An Homeric element indeed exists in the heroic dimension and commitment of his characters, also in the self-knowledge which they gain through suffering. But beyond stands the unhomeric element of a goal to suffering, which is the sight of a new order won from time, a transvaluing of heroism into progress. Aeschylus' main title may not be as the creator of tragedy but as the inventor of the idea of meaningful time.

These ideas of conflict and of time divide Aeschylus from Pindar, marking him as the spokesman of a new society which accepted revolutionary change. Democracy works through the struggle of opinion, and Pericles in the Funeral Oration praises competition as necessary to progress.

Yet a mood can arise in which change begets only more change, and a standard of judgment or prospect of a goal disappears. Therefore, at some point Aeschylus necessarily sought common ground with Pindar in the vision of something stable and final. The great theme to which the two men equally rise, though in very different ways, was discussed in connection with *P.* 1: it is the theme of the divine harmony which dissolves strife in lucid order and makes the world intelligible. All the optimism of the age speaks in this splendid confidence that mankind can share the Olympian peace. The two men conceive its attainment from very different circumstances: Pindar from moments of contemplative repose which rise on effort revealing its beauty and meaning; Aeschylus from an historical vision of society's painful ascent to a state of justice and peace. Pindar's sense of harmony is personal and private or, if not quite private, to be shared with friends and men of like mind. Meaning to him surrounds the known, recurrent events of life, and if a victor saw the flash of highest brightness only once or twice, cult could reveal a similar light more often. This divine meaning shone for him above the present like a sky above the common earth. Aeschylus was less at home in the present, more morally impatient of it, far more sensitive to evil. His moral urgency postponed the sight of peace and order until society as a whole could share in them. When at last the vision came, it wore the apocalyptic colors of a new society, and the revelation drew power from the moral scruple which had postponed it. This difference of outlook betrays again the difference between two societies. But revolutionary as was the Attic democracy, it was at first conceived as subsuming rather than as destroying the former order. Though Plato, Aristotle, and even Thucydides in the second half of his *History,* came to see democracy as simply a new form of despotism, that of the poor instead of the rich, the authentic and older view of Aeschylus and Pericles saw it as the constitution which reconciles rather than divides, which elicits rather than redistributes. Hence Aeschylus' view of the final harmony was not wholly different from Pindar's. Though drawn from deeper moral sources and though public rather than personal in tone, it is equally a religious vision, giving meaning to the life of the whole state as Pindar's did to that of narrower circles. Aeschylus asserts far more powerfully even than Pericles that the democratic society is not merely the society of competing interests but of a higher unity and more generous reconciliation. As such, further, it is not an unnatural society. The final understanding of Zeus and Prometheus and the final transformation of the avenging Furies into spirits of blessing and plenty carry a view of nature as crowned by divine order and beauty. As we have repeatedly seen, this is also Pindar's view. In *N*. 6 men's great mind and form share affinity alike with the fields and with the gods, with process and with being. So with Aeschylus the long process of history attains to justice, in which shines the divine being. However conscious of the bitter fact of conflict, Aeschylus found in the idea of time a bridge to the divine timelessness, and this final repose invests his view of the new society with a harmony which is the two men's common vision.

In turning to Aeschylus one meets antitheses which are absent from Pindar. The energies released by freedom inspire fresh possibilities and raise fresh problems for which new forms of reconciliation are continually asked. Judged by the standard of willingness to face diversity, Pindar can appear provincial, and if this standard were all, his art would seem outmoded by tragedy. In fact it became thus outmoded, and Aeschylus supplied the need of a new age for a more complex art which would recognize openly the savage diversities of the world. But it is the secret jewel of provinciality that the mind is not so distracted by conflicts as to lose grip on the unity of experience. This wholeness of per-

ception is the life of poetry. Analysis and the awareness of
problems lead eventually to prose, and it is no accident that,
as an Athenian vehicle, tragedy was itself presently super-
seded by philosophy. Pindar's comparative simplicity of
mind is therefore not a defect, though it could have been,
had it tied him to his narrow standards of time and place.
As it was, because he rose from these to a persistent sense of
radiance and meaning, he passed in a single leap to the same
kind of solution that Aeschylus painfully reached out of his
conflicts. In that leap Pindar's seeming simplicity ceased to
be simple, or at least no longer appeared so to generations
which had begun to think analytically. It perceived divine
presences rather than ideas, moved toward meaning by association rather than by reason, continually sought immedi-
acy of experience, would not discerp the unity of sense,
mind, and feeling. The strength of Pindar's symbolic art
is in that sense of wholeness which alone prevents life from
declining into a sequence of random particulars.

In conceiving history as conflict Aeschylus drew nearer
the analytical outlook which would one day issue in prose.
His characters represent two sides of a situation and, because they take competing positions, become more than characters, carrying elaborate burdens of symbolic contrast. Yet
the fact that he sees them as characters and sets them on the
stage shows that, like Pindar, he saw the world through living beings, not through ideas. His difference from Pindar
is to have pressed this sense of life farther toward analysis,
using it not only, as Pindar did, to catch final states of being,
but to portray the oppositions and strains which precede
these. This step is paradoxically both a step downward into
darkness and upward toward light. It is toward darkness in
the sense that Aeschylus uncovers layers of fear and hate
that Pindar did not contemplate and which would probably
have struck him as superstitious, certainly as repugnant. His
imagery can be much more lurid and harsher than Pindar's;

the struggle between male and female that runs through the plays destroys any easy harmony; even heroism is dangerous to him because it drives the violent male will to achievements mixed with destruction; Orestes' and Prometheus' return to sanity is bought by a retirement from the world which is nearly the loss of reason. Archaeologists say that a new technique commonly wins its advances by disrupting the grace of older forms, and something of the sort is visible here. Though he writes in the spirit of progress, Aeschylus begins by presenting more primitive states of mind than appear in Homer. The upward step may be in part the mere acknowledgment of these; it is at least the sense that this avowal is the first step toward any triumph over hate, hence to any true peace. The popular origins of tragedy speak in the darkness of his legends. It is as if the disturbed consciousness of a people, so far only half expressed in the aristocratic art of a Homer or Pindar, now fully spoke for the first time. Unlike Apollo, Dionysus was a god of the people, and his triumph in tragedy was their triumph. But conversely Aeschylus' intense faith in the advances won by the new democracy is a popular faith, and the hope that created the democracy is clearer through him than from any Greek source. In taking much longer steps than Pindar toward the analysis of problems, he moved nearer the age of reason and prose. Yet, because of his very urgency, he felt with as strong poetic presentness as Pindar the harsh forces of history that led on to progress.

So far we have considered the outer and social forces which gave rise to tragedy: the conflicts implicit in democracy, an experience of change which evoked ideas of time and progress, popular origins which supplied franker myths. But recent writers have justly dwelt on an accompanying inner change, of which something was said earlier. Pindar's odes were seen as an extended metaphor in which ideas appropriate to heroes were applied to victors and the two

merged, or nearly merged, in a common light. Such an outlook was found radically distinct from Homer's way of seeing things singly, each in its own identity, and this method
of taking things together seemed to show the mind's new
confidence in its own synoptic powers. This heady self-trust
of the mind was in turn declared the common impulse behind
Pindar's and Aeschylus' bold styles. They composed im-
periously because they saw a flashing allusiveness in things,
which hinted at one another, carried common meanings, and
joined to reveal new simplicities. But it is obvious that a
mind which feels this synoptic power can feel its burden also,
and tragedy has been described as expressing this new weight
of choice.

Homer, it has been argued by Bruno Snell,[109] has words
for parts of the body, but not for the whole body, except
dead, and likewise for faculties of the soul, but again for the
united soul only after death. Homer evidently lacked any
such notion as Aristotle's of the central and controlling mind.
The conclusion follows that it was the gods who were felt to
explain those decisive moments when the mind feels itself
united and acts with heightened power. Through a god's
presence Glaucus forgets his wound to help Sarpedon,
Achilles stops short of killing Agamemnon, Telemachus
loses his shyness to address Nestor.[110] The Olympian religion, this argument goes on, originally explained those concentrated moments when men do the unforeseen and for better or worse momentarily stand outside themselves. But it
evidently could not and did not explain failure, though times
when a man stood alone unstrengthened by any god could
show him not less a hero. Thus in his last moments Hector
perceives that Apollo has left him, but fights nevertheless.[111]
One mark of Homer's greatness is that he seemingly modi-
fied the inherited epic view that the gods inspire and explain
heroism — which is to say, came to see in men a courage and
fidelity which were not less characteristic of heroism than

was divine support. This double motivation for great acts
runs through the *Iliad,* which sees alike those radiant deeds
that betray a present god and those other deeds, stubborn
and desperate, which show a man alone. But with Aeschylus
this sense, nascent in Homer, that a man himself carries final
responsibility is full-grown. Tragedy as a form may be seen
as a way of giving it speech.[112] To set men on the stage
without such comment as the epic poet gave, hence without
that frame of divine presences which in the *Iliad* surrounds
the heroes' acts, is to show them in their isolation. Aeschylus marks very sharply the moments when his characters
make their lonely decisions. Agamemnon strikes his staff on
the ground in pain that he must choose between holding the
fleet at Aulis and sacrificing his daughter; the sight of his
mother wrings from Orestes the desperate cry "What shall I
do?"; Atossa maternally but vainly explains the taunts that
led Xerxes to try to excel Darius; Eteocles' resolution to fight
his brother is the third in a series of violent decisions going
back to Laius' disobedience of the oracle; Pelasgus in a
memorable speech calls his mind a diver which must plunge
deep into the decision whether to protect the Danaids; the
Prometheus is in effect a long explanation why the Titan re-
sisted Zeus and it closes with a crowning defiance. In all these
cases the central fact is a man's responsibility. If tragedy is
analytical in showing a conflict of forces, it draws presentness from the sense that a man is more than their creature
and product, but himself acts on them, creating his own future. Playwright and audience are drawn to participate in
these moments of decision, and the fearful attention that
beats on the stage is the mind's acknowledgment that even
as it has the power to understand so it has the obligation to
act.

   Pindar did not share this feeling for decision. Though
his synoptic style shows the mind's new sense of its power
which was the mark of the age, he shrank from pressing this

sense of power to a sense of responsibility. Or perhaps this is only to repeat that his guiding impulse was religious, not like that of Aeschylus, strongly ethical as well. His doctrine of a right nature natively implanted in a man (for example, in the infant Heracles of *N.* 1), his sense in such figures as Eleithyia, Youth, and Quietude of enfolding presences that foster and guide such a nature, his feeling for victory as enveloping a man in the divine radiance, his emphasis on music and repose, all show a contemplative mind which feels that the divine order lays hold on us, not we on it. He of course often speaks of the pain and effort which precede victory, but in such a way that they are largely anticipatory. They inhabit a semidarkness which scatters when the light of true being dawns. His discomfort in the odes, *P.* 2, *N.* 4, and *N.* 7, in which he feels himself misunderstood, suggests how loath he was to think life characterized simply by personal choice and how passionately he wished to regard even his own abrupt and allusive thought as describing things divinely given and widely visible, rather than lonely things discerned by private eyes. In spite of his metaphorical style he was nearer to Homer in seeing the brightness of the world as god-given and in avoiding, frontally at least, the problem of human responsibility. But tragedy as Aeschylus created it was this frontal vision of responsibility. The contrast between the two forms and the two men thus becomes a contrast between deeply representative outlooks. The older attitude looks toward the outer world; is comparatively unconscious of the self, which seems borne in the hands of great natural forces; draws strength from this bond with nature and finds freedom and happiness in a sense of unity with the great whole. The newer attitude brings the self sharply forward; hears the bracing imperative that a man can and must act by his own resolution; being morally roused, is intellectually roused also and becomes absorbed in problems which its moral urgency revealed. At this point the newer attitude strikes an obstacle which was not at first apparent; for having originally felt a oneness with the world which the emphasis on self only made more intense, it presently runs the risk of losing this sense of oneness as it turns to more purely intellectual problems. Such at least was the evolution of Greek poetry in the fifth century. Despite the headier consciousness of self which is implied in his meta-phorical style, Pindar lingered in the untroubled view which lost the self in the surrounding world. In the invention of tragedy Aeschylus put this self forward to a crucial place, clothing it with the fearful necessity of decision and present-ing it with choices which roused its analytical powers. Only Sophocles thereafter was able to keep the delicate balance between life as sensed participation and life as idea. But having once felt the power of ideas, the Greeks turned in-creasingly to those intellectual conquests which indeed give the world shape and order but at the cost of freshness and oneness. The path is straight which leads from Aeschylus to Aristotle and thence to the analytical conquests of the West. The tone of these future conquests is already visible in Aeschylus: political justice, rational inquiry, moral obli-gation. These goals reflect their humanistic source, and if they have a weakness, it is the weakness of this source, that it tends to overvalue the conscious self, hence to weaken in-tuition and to dissolve the sense of bond with nature. In Pindar one catches sight of what Greece and the West might have become if there had been no Athens, something closer to the symbolic and formal cultures of the Orient, less analytical, more conscious of the enfolding whole. But since no developed culture is so uniform as to preclude outlooks at variance with its main tendency, Pindar and Aeschylus can express competing strains within the West itself: the sense of being and the sense of process, the static and the emergent, life as an intuitively felt present, and life as an analyzed complex of past and future.

Tragedy thus reflects more than the outer changes incident on the new democracy; it reflects also an interior change of feeling. But this wakened sense of personal responsibility, however important, is not quite enough to explain the special tone of tragedy. Something expiatory remains over, something that suggests the necessity of suffering. This element too has been brought forward in recent years. Logically considered, it is the obverse of the sense of responsibility. The latter expresses a man's freedom; it moves toward Aristotle's ideal, in the *Ethics,* of a perfect power of intelligent choice; hence it posits at bottom the thorough victory of intelligence. The sense of expiation, by contrast, feels something dubious and half-wrong in this confident freedom, as if the man who espoused it were bound to work harm as well as good. E. R. Dodds[113] has adopted for Homer's and for Aeschylus' worlds the terms respectively of shame-society and guilt-society, the former meaning a state in which a man's opinion of himself depends on his reputation among others, the latter signifying a time of men's lonely self-judgment, and he asks why the former state should have changed into the latter. His answer is that poverty kept driving the Greeks of the archaic period to inventive efforts, chiefly migration overseas and creation at home of more complex and productive forms of society. But these efforts in turn strained the traditional bonds of place and family and of a religion heavily based on them. Innovation, always difficult, was doubly so for the Greeks because of the ancestral and local color of their cults. Hence arose, the argument concludes, the Oedipus-like guilt which haunts innovation, and it is this which gives tragedy its distinctive tone. The tragic man is at once great in his lonely decisions, yet guiltily conscious of destroying something in order to reach them. This view draws on the immense discussion that has grown up since Freud around the idea of guilt. It was said a little earlier that Aeschylus' mind is paradoxically both darker and more hopeful than Pindar's. He acknowledged savage impulses in order by transcending them to reach a higher healing. It is clear in any case that the conflict which marked democracy took on for him the tone of this inner conflict, and his subject is simultaneously the state and the mind. The idea of time then came to involve more than an historical evolution; it concerned the mind's living with its guilt until, like Orestes, it could sense its ancient sore subsiding and feel itself free. So Prometheus in a Latin version of a speech from the lost second play of the trilogy (fg. 193) says that his once-violent will to live and resist has died. He has lost a strain of self-will which was mixed with his heroism and which in the first play implied guilt through extreme need for self-explanation.

These two sides of tragedy, the sense of responsibility and the sense of guilt, merge and find their solution in the idea of time; therefore go far to explain the invention of the theatre as an experience in time. Early in the *Prometheus* Oceanus offers to reconcile the Titan with Zeus, but is scornfully dismissed by Prometheus and appears slightly ridiculous. Yet the trilogy ended in exactly such a reconciliation, and Oceanus' original offer was justified. Why then did he appear ridiculous, and what happened in the course of the three plays that a state of mind at first unthinkable should later become possible and just? The change contains Aeschylus' doctrine of learning by suffering, and time is the medium in which learning takes place. The need for expiation is not, as it might at first seem, merely an irrational survival, the result of subconscious unwillingness to accept change. It is the sign rather of a certain heat of egotism that was mixed with the original act of courage. Though courage nerved Prometheus, as it does the other heroes, to his great decisions, a stubborn alloy of self-absorption and self-will worked also, and this second impulse, to the degree that it remained operative, would mark the results of his

acts. Time and suffering discovered what in an act did not
spring from motives of self and hence contained the promise of general good. A chief trait of Aeschylus' style is his
absorption with wide spaces. The *Suppliants* gives on great
distances; the *Persians* is the lament of an empire; Prometheus tells Io's past and future wanderings, he addresses the
elements and seems to see the world from his rock; the
chorus of the *Agamemnon* still spy the army leaving for
Troy, Clytaemnestra sees the city's last night and traces the
returning beacon; Orestes travels by land and sea until his
stain is old. This sense of space, which may be Aeschylus'
truest hall-mark, is related to the experience of time and
suffering because it evokes a wide freedom which is the escape from obsessive self. The trilogy may be thought of
as opening spatially on free horizons, while the characters
climb temporally with pain to the possession of freedom.
Space is the language and promise of freedom. The lonely
deciding self, though central to tragedy, thus did not remain
isolated. Though necessary to all desirable ends, it was rather
a beginning than an end, in that on the step of self-awareness followed a second step of self-transcendence, which was
a merging with the general good. This progression applied
also to the audience, and most fully to them, since some of
the characters, for example, Agamemnon or Eteocles, die to
take their place in a longer evolution. The audience attests
the relevance to the new democracy of the ideas of conflict
and of solution won through time. These ideas inspire the
historical and social progression of the trilogies. But the
same ideas, inwardly experienced, involve private evolution,
and the audience is both corporate Athens and a gathering
of isolated and separate persons. In this second and inward
sense, conflict contains both responsibility and guilt, the former as a step toward achievement, the latter as the sign of
the impeding self. What higher state could emerge as a
private or a public gain would then be bought by some expia-

tion of the merely assertive self. The knowledge of this further gain and true solution is the knowledge which comes through suffering. It is the experience of justice both as punishment and as an ideal. The trilogy contains this movement through time out of conflict to solution, seen by the audience as a single process necessary alike to the individual and the state, seen only partially by some of the characters whose responsibility and whose guilt are their imperfect and tragic experience of the process.

Aeschylus lacked the difficult mystic idea that serenity can exist beside evil and pain and by existing know something of the final good even in the imperfect present. Pindar was close to this idea in feeling that victory and poetry, act and thought, can momentarily lay hold on the divine timelessness. In this sense his guiding impulse may properly be called religious. He felt the presence of the gods in life as it is, and the Odes have their uniting theme in this awareness. The strong social bent of Aeschylus' mind forced him to postpone the state of peace and harmony until society itself possessed them; and he sought the coincidence of private and public happiness. The *Oresteia* culminates in such a vision of an ideally just Athens; the conclusion of the Danaid trilogy sees the union of Heaven and Earth in Hypermnestra's marriage; Prometheus' reconciliation with Zeus merges creativity with justice. This optimism reveals the high mood of Athens and proclaims that the divine justice is realizable and at hand. To the degree that the plays thus express an ideal attainable on earth, Aeschylus stands apart from Pindar, not so much waiting on the divine as seeing it possessed and embodied. The confidence of the West in morals and intellect speaks in this faith. But to the degree that the plays have to do with an inward, not an historical progression, the ideal Athens of the *Eumenides* signifies a spiritual rather than a social state. It describes the mind's release from self-absorption and its recovered joy in earth and community. Certainly the plays have largely this inward meaning, in the light of which Aeschylus and Pindar do not after all stand far apart. Both see the divine freedom and harmony as touching life, and inwardly find the gods in the world. Pindar feels the radiant fact of the gods' presence; Aeschylus, men's slow emergence toward it. He begins with bitter conflicts which confine characters to their private passions; reveals as they face their decisions both their heroism and their confinement; finally brings into being from their suffering the results of their heroism alone, purged of confinement and visible as the new order, saving alike of the state and the mind.

THE SUPPLIANTS

THE *Suppliants*[114] opens a trilogy of which the last two plays, the *Egyptians* and the *Danaides*, are known only conjecturally and in outline. Because the chorus consisting of the fifty daughters of Danaus has by far the chief part and its lyric and corporate tone contrasts sharply to the developed characterization of the *Agamemnon*, the play has been thought the first extant tragedy and from Aeschylus' early period. But this criterion which makes characterization the mark of his growth suggests nineteenth-century rather than Greek feeling. It is incompatible with the abstractness of the *Prometheus*, which has been argued to be the latest of the plays,[115] and even with the *Eumenides*, which merges the individualism of the *Agamemnon* in the corporate light of the Areopagus and an ideal Athens. It is by no means clear that in his middle or late years Aeschylus could not have given chief weight in the older manner to the chorus, as he comes near doing in the *Eumenides*. A recently published papyrus[116] fragment of an hypothesis to the trilogy, stating that Aeschylus won with it over Sophocles, may force revision of the older view.

The hatred for their cousins, the sons of Aegyptus, which drove the suppliant Danaids from Egypt to Argos and gives the setting for the first play, did not persist in one of them, Hypermnestra. The sons of Aegyptus, who are off shore at the end of the first play, landed in the second. Apparently after a battle in which the king of Argos was killed, Danaus expounded his famous scheme whereby his daughters shall marry their cousins and murder them on their wedding night. All do so except Hypermnestra, who spares her bridegroom Lynceus through love and is tried before a court in the third play. The trilogy ended with her acquittal after a defense

by the goddess Aphrodite herself, part of whose speech is
preserved. "Pure heaven yearns to wed the earth and love
solicits earth to meet his wooing. The rain descending from
the bridegroom sky impregnates earth, and she bears for
mankind pasturing flocks and the life-giving grain. Green-
fronded springtime from the showery union is wrought, and
I of all this am part cause." (fg. 44) Hypermnestra's love
for Lynceus thus signifies the love which frees earth from
her sterile isolation, uniting her with the sky and giving her
a fruitfulness which attests the gods. This bond with the
gods through the life of nature recalls *N.* 6. But the point
to be noted here is that this conclusion of the trilogy[117] in a
new and divinely sanctioned order is close in spirit to the
conclusion of the *Oresteia* and, so far as we can imagine, of
the Promethean trilogy. In the *Prometheus Bound* (869)
the Titan predicts the happy results of Io's sufferings which
will come after generations when her descendants return to
Argos and from their line will spring the demigods Perseus
and Heracles. The present trilogy shows a step in a similar
progress. The king Pelasgus having died in battle, Danaus,
and from him Lynceus and Hypermnestra, will rule in
Argos, and the new line will contain through Io the blood of
Zeus. Hypermnestra's love for Lynceus initiates a state
radically distinct from the mood of fear and flight in the
first play. This better state stands clear of two equally unhappy possibilities: of a rooted localism which contains nothing of the divine scope, and of a wandering and search which
contains nothing of localism. Hypermnestra dissolved both
defective choices by a commitment through love which,
in Aphrodite's speech, is itself the bond of the free gods
with earth. If the *Suppliants* is part of an early trilogy, one
could only conclude that Aeschylus' thought emerged nearly
full-grown. If so, it would resemble Pindar's, which, if
marked by detectable periods, shows in the earliest ode, *P.*
10, traits of the latest ode, *P.* 8. But questions of date are

secondary, and what is notable in this trilogy is that, despite
a lyric tone in the *Suppliants* quite distinct from the dramatic
clarity of the *Agamemnon,* the movement of Aeschylus' mind
toward resolution of conflict in harmony is the same.

The opening lines announce the conflicting themes of
placelessness and place which are resolved only at the end of
the trilogy. "May Zeus who protects arrivals look merci-
fully on our ship-borne troupe, that put to sea from the
smooth sands of the mouths of the Nile. We flee forsak-
ing the sacred country bordered of Syria. ―― What happier land than this could we reach, bearing our wool-decked
suppliant branches? O city, o soil, o water clear, o gods of
heaven and vengeful gods who inhabit tombs underneath
earth, and third, o saving Zeus, who watchest righteous
men's houses, look with the land's sweet influence on our
fugitive band." (vv. 1-5, 19-29) The wide sea and remote
places of Egypt and Syria are balanced by the security of
Argos, the former evoking space and movement, the latter
fixity and rest. The girls' motives in their flight remain obscure after much discussion. They say that they left Egypt
for no crime, but in what they call "kindred man-flight"
(v. 8) namely, from their cousins, the sons of Aegyptus,
whose intentions they call impious. A later dialogue with
the king, Pelasgus, somewhat illuminates their minds. "Why
do you say you seek these gathered gods, proffering newly-
plucked your white-wreathed garlands?" "To flee subjection to Aegyptus' sons." "From hate or do you mean it is
unholy?" "Who could enjoy connections which possess
them?" "But this is how the strength of families grows."
"Yes, and divorce is easy when they founder." (vv. 333-339)
The girls evade the question whether such a marriage with
first cousins is illegal, as it was not in Attic law. A textual
difficulty slightly obscures their reply, and they ask either
who could enjoy or who would buy connections which own
them. (v. 337) In either case they foresee servitude to their

husbands' financial authority, and when Pelasgus answers that this is the way by which a family's property is kept intact (i.e., by kinsmen marrying heiresses), they reiterate that a woman is then helpless when her husband wants to divorce her. It has been argued from this passage that Aeschylus understood the freer position of women in a tribal society which was destroyed by male control of property in the mercantile age.[118] He obviously felt a cleft of interest between the sexes, and it is reasonable that legend and popular memory should have conveyed to him a sense of happier times before the competitive present. Throughout the plays male ambition is dangerous even when it is heroic, and the Egyptians' menace for the Danaids resembles that of the conquering Agamemnon for the peaceful Iphigeneia or of the warlike Eteocles for the pious women of Thebes. Aeschylus wants a community in which female peace and abundance shall not fall prey to male will and intellect, and the luxuriant blessings which the Danaids presently invoke on Argos are similar to those which the Eumenides bring Athens at the end of the Oresteia. But Aeschylus' interest is hardly antiquarian. If the Danaids evoke a bygone age in rejecting marriage customs currently sanctioned, they do so because they express the deeper question of freedom and commitment. As descendants of Io, who had herself been uprooted by Zeus and carried to a higher if harder destiny, they will not willingly relapse into a fate even more bounded than hers before her change. Their dislike for their cousins is a dislike for dull and servile limits. In their trailing clothes and sunburnt skin they are several times likened to Oriental women (vv. 71, 234, 279), but they are Greeks at heart and their Greekness is their passion for scope. Aeschylus manages to forget, at least in this first play, that the sons of Aegyptus are likewise descended from Zeus by Io. Their name made them foreign, and they have become Egyptians as the Danaids have not. Hence the conflict between the

girls and their suitors is a conflict between Greek liberty and
Oriental subjection, and liberty carries implications of the
wider mind which is Zeus. The paradox of the play is that
the character of the girls as women conflicts with their character as fugitives and descendants of Zeus. As women they
ultimately imply commitment and love, the traits which are
vindicated in Hypermnestra by Aphrodite and which resolve
the trilogy. Yet as fugitives they seek at the beginning an
entire uncommitment, and their hatred of the Egyptians
drives them to a mood of flight which shares the spirit of
Io's wanderings but lacks that of her final release.

The question, like all the main questions in Aeschylus, involves Zeus's will for mankind, and the Danaids presently
break into a superb and deeply agitated hymn to Zeus. They
have returned to Io's haunts; one who heard their cry would
think it the sad nightingale's who killed her son (their later
murder of their husbands speaks in this lament, which is that
of placelessness and lost ties) ; yet the gods hate violence;
"even for the oppressed of war there is an altar, refuge for
war's fugitives, the awe of heaven" (vv. 40-85, here speaks
the justice of their claim to resist subjection). Their
hope both for the safety that they seek and for the deeper
accord which they do not yet understand is Zeus's will. "It
blazes on all sides, even from night, with issue dim for men.
Tangled stretch the pathways of his mind and shadowy, invisible to eyes. He hurls men ruined from their high-tow-
ered hopes, yet wears no violence. Effortless is all that is
the gods'. Seated, he yet from where he is fulfills his will,
from his untouched repose." (vv. 88-103) Their cry resembles the famous prayer to Zeus in the *Agamemnon* (160-
183) both in language and in position just after the king's
half-right, half-wrong decision for the army and against
Iphigeneia has been presented. So here the Danaids' isolation which was in their likeness to the nightingale conflicts
with their just search for freedom, and only the incalculable

mind of Zeus will find the solution. They are consciously
praying that their own wishes be enacted, and they go on to
describe the violence of the Egyptians and to invoke Athene
as the protectress of girlhood. But time to Aeschylus begets
the unforeseen, and their conscious hopes are not the end.
Even they subconsciously know this, and the incalculability
which they ascribe to Zeus contains, like the comparable lines
of the *Agamemnon,* a dim awareness of the further state
which Hypermnestra, like Orestes, will reach through pain.
This evolution was revealed in Io, to whom they revert at
the end of the ode. Her suffering was inseparable from her
destiny as bride of Zeus, but though they know her final rest,
they cannot conceive a like mood for themselves, understanding as yet only flight and rejection.

Danaus now announces the approach of the Argives, and
all the warlike masculinity which Aristophanes later felt in
Aeschylus is in this description of dust, shrieking wheels,
spears, and marching men. In this passage and in the
speeches of the king, Pelasgus, is a quality of unspoiled
native force descriptive of a people who had not yet felt the
complexity of the world. The Danaids gather by the images
of the gods which adorn the precinct where they have taken
refuge, and Pelasgus, after marveling at the girls' barbaric
clothes, explains himself, his city, and the wide extent of his
early kingdom. They reply by expounding their claim
through Io on Argos, recalling how she was wooed by Zeus,
hated by Hera, changed into a heifer, driven over much of
the earth by a gadfly, and finally in Egypt was delivered of
a son, Epaphus. By Libya he in turn had a son Belus, who
had two sons, Danaus and Aegyptus, the fathers respectively
of the girls and their pursuers. At this point occurs the dialogue quoted earlier in which the king tries to discover the
girls' motives for flight. But though they prove to lack clear
grounds in law, they have the authority of the shrine in
which they stand, and their interchange with the king be-

comes a conflict between worldly and religious claims. Pelasgus is entirely Greek in feeling both claims acutely. Though the girls insist that as king he has authority to decide in their favor, he protests that he cannot act without appeal to the people. Aeschylus is evidently describing early Greece in him, and if the picture is anachronistic, it conveys both native force and native sense of liberty. In its political aspect, the trilogy will show how these virtues emerge on a wider stage. Sensible as the king is of the girls' religious appeals, he is equally horrified at the prospect of war in Argos if he heeds them. "The judgment is not clear. Call me not judge. I have already said, without the people I cannot act, though sovereign, lest with time citizens murmur if disaster fall, 'Honoring strangers you destroyed the state.'" (vv. 397-401) He stands at the lonely moment of decision which all Aeschylus' heroes face and in which Hypermnestra will follow him. "Now must the seeing and undrunken gaze of deep remedial intellect descend bottomwards like a diver, so that first the city be undamaged and events ensue benign for us, and yet that strife seize not on you as victims nor by shunning fugitives to these sacred images we plant among us the pursuing god who still in Hades remits not the dead. Think you I have no need for saving thought?" (vv. 407-417)

What then do the Danaids bring Argos? The answer is rather implied than stated in this first play of the trilogy. In describing himself and his kingdom, Pelasgus made no claim of divine descent. The Greece over which he rules, though vigorous and uncorrupted, is parochial. Zeus's love for Io was the hand of divinity touching Argos, and the destiny which it imported was at once higher and harder. The sense of space which was in the Danaids' opening lines returns in all references to Io, and something of the placelessness of Zeus himself surrounds her. In the question whether to repatriate her descendants, Argos confronts an element of immensity in things which endangers its earlier security, and the troubling destiny which had been Io's alone now touches the city. Similarly in the *Oresteia* the Trojan expedition, while great and partly just, disrupts the life of Mycenae and leads eventually to a new view of the state. Pelasgus is so disturbed by these dangerous prospects that after the troubled speech just quoted he ends by disclaiming responsibility. Wealth, he says, can be restored, but life cannot. "I'd rather be untutored in disasters than expert." (v. 453) The turning point in the simple action of the play comes as the girls threaten to hang themselves in the sacred precinct if they are rejected. Pelasgus is horrified. "The words I hear are lashes to my heart." (v. 466) He sees the future now as deeply uncertain, but feels no choice but to avoid the worse evil of sacrilege. "Unless I pay you our indebtedness, no arrow can outshoot the curse you utter. And yet if stationed at the wall I try issue of battle with Aegyptus' sons, your cousins, is it not a bitter price that men for women's sake corrupt the earth?" (vv. 472-477) The statement of conflict between the sexes well expresses what the Danaids have to offer Argos. It was noted that they have a double character, as fugitives and as women. The one side of their nature conveys the disturbing quality of Io's wanderings. They disrupt security much as Helen disrupts the peace of Greece and Troy, though they are not guilty as Helen is guilty. They are figures of unrest, partly through their own timorous and emotional natures, but partly also because Zeus has shown his hand in history through them and they in turn are more sensitive to his will. But in their second aspect they resemble Penelope rather than Helen and imply rest rather than unrest. This side of the Danaids appears only indirectly in the present play, which nevertheless looks to it as a solution. The Danaids' quality of unrest is ended in Hypermnestra, whose act of commitment replaces their mood of wandering. Three states or

stages of mind thus emerge: first, the confident and masculine but limited and even youthful security of Argos before
the Danaids' arrival (a state corresponding to Io's before
she was loved by Zeus) ; second, the loss of this security by
awareness of remote places and peoples and even of the
hitherto remote gods (the condition corresponding to Io's
wanderings) ; and third, the recovery of something like the
first peaceful stage, but after events which have brought
much deeper understanding of the world and the gods and
which consequently force a new definition of place and peace.
Pelasgus' reluctance to endanger men on behalf of women
is his reluctance to surrender the order and intelligibility of
the first stage for the uncertainties of the second. The tone
of vigorous and martial confidence which was in the description of the Argive army has been made less secure in his
lonely choice.

The Danaids have in effect won their point, and the action verges toward its consequences in the later plays of the
trilogy. But as Pelasgus could not avoid endangering
Argos' first state of sheltered peace, so the Danaids cannot
linger, as they hope to do, in the second state of flight and
negation. Two fine odes express their mood, the one sung
after Pelasgus leaves to urge the people on the girls' behalf,
the other after Danaus returns to announce a favorable decision. They sing the first ode, about Io, while some uncertainty still remains. They fervently seek Zeus's protection
both as Io's descendants and as women. "Lord of lords, of
blessed most blessed, power perfectest of perfections, serene
Zeus, heed and may it be. Fend in loathing off the lust of
men; cast in the purple sea their black-benched folly. Look
on our storied breed, the women's cause, and happily renew
our forebear's praise, the woman thou didst love." (vv. 524-
534) They describe her wide travels and the reverence
which she received in Egypt, then come to her deliverance.
"By his unwounding strength and breath divine her trial

subsided and she welled away her tears' sad shame. She took
a burden justly named of Zeus and bore a blameless son . . .
What god then may I fitly hail for righter acts? By his
mere touch our sire, progenitor, and lord, our breed's great
builder brooding anciently, Zeus of fair winds, in all
remedial. Enthroned beneath no other's rule, he the greater
sways the less. None seated higher heeds he from below.
His acts are as a word, to bring to pass his pondering mind's
intent." (vv. 576-581, 590-599) All Aeschylus' distances
are in this ode: geographical in the reaches of Io's travel,
speculative in the reverence for Zeus's creative will, temporal
since he reveals himself darkly and at his own pace. From
the point of view of the action, the girls' claim through Io
on Zeus is their claim on Argos as suppliants, but as in the
earlier ode, their sense of Zeus's vastness gives their
thoughts a wider dimension. They convey a kind of listening for Zeus's will, and their character as women fits this
role, in that their impressionability intuitively rejects both
the harsh authority of the Egyptians and the secure prudence
of Pelasgus. The conflict between male and female widens
into that between place and placelessness, and the claim
which the girls make on Argos is a demand that the state,
however fixed and rooted, somehow accommodate itself to
the freedom and change which are Zeus.

In announcing on his return that the assembly has acted
favorably, Danaus quotes the king as foretelling immense
disasters if the rights of suppliants are neglected. (vv. 616-
620) These evils resemble the wasting sickness with which
Apollo in the *Choephoroe* (269-296) threatens Orestes if
he shall fail to avenge his father. Both threats express the
impossibility of refusing change and of lingering in a sheltered state when the painful time has come to leave it. The
vote of the assembly confirms the earlier impression of the
Argives' native strength and sense of freedom, and these
virtues are about to emerge into history. At this point the

Danaids sing the second of the odes just mentioned, invoking blessings on Argos. This is the ode that closely resembles the brilliant closing passages of the *Oresteia* in which the Eumenides in the presence of Athene pour out blessings on Athens. There these benefits are the culmination of Orestes' painful act, at last healed and translated into a new order. Here the end has not yet come, but the peaceful fruitfulness of land and people which the Danaids invoke is precisely that which Aphrodite sees in Hypermnestra's love for Lynceus. The ode is a vision of the solution, though the Danaids themselves have not reached it. And as the Eumenides are women who until their final conversion had fiercely upheld Clytaemnestra's cause against Orestes, so the Danaids' blessings convey a final harmony between the sexes, and Pelasgus' acceptance of the Danaids implies Hypermnestra's union. "They did not set their vote with males, dishonoring women's pleas, but spied pursuant Zeus, watcherlike, incontestable. What house is glad with him against its roof? He presses heavy . . . Therefore prodigal blessings shall take wing from our bough-shaded lips. Never may plague drain from this state her men, nor civil war corrupt her fields with tumbled sons. Unharvested be flowering youth, nor may harsh Ares, Aphrodite's bridegroom, reap its bloom down." (vv. 643-651, 656-666) They pray for smoking altars, fruitful fields, herds, music and singing, justice at home and abroad, and piety.

Yet the Danaids have not themselves inwardly reached the state of peace corresponding to these prayers, and the end of the play casts them back into their original agitation. When Danaus sights the Egyptian ships off shore and goes for help, leaving his daughters alone, their fears show themselves again in images of space and flight. "How could I find some skyey seat where drift the dank clouds into snow, or some precipitous hanging cliff outranging goats, beyond sight, lonely-thoughted, where vultures haunt, that it could

witness to my sinking leap before I violently meet heart-cut-
ting marriage?" (vv. 792-799)   They repeat their cry to
Zeus.   "The males of Aegyptus' lewd outrageous breed
hunt me with shouting follies as I run, to clutch me with
their strength.   But thine the scales are balanced over all.
What for mankind is wrought apart from thee?" (vv. 817-
824)   There is obvious provocation for these fears, which
nevertheless contain something excessive, and it is this excess
which will end in the murder of their husbands.   The sexual
conflict has bred an emotional disturbance hostile to the harmony of Zeus, to whom they at the same time pray.   Hence
the political problem confronting Argos is matched by an inward problem confronting the Danaids, and neither will be
solved without the other.   In this interpenetration of public
by private states is the deep sources of Aeschylus' power.
Egyptian heralds, though not the pursuers themselves, finally
enter talking a wild half-Greek, and they are dragging the
girls off when Pelasgus and Danaus return.   When the king
states the city's will to protect them and the heralds threaten
war, the situation of the next play is presented.   Danaus directs the girls to Argos with minute advice about their be-
havior, a passage which amusingly shows the contrast noted
in the first chapter between idea and detail in the late-
archaic style.   In the choral odes Aeschylus had presented
the Danaids as almost pure idea, figures sensitive to Zeus,
deeply inward, associated with space and change, but here
they are simply eligible girls.   In the same way, the Oceanids
are partly seen in the *Prometheus* as sympathetic spirits of
earth and sea but partly also as the hero's young sisters-in-
law.   As the Danaids leave with prayers to the virgin
Artemis, their servants have the last word.   "But this glad
song shuns not the Cyprian.   With Hera she holds power
most near to Zeus, devious goddess honored for sacred acts.
Jointly on their mother wait Desire and winning Persuasion
undenied and Harmony partakes from Aphrodite the whis-

per and the touch of love." (vv. 1034-1042)   Though the suppliants protest their continuing hatred of the Egyptians, the suggestion has been made that leads beyond the murder of their husbands to Hypermnestra's act of love.   Alone she will outweigh the others and prove Io's true heir by bringing flight to rest and changing loss to possession.   As for the city, the return of Zeus's line will inaugurate its destined greatness.   Through the touch of Zeus place and fixity will lose their boundedness by harboring the unbound traits of justice and mercy.   As for the quarrel between the sexes, it will have been solved in favor of the male, yet with a harmony which alone can produce the blessings invoked in the Danaids' prophetic song.

To return briefly to Pindar, the flaring night-fire of Zeus's will which the Danaids proclaim in the first ode is both like and unlike the night-fire of heroism in $O.$ 1.   Both men see in the divine the same blazing vitality, but whereas for Pindar it shines from the night of common life in the flash of joy and glory, to Aeschylus it is the blaze of justice guiding to the future.   Insofar as it acts for him in the present, scattering, for example, the darkness of the Egyptians, it has the violence of lightning, and even the Danaids who invoke it cannot grasp its power, which will singe them in their resort to murder.   This is only to say again that Aeschylus' blazing vision of justice wakens proportionately black shadows, blacker even than those in Plato's cave, because the light of justice shines directly against the passions of the world.   Pindar, because he lacks this ardor for justice, is able to see finality already about him.   He is the visionary of the present, Aeschylus of the future.   A similar difference colors their feeling for women.   Cyrene and Evadne in $P.$ 9 and $O.$ 6 resemble Io to the extent that their fixity in earth and place is likewise broken by the intruding god.   Yet in Cyrene there was a willingness for his coming, and for both women the intrusion soon brings a bright completion beyond

their hopes. Only Thetis in the sorrowing *I*. 8, written just
after the Persian invasion, conveys the tragedy which haunts
the union of mortal with immortal, in that her glorious son
Achilles must die. But the emphasis is different there;
Thetis is the immortal who by her union with the mortal
Peleus sacrifices something of her bright permanence. From
the opposite point of view, Peleus reaches his highest happiness in her, as do Cyrene and Evadne in Apollo. The gods
for Pindar complete rather than jostle the actual world,
which thus from the first shows a latent harmony with them.
In Aphrodite's speech Hypermnestra's marriage also finally
reveals this harmony, but only after the sufferings of Io, the
Danaids, Argos, and herself. The Danaids perpetuate the
spirit of Io's unrest because Zeus for both was of scope too
vast for common limits. The destiny which he implants corresponds to Aeschylus' vision of wide space; it bursts rooted
ties and leads to remoteness. It is true that a second and
ultimately stronger side of Aeschylus' mind accepted place,
fearing the limitless horizons on which the divine presence
opens. His problem was therefore to conceive a return to
mortal limits which would yet be compatible with boundless
space. This return comes near being his definition of freedom. It is a state like Hypermnestra's which is finally able
to recognize the unbounded and divine in the bounded and
mortal. But the difficulty of reaching this state is to be felt
in the initial conflict between space and earth. Place and
commitment do not, as they do in Pindar, find ready and
natural fulfillment in the pure being of the gods, but accord
between earth and sky follows a chastening tuition.

THE PERSIANS

THE *Persians* also has to do with freedom and in a more purely political sense. Produced in 472 with the young Pericles as choregus it treats the great events culminating in Salamis which Phrynichus with Themistocles as choregus had treated in the *Phoenician Women* four years earlier. To the generation of Aeschylus the line which divided history from legend was dimmer than it later became. Phrynichus also dramatized the fall of Miletus; Bacchylides' fifth ode substitutes an account of Croesus for the usual myth; *P.* 1, which begins with the divine harmony and Zeus's punishment of Typhus, goes on to Salamis, Plataea, and Himera and ends with Croesus and Phalaris. The argument of the *Persians* gives it as the second play of a tetralogy which included the *Phineus,* the *Glaucus at Potniae,* and the satyr-play *Prometheus Firelighter,* and since Aeschylus seems otherwise to have composed in sequences, it has been imagined that the *Phineus,* which was laid in Thrace, may have foretold the advance of Persia much as the *Prometheus Bound* foretells the eruption of Aetna, while the *Glaucus at Potniae,* a town in Boeotia, may have looked in the same way to Plataea.[119] But this is pure conjecture, and the play differs from the others in being self-contained.

From a dramatic point of view it is easy to see why the scene is laid in Persia, presumably at the royal palace in Susa. The news of the defeat coming from a great distance breaks more sharply on the previous silence and is more devastating. But this remoteness serves further purposes. By showing Greece and Athens from far and through alien eyes, it sets them in a perspective which allows comparison and even praise but is at bottom strangely equalizing. This effect is enhanced by the arrangement of the Persian characters as father, mother, and son. The family is both a common standard and the simplest setting for any question of change and creativity. In her unimpaired love for Xerxes, his mother Atossa acts to soften the harsh judgment made of him by the ghost of his victorious father Darius. The two parental figures have been described as standing on either side of necessity,[120] the one with gentleness and sorrow, the other in condemnation. Xerxes in defeat is thus seen at once in his humanity and in his folly, and if he failed, it was not so much because any effort of a son to act otherwise than his father — any effort, that is, toward fresh achievement — was bound to fail, as because Xerxes lacked the true grounds of achievement. What these are appears in the persistent comparison between Persia and Greece. Gold contrasts to silver, pomp to piety, conquest to self-defense, imposed authority to the discipline of freedom. Xerxes thus appears as having relied in his youthful folly on wealth and power only, and his final lament is his acknowledgment of the necessity that humbles him. This law that wrecks falsely conceived ambition is then tacitly felt to apply to Athens and to all men. If the Athenians have escaped its working, it is because they have recognized the limits within which achievement is possible. "Sons of Hellenes, on. Redeem your fatherland, redeem your children, wives, seats of ancestral gods and forebears' graves. The prize is all of them." (vv. 402-405) This battle cry at Salamis is to be compared to the speech in which Atossa explains Xerxes' decision to his father. "Haughty Xerxes was corrupted by the talk of wicked men, telling how you took from battle huge enrichment for your sons, while he at home supinely warring furthered not his ancient wealth." (vv. 754-756) Country to the Athenians carries common ties and inherited pieties, and their courage at Salamis flowered from old roots in the kind of creation that Pindar recognizes, in which the divine energy crowns and transfigures mortal efforts. Solon had stated the working of a law which cuts down self-aggrandizers (fg. 1), and this law operates against Xerxes. He illustrates the necessity of retribution; the Athenians reveal the freedom into which the same law issues when it is heeded.

Aeschylus' characters seem to fall, morally speaking, into three classes: those who are dominantly moved by imperiousness and self-will; those who though still consciously or unconsciously self-willed have nevertheless clear grounds of justice; and those who are entirely just. The first class contains Aegisthus, Helen and Paris as they are seen in the choruses of the *Agamemnon,* Polyneices of the *Septem,* the Egyptians of the *Suppliants,* and Xerxes of this play. If we had the other plays of the Danaid trilogy, the Egyptians might appear somewhat differently. Lynceus' claims at least were sufficiently just that Hypermnestra's marriage to him resolves the trilogy. Polyneices also has some right in seeking to recover his patrimony, as has Xerxes here in trying to extend Persia's ancient conquests. None of these people are largely evil, even Aegisthus, the evilest, having some shade of justification; their common trait is their blindness to anything but their own interests. The second class contains the great Aeschylean protagonists, heroic and creative figures acting from generosity and a sense of justice, lacking only that apperception of final justice which Zeus alone has (or attains in the *Prometheus*) and which alone cleanses a residue of wrong even from preponderant right. Agamemnon is such a figure in seeking to vindicate his brother's honor by punishing Paris, and Clytaemnestra, though harsher, feels no less generously toward Iphigeneia. Eteocles presumptuously identifies Thebes' advantage with his own, but he has courage and patriotism which his death clears of this one stain. The Danaids, as we have seen, flee to Argos in justified passion for freedom; the weakness of their position is that, like Clytaemnestra's, it leads to murder, which only

Hypermnestra has the purer impulse to refuse. Prometheus is the archetype of these heroic characters, the figure who supremely combines Aeschylus' feeling for progress and creativity with his still stronger scruple that these great ends are incompatible with pride. The third class of characters, consisting of the wholly just, is represented almost alone by Athens. Orestes reaches this stage by obedience to Apollo, by his later sufferings, and by Athene's final acceptance of him. But he drops out abruptly at the end of the *Eumenides,* and the state of justice that he reaches is rather seen in the city and the court which validate it. If we had the Danaid and Promethean trilogies, we should see a like stage of final attainment in them. But as among the extant plays only the Athens of the end of the *Oresteia* and the Athenians of this play illustrate the entire justice which is also freedom and pure creativity. The *Persians* is the simplest of the plays in juxtaposing the quite mistaken Xerxes to the quite just Athenians, and Aeschylus is swept by the glory of Salamis into a sense of complete and present achievement. Yet in the background remains the operative law of Zeus's perfect justice, which because the play chiefly concerns Persia, shows more fully in its destructive than in its liberating force. The great description of Salamis is the flash of pure creative justice, seen against the dark weakness of delusion. The play is the least Aeschylean in the sense that it avoids the second class of characters and actions, which are the troubling ones. The Pindaric glory of Salamis is the direct possession of an end which is elsewhere reached only through time — unless the past is as fugitive as the future, and Salamis, eight years distant, already wears the remoteness of the perfect.

The opening, sung by Persian elders, is in the lyric and corporate manner of the *Suppliants.* "We are entitled the trustworthy men of the Persians departed all to Greece, the protectors of these felicitous halls, this golden seat, whom

the king himself, Xerxes the son of Darius, chose to keep
watch on the land." (vv. 1-7) The gold that here describes
the Persians keeps recurring until it shifts to the Greeks in
the morning sunlight of Salamis. The elders go on to name
the lords and commanders who have accompanied Xerxes,
describing them by country, Persia, Egypt, Lydia, Lycia,
Mysia, and Babylon. This vast host, they say, has poured
across the bridge of the Hellespont, and nothing checks it.
Yet they are anxious. "A god-sent destiny holding from of
old gave to the Persians to follow tower-shattering wars, the
press of battle-steeds and wreck of cities. They learned to
view the plain of the passaged sea when it froths white with
hurricane and to trust their cables' narrow house and army-
wafting arts. Yet what mortal man shall shun god's subtle
deception? Who with supple foot shall master that light
leap? Folly, flattering at first and bland, deflects men to her
snares, whence never a mortal struggles out to freedom."
(vv. 93-114) It is unspecified what this ancient destiny is;
what is clear is that, descending to Xerxes, it has offered him
in turn a revealing act of choice. The queen enters to describe a dream which, like Clytaemnestra's in the *Choephoroe,* deepens foreboding. She saw Xerxes yoking to his
chariot two figures, first women, then horses; one was docile
but the other struggled, finally breaking the chariot and
throwing Xerxes to the ground, while Darius stood by and
wept. When she tried to placate her dream by offerings,
she saw a hawk putting to flight an eagle, and she seeks the
elders' advice to quiet her fears. But they can suggest only
further offerings to the earth, the dead, and the shade of
Darius, and she turns to questions about Athens. Where is
it? Far to the sunset. Why does Xerxes attack it? Because he will then possess Greece. Is it so populous and rich?
It harmed Persia before and possesses a rill of silver, a
treasury in the earth. Are they bowmen? They fight from
close with spears. Who is their king? They are free, no

one's subjects. How then can they stand invasion? In such a way as once cost Darius an army. (vv. 231-244)

The dialogue presents Athens with a clarity that only distance and foreign eyes can give but, after the elders' talk of their friends and the queen's of her son, carries little exultation. Aeschylus invokes his characteristic sense of space differently here from in the *Suppliants*. In both plays space is the mark of Zeus, the frame and element of his brooding will. But whereas the Danaids as his descendants carry something of this space with them, and its adjustment to fixity is the problem of the play, Xerxes, the distant Persian, is paradoxically seen from home and it is Athens which is remote. Unlike gods, men must make their terms with place also, and seen as remote yet fixed in their ancestral ways, the Athenians seem to fulfill both demands. Athens is what early Argos evidently becomes at the end of the Danaid trilogy, a city in which piety and honor imbue local habits with something of the divine freedom. The queen's ignorance of Athens, if illogically extended to Xerxes, yet in fact becomes characteristic of him. He is so hedged by pride of place as to have forgotten the divine scope which makes place insecure, and Aeschylus' judgment of him is chiefly expressed through the settled pomp of Susa. Correspondingly, the shock of Salamis when thus seen from the Persian side transforms, if it does not dim, the audience's sense of triumph, inducing awe before the divine will which laps all fixity in change.

It is in the spirit of such a revelation that the messenger enters to announce the great defeat, fittingly beginning with the deaths of men whom the elders had named at the start. The Greek ships, he says, were fewer, three hundred and ten against a thousand. "Appear we then outnumbered in the battle? No, some divinity destroyed the fleet, weighting the balance with no poised luck. The gods protect the goddess Pallas' city." (vv. 344-347) He describes Themistocles,

not by name, as the spirit of ruin whose message deceived
Xerxes into guarding the straits of Salamis on the eve of the
battle. "The night advanced while never the Greek fleet
showed slightest overture toward secret flight. But when
the white-horsed morning radiant before our eyes recovered
all the earth, a rushing sound like joyous singing rose in
omen from the Greeks, and instantly answering from the
island's rocky cliffs echo rang high." (vv. 384-391) On this
paean and with the battle cry quoted earlier the Greeks
move toward the Persian squadrons, now caught in the nar-
rows and unable to avoid the rams of their quicker opponents. The well-known description follows of shattered
hulls, floating wreckage, men speared or struck with oars as
they swam, escaping ships, and carnage on shore. From his
throne on the Attic cliff Xerxes watched the annihilation of
the force which had been landed on the island of Psyttaleia
to destroy Greek fugitives; then with a groan he gave the
command to retreat. The recital ends with the sufferings of
the army through hunger, thirst, heat, and cold during the
long march through Greece and Thrace to the Hellespont.

This is the event; the next scene is its interpretation. It
is later said (v. 792) that the earth herself aided the Greeks
(as was seen in the events of the retreat), and the queen,
consciously foregoing her earlier pomp, now brings milk,
honey, water, and wine as simple offerings of earth to the
shade of Darius. In his effort to contrast Darius to Xerxes,
Aeschylus somewhat neglects Marathon, and Darius is invoked by the elders as formerly flawless and now a king
among the dead. Presently he rises from the tomb, and
when Atossa reveals the disaster to him, the two as mother
and father take deeply contrasting positions toward their
son. Darius, who knew from oracles that Persia would some
day falter but had believed the time far off, recognizes that
it has come through Xerxes' pride in bridging the Hellespont and his impiety in profaning temples. He condemns

him for blind and imperious willfulness, applying to him
Solon's old adage of the flowering of insolence into ruin.
(vv. 821-822) Atossa does not so much judge as pity. She
seeks in the lines quoted earlier to excuse Xerxes as the victim of bad advisers, and as the scene ends, her concern is for
the rags in which he will enter. Her offerings from the
earth describe her. She is a figure of place and commitment,
as Darius, both as man and as ghost, is a figure of Zeus's
spacious time. These two positions serve to describe the
Greek triumph. The Athenians' veneration for place, kindred, and local gods is as great as Atossa's, and these ties
temper and direct their creativity, as to Darius' mind
Xerxes' creativity was not tempered. Aeschylus escapes the
negative and forbidding tone of Solon's preachment in recognizing the freedom which springs from the union of place
with scope and which creates a mind both tempered and
creative. Atossa and Darius respectively witness Xerxes'
defect in both elements of this union, and he enters as a figure of failure toward both home and the gods. The Athenians by contrast reconcile fixed home with free gods.

There is a tone in tragedy of pure lament for transience,
and this tone is strong at the end. As Darius leaves with
warning to the elders to enjoy life while they can, the chorus
celebrate his great former triumphs even over Greece and
the islands. This feeling for the majesty of the Persian empire at its height is natural to the elders, but even Aeschylus
seems swept into it, partly through marvel at the divine will
which brought the empire's downfall through Athens, but
partly also from the sheer impressiveness of things vast.
Xerxes, the chorus say, has undone the fear that once bound
Asia and has ended the awe of kingship. When he enters
in rags, the chorus join him in an antiphonal dirge, and the
play rounds to its beginning in a lament for the lords and
counsellors there seen as setting forth. "Where is my host
of friends and where your men at arms? As were Pharan-

dakes, Sousas, Pelagon, Dotamas, Psammis, Sousikanes, and Agabatos, gone from Ecbatana?" "I left them dead and drifting from a Tyrian ship by the cliffs of Salamis, rolling against the heavy shore. —— Unhappy all, they saw that hoary city, hated Athens, and in one single crest gasped on her strand." (vv. 956-966, 974-977) The antiquity of Athens attests the age of the law that is manifest in her. Xerxes is what she would be, if her ancient pieties were not her present support. Her freedom is a kind of acceptance of limitedness which, by recognizing gods in one place, is aware of them in all places.

To return again to Pindar, the *Persians* of all the plays is most nearly in his spirit, not only in its feeling for the sheer glory of achievement, but in the absence of conflict, both in Athens and the figures of Darius and Atossa, between gods and land. The fact that Xerxes is disloyal to both removes the strain between them that Aeschylus' great characters feel. If the king being a mortal is seen more sympathetically than Typhos, for example, in *P.* 1, he resembles Typhos in unwillingness to wait for the divine will and in lacking the repose which the sight of it brings. Other Aeschylean heroes lack this repose, but they at least see signs of Zeus in mortal justice, and their miseries, unlike Xerxes', follow from the fact that their partial sight is still imperfect. Xerxes first sees the gods' will in defeat; Agamemnon sees part of it from the start. And yet the two poets remain very different even here, and their positions as Theban and Athenian toward the war seem to fix this difference. The bold, majestic, and metaphorical manner which they have in common marks a spirit in the age which they equally felt. It was argued earlier that the great political and military events of their time do not adequately explain this bond, though Pindar was in Athens as a young man and must have felt the city's headiness. Rather their bond is in the metaphorical style itself which reflects the inner mind's new sense

of power.   But granted this intenser vision, they show it
diversely.   The fact that the Athenians rose to the menace
of Salamis as the Thebans did not marks a power of action
in them, a translation of new freedoms into new decisions,
such as, for example, the decision in 483/2 to spend on the
fleet the revenue from the fresh vein of silver discovered at
Laurium.[121]   This Attic bent toward action shows in Aeschylus.   In the present play, the fate that will some day close
Persia's greatness is not felt as automatic, but lies in Xerxes'
hands to be hastened or deferred.   Aeschylus' scope is related to this feeling for action, since the responsible mind
must survey the world to find its proper course.   His space
is the language of his freedom, which then must face the
divine freedom and accommodate it in the end to something
less than all space.   Aeschylus' likeness in his sense of scope
to the spokesmen of other emergent peoples, notably to Mar-
lowe and to Melville, is striking.   Faustus and Captain Ahab
are haunted and finally ruined by the vision of the world as
sheer potentiality, and so are Xerxes, Agamemnon, and the
family of Laius.   But Orestes returns home, Hypermnestra
finds place in Argos, Prometheus and Zeus are reconciled,
and Athens shows a possible union between scope and place.
Aeschylus superbly matches this sense of the mind's power to
a sense of its responsibility, and Salamis is the bright validation of his faith. Pindar characteristically lacks this geographical width.   He tends, so to speak, to vertical rather than
to horizontal lines, rising straight from particularity to essence.   Less aware of the width of the world, he is less sensitive to its clashes, hence to the perils of decision and the
chances of error.   His metaphors tend to be static, composed of nouns and adjectives that convey flashing or reposed states of being.   Aeschylus' metaphors tend fiercely
towards movement, and seek participles and verbal forms
expressive of change.   Though in *I. 5* Pindar knows the
hail of death that beat at Salamis, he chiefly sees in the bat-

tle the brilliance of the goddess Theia, author of all coruscation of act or spirit, and though Aeschylus too knows this coruscation in the morning sunlight of victory, he chiefly sees the hail of death. Their emphasis is opposite. The *Persians,* though marked by the flash of victory, is a threnody for defeat, full of the sufferings of nations, intensely aware of evanescence, conscious of the inexorable gods. It has no true parallel even in Pindar's dark poems, *P.* 8 or *N.* 11, in which the strong sense of evanescence reflects not so much the mistakes of men as the unpredictability of the gods. Pindar waits on the gods; Aeschylus would meet them by scope of thought and rightness of act.

THE *PROMETHEUS BOUND*

ONE hesitates at the *Prometheus* as at no other Greek work except the *Iliad,* partly through perplexity at certain statements: for example, that new power is always harsh. Is this an historical judgment of the Attic tyrants and, more broadly, of any past authority in its first stages, for instance, Agamemnon's in his decision to attack Troy? Or does it look to the present as comment on a certain harsh one-sidedness in the democracy? Or is it at bottom non-political, having to do with the creative mind's concentration on its own ends and unwillingness to be checked? It could be at once an historical, a contemporary, and an inward judgment, and this kind of ambiguity is one reason for hesitation. But the main reason goes deeper, that the play like very few other works, perhaps *King Lear* or the *Brothers Karamazov,* has the quality of touching final doubts. Dante approaches questions as final, and perhaps no one, not even he, could conceive them except from some region of doubt. But if so, he has already moved far toward affirmation, as in this first play of this trilogy Aeschylus has not. Though Zeus and Prometheus are reconciled in the last play, the spectacle meanwhile exists of a world in which moral standards have no means of appeal, hence of a world where only force decides.[122] This spectacle is not inherently affecting; certainly such a view of the world has often been expressed. But it remains tolerable only so long as human nature appears in uncertain colors. When, by contrast, characters speak with the authentic accents of mind and sentience and an atmosphere of the virtues is created, the view of the world as force collides with the view of the world implied in these virtues, and the mind loses its familiar bearings. This is the case in the *Prometheus* because Zeus is himself imperfect.

The other extant plays offer no parallel. If Agamemnon dies after his half-wrong, half-right choice for the Trojan expedition, it is because he is partly unjust, not because Zeus is. His son Orestes can reach a higher stage nearer Zeus's perfect justice, and history will be intelligible. So Hypermnestra will fulfill the good and escape the evil in the Danaids' original decision for flight. But when in this first play of the trilogy Zeus is forced like Agamemnon into half-injustice, history is condemned to meaningless evil before the good is reached. This prospect is fearful because the present is not to be seen only in the last play but partly through this play also, which would otherwise be simply antiquarian. The prospect removes from tragedy any secure confidence in the existence of justice, leaving only the spectacle of strength and courage. The Promethean myth evidently set free Aeschylus' most contradictory speculations, and the result has a quality of candor which transcends ordinary reasoning. Sophocles may be thought of as taking on from this play, in the sense that, once evolution was ruled out as an answer to the question of pain, and a man cannot be said to suffer justly by standards which do not yet exist, then virtue must find a present meaning. Sophocles accordingly turned from heroism as evolutionary to heroism as carrying its own credentials, and he gave up the trilogy as a form in favor of single plays which accept the present moment in time as containing all the meaning in life that can be had. But Prometheus is the primal tragic figure, and in him tragedy is the expression not of a secure and visible justice but of an impulse toward justice which survives even its own contradictions.

In Hesiod Prometheus is closely if obscurely connected with mankind, which is punished for his theft of fire by loss of easy livelihood from the earth's abundance.[123] Aeschylus changed this version in keeping with the progressive mood of the fifth century, reporting early man not as happy in an original Eden but as brutal, wretched, and uncouth. (vv.

442-458)   Prometheus not only gave men fire, he taught
them to build houses, foretell the seasons, write and calcu-
late, travel by land and sea, cure diseases, and recognize
omens. (If this last gift raises the smile that one illogically
directs to the past as if the present were perfect, there is a
sense in which divination is not purely superstitious, but represents subconscious self-questioning.) A similar feeling for
progress speaks elsewhere in the famous ode of the *Antigone*
on man, in the so-called Archaeology of Thucydides and in
the Funeral Oration, in Euripides' *Suppliants,* in the Promethean myth of Plato's *Protagoras,* and in the Hippocratic
tracts *On Ancient Medicine* and *On The Sacred Disease.*[124]
These writings in turn reflect the progressive temper of the
democracy itself, the optimistic view that a people is capable
of self-government being both the cause and the consequence
of Athens' enormous expansion during Aeschylus' lifetime
and for a few following decades. Thus Prometheus was far
more admirable to Aeschylus than to Hesiod. His inventive
arts were not suspect as having cost mankind an earthly
paradise, but on the contrary were to be seen in Athens'
present flourishing. Hephaestus' reluctance in the opening
scene to bind Prometheus to the rock expresses the sympathy
of an innovating age for the inquiring and inventive mind.
Considered theologically, Prometheus is equally progressive.
He helped Zeus overthrow the rule of the Titans, being
partly moved, he says, by his mother's prophecy that Zeus
would triumph by mind rather than by force. (vv. 209-213)
It was said earlier that Hesiod had failed to apply to men
the progressive evolution that he proclaimed among gods,
and it is in Prometheus that Aeschylus most clearly asserts
this second step. If order and intelligence emerged in
heaven with the Olympians, so did they on earth with Prometheus. He is the extension of the process begun with
Zeus, and he falls out with Zeus not because he is unlike him
but because he is like him. Thus his encounter with Zeus is

at bottom his encounter with himself, his realization that progress and change have meaning only in relation to something unchanged. In this sense the trilogy represents his struggle to admire and accept the world for reasons other than his power to improve it. This same struggle is evidently in Zeus, and he too must pass from a state of becoming to a state of being. But as we see them in this first play, both are flushed with the excitement of recent innovation. The question of the trilogy is not whether such innovation is good but whether it is all.

But if Prometheus has ties of intellect with the Olympians and if he helped bring about their triumph, he has ties also with earth. Aeschylus further changed Hesiod's myth by making him the child of Earth, who is further identified with Themis. (vv. 209-210) It will be recalled that in Pindar's hymn on the marriage of Zeus and Themis she becomes the mother of the Horae, the Seasons, and through them of the benign order of nature. (fg. 10) Though nothing is said here of this marriage, she carries the same implications of natural order, and her identification with Earth expresses the latter's inborn wisdom. In *N.* 6 Pindar feels the presence of the Olympians in the life of earth, as does Aeschylus in Aphrodite's defense of Hypermnestra, the gods being Earth's remote progeny through her union with Sky. Yet her periods of sleep and fallow do not for Pindar contain the Olympian brightness as do her seasons of blossoming, and men, who know both seasons, are therefore like and unlike the gods. Something of this mortal duality evidently descends to Prometheus also from his mother, though he is immortal. His first words are to greet the bright sky, winds, rivers, the sea, the earth, and the sun. The chorus of Oceanids in whom he finds sympathy are water spirits of earth and ocean, and their father Oceanus feels bonds with him.

Though Prometheus sided with Zeus against the Titans,

he yet laments the sufferings of Atlas and the imprisonment
of Typhos, whose outpourings from Aetna do not express,
as in *P.* 1, the relic of the world's disorder now tamed by
Zeus, but the earth's protest against Zeus.   Similarly the
chorus state the lament of the peoples of the earth for Prometheus and the Titans.   This double tie at once with the
Olympian intellect and with Earth and the Titans conveys
his kinship to men.   He embodies Pindar's feeling that we
are like yet unlike the gods.   But whereas for Pindar this
partial resemblance is grounds for joy in that it imports
brightness and permanence into what would otherwise be
the shadow and change of mortal life, to Aeschylus Prometheus' half-Olympian, half-earthly nature is a source of conflict.   One of his gifts to mankind, he says, was to take away
their foreknowledge of death, which he did by substituting
blind hopes. (v. 250)   He took away, that is, the instinctual
prescience which animals have and gave in its place the conscious mind's hope of perpetually finding solutions.   If the
Titans represent force, they also represent instinct, and Prometheus' opposition to the Titans, yet sympathy for them
shows a conflict between the Olympian intellect and the ob-
scurer ways of thought of Earth-Themis.

This conflict, as already noted, has no solution in our
first play, the power of which is in its awareness of these
antagonisms.   The reason why a solution is impossible is that
Zeus does not yet include, as he does in the other plays, the
idea, feminine in its implications, of place and nature.   To
the degree that Prometheus resembles him he too is drawn
on to a male creativity which, important as it is in him, is
not only at odds with other parts of his nature but does not
adequately explain his actions.   Though he has become a
figure of mind, he is in fact largely a figure of feeling.   His
loyalty to man, the source of his pains, was such an emotional impulse.   In the play his proud fear that visitors to his
rock have come to mock him, his quick responsiveness to the

Oceanids, his scorn for Oceanus, his curious mixture toward
Io of satisfaction that her treatment by Zeus resembles his
own, yet of sympathy for her sufferings and of candor in admitting that they will end happily, and above all, his stubborn intransigence toward Zeus, all show the complexity of
his nature.

Zeus is seen in the play through hostile eyes, much as the
Egyptians are seen in the *Suppliants,* but he too is evidently
not moved by intellect only, but by will to dominate. His
difference from Prometheus is that he is less moved by motives of sympathy. This is not absolutely certain because of
the hostility through which he is seen, and his intention before Prometheus intervened of destroying mankind and
starting fresh (vv. 232-233) may have had a benigner impulse than is reported, as his love for Io may have harbored
the high plans for the future that appear in the *Suppliants*
rather than the mere passion that appears here. But it is
impossible not to accept Prometheus' view of him as a brutal
tyrant. This harshness, as noted at the start, is repeatedly
ascribed to the newness of his power. The explanation certainly contains Aeschylus' observation of history, but since
this play and all the plays move at once in the sphere of history and that of the mind, the explanation is more than historical and must be connected with the impulse of creativity
itself. The male will to achievement is almost pure in Zeus,
and he founds a new era in which the fruits of such achievement will be manifest in intellect and created order. But as
he limits Prometheus, so he is himself limited by the Fates,
and Prometheus' foreknowledge of the Fates given him by
his intuitive mother Earth is his one weapon against him.

In *I.* 8 Pindar describes the quarrel between Zeus and
Poseidon over the Nereid Thetis, from which Themis dis-
suaded them on the ground that she was destined to bear a
son greater than his father. She was accordingly given to
the mortal Peleus, to whom she bore Achilles. For Pindar

the myth is a lament that even the divine brightness in men is mixed with mortality.   But for Aeschylus, who knew *I*. 8 and uses a line from it,[125] the myth came to mean something else.   It prophesied a possible overthrow awaiting Zeus like that which he had inflicted on his father Kronos.   (vv. 907-927)   The future would accordingly contain, like the past, a series of powers upset by stronger powers, and time would remain warfare.   This is clearly a condemnation of male creativity as a sole and guiding principle.   The Fates which stand behind Zeus are the necessity that intellect and will make terms with order and rest if they are to survive, that becoming pass over into being, and that creativity cease to assert the part against the whole, but somehow emerge from and express the whole.   It is in this sense that Prometheus' problem is identical with Zeus's problem.   Both must reconcile their brilliant impulse toward creativity with a peace of mood which will find fulfillment in the present rather than in a forever novel future.

Thus the play like the other plays, except the *Persians,* is to be seen through the rest of the trilogy.   When in the last scene Prometheus still refuses to divulge the secret of Zeus's overthrow, he is overwhelmed by lightning and falls like Typhos into the depths of the earth, whence he will be brought back, Hermes says, after huge time to hang enchained on the Caucasus and preyed on by Zeus's eagle. Much more is preserved of the second play, *Prometheus Freed,* than of the third, *Prometheus Firebearer.*[126]   The *Oresteia* is our one model, conceivably deceptive in many ways but all that we have, for the general tone of Aeschylus' solutions and for his procedure by recurrent themes.   In the second play the Oceanids are replaced as chorus by the Titans, now freed, and Oceanus and Io are replaced as visitants by Earth and Heracles.   These latter figures complement those of the first play, Earth as a primal deity akin to Oceanus, Heracles as Io's descendant, and they carry a like

recurrence of idea, Earth urging reconciliation with a cogency
at this stage which Oceanus originally lacked, Heracles attesting the longer purpose which lay behind Io's seemingly
purposeless sufferings.   A scholiast on our play (v. 180)
states that Zeus pursued Thetis in the Caucasus, and it has
been inferred that Prometheus had only to keep his secret
a little longer in order that the fearful consequences which
would follow from Zeus's union with her would in fact take
place.   If Prometheus freely divulges the secret at such a
time, it is because he has changed.   The Latin fragment has
been mentioned in which he states his weariness with suffering and his longing for death (fg. 193).   Yet he is hardly
to be conceived as yielding to force.   He is weary not so
much of life as of conflict, and Zeus's release of the Titans
gives evidence of a similar change in him.   Even so Prometheus might not have yielded except for a sign of suffering
in Zeus comparable to his own and a sign, moreover, which
betrayed ties with earth and man.   This evidence comes not
from Zeus himself but from his son Heracles.   Zeus's suffering is in part vicarious in Heracles' life of labor, in part
his own in his love for his son.   Some fragments (195-199a)
remain of a speech in which Prometheus prophesies Heracles' wanderings and labors in the north and west, as he had
prophesied those of Io in the east and south.   The earth un-
rolls in these complementary speeches, and Prometheus' mind
encompasses the earth.   If the speech follows Heracles'
shooting of the eagle, the play would leave his destiny incomplete as Io's is left in the first play, and the end of the
trilogy may have united his release from toil with that of
Prometheus.   Whether the secret is delivered to Zeus in the
second or the last play is unknown, but when Zeus ceases to
pursue Thetis, he makes a kind of amends for his pursuit of
Io.   If Heracles is rewarded in the third play with Hebe,
the child of Zeus and Hera, Zeus will no longer be the violent dominator of women, but will express with Hera the kind

of willing union which Lynceus and Hypermnestra reach at
the end of the Danaid trilogy.   It is said in our play that
Prometheus will not escape his torments until someone vol-
untarily dies in his stead. (vv. 1026-1029) The mythologist
Apollodorus (ii 5.4) gives this substitute as the centaur
Chiron, who had been accidentally wounded by Heracles and
longed to die.   It is added that Prometheus wears a crown
of olive in memory of his fetters.[127] He was worshipped as
the Firebringer at Colonus together with the two other gods
of handcraft, Athene and Hephaestus,[128] and unless the
model of the *Oresteia* is deceptive, there was notice in the
third play of this Attic cult which Sophocles praises in the
Oedipus at Colonus and which was celebrated with torch
races. If so, Zeus would at last approve progress and invention, and the trilogy would round to its beginning in the
sympathy between Hephaestus and Prometheus, much as in
the *Persians* the final lament for the lords and commanders
rounds to the description of them at the beginning, or as in
the *Oresteia* the final torchlight which guides the Eumenides
to their seat of worship fulfills the watchman's waiting for
the light at the start of the *Agamemnon*. Zeus and Prometheus would be in accord, the former's abandonment of
Thetis attesting the stability of his rule, the latter's crown
of olive remaining as the token of his sufferings. The liver
was anciently held the seat of the passions, and the eagle that
devoured Prometheus' liver may express the quelling of passion. In any case, this is the effect of Prometheus' long pains,
and his freedom from his fetters is his freedom from the
obsessive heat of his creativity. Earth, who had given him
the secret that he at last willingly surrendered to Zeus, is
herself in that act reconciled with Zeus, and mind and intuition, male and female, creativity and changelessness, resolve their discords.

To return to our play, if the present is to be seen only in
this final reconciliation, the original conflict is long over, and

the play has meaning only in recalling a troubled past.   If
on the other hand the conclusion represents not so much an
actual as an ideal harmony in the world and the mind, the
conflict of the first play is not wholly past but still being enacted.   Aeschylus' ambiguity of subject is in this question.
Insofar as his subject is society and society develops histori-
cally, the trilogic sequence not only here but in the *Oresteia*
and the Danaid plays does in fact express a triumphant present which has at last struggled clear of the bitter past.   But
insofar as his subject is states of mind and history is chiefly a
language for them, then the past is forever relived in the
present and the trilogic progress is spiritual.   One cannot,
and need not, decide the exact weight of emphasis as between these purposes.   So long as the latter purpose weighed
at all with Aeschylus (as it did and heavily; for how otherwise explain the power and presentness of the first plays in
any trilogy?), he saw bygone struggles as still present and
their consequences as still felt.   Hence the *Prometheus
Bound* did not wholly take place aeons ago, and to Aeschylus
peace has always to be rewon between the innovating intellect and something in the world which is not subject in the
same way to innovation.   Prometheus is vastly heroic, and
the Oceanids' loyalty to him in the face of Zeus's threats
shows the devotion which his virtues inspire.   Yet even they
warn him against his obduracy, and his scorn of Oceanus'
conciliating mood, if justified at the time because Zeus is
equally obdurate, is in the end unjustified.   There is no escape in our play from Zeus's imperfection, and the question
becomes whether after all it does justify Prometheus.
Shelley,[129] believing passionately in progress, would say that
it did.   History will accordingly show the triumph of the
suffering and courageous human spirit, and Prometheus may
be admired without reservation. Aeschylus, despite his nearly
equal faith in progress, was more guarded.   To him the very
act of obduracy, however provoked, harbors an evil which

cannot beget final good. The resemblance between Zeus and
Prometheus is the state of mind which conceives life as warfare. It follows that heroism, even when consciously benign
and innovating, is not in itself for Aeschylus an adequate
state of mind. Prometheus has indeed brought enormous
gains, as had Zeus in his victory over the Titans, but these
will end by producing only vaster conflicts if Prometheus
withholds his secret through hate and Zeus then comes into
conflict with some stronger son. The progress which Prometheus gives is delusive so long as it is corrupted by self-assertion. Nor will intellect solve the difficulty, being rather its
cause, since both antagonists are notable for mind. Aeschylus profoundly differs from Homer, in that heroism, even
with the addition of high intellect, can result for him only in
tragedy. Perhaps this is not a difference and the *Iliad* says
the same. But Aeschylus wants more from life than did
Homer, is less solaced by the masculine flash of heroism, and
felt in the city-state's rootedness in land and place a necessary complement to heroism. This complementary force is
from the first implicit, if unrealized, in Prometheus through
his mother. Whether one conceive it, in the spirit of Heraclitus and indeed of Whitehead, as an instinctual sense of involvement with the whole or whether it is the capacity for
joy and rest in the present, Prometheus' gifts of mind are incomplete without it. Zeus too makes terms with earth
through his son Heracles only as he acknowledges his deep
bond with what is. Zeus then takes the world into himself,
rather than superimposes his superior will on it. Athens to
Aeschylus implies such a healing of old conflicts. To that
extent the evolution of the trilogy has led to an actual present. But to the extent that a desirable present can never
come about except as the mind through suffering loses its
creative self-assertion in a harmony which both transcends
and fulfils the self, the first play is never escaped, at least as

an initial stage.   Tragedy and heroism to Aeschylus are
paradoxically only a beginning.

If one consider the end of the trilogy, Aeschylus and Pindar stand very close; if the beginning, very far. *P.* 4 (291),
for the exiled Damophilus whose return to Cyrene Pindar
urges on the tyrant Arkesilas, gives Zeus's release of the
Titans as the mark of a final stage of peace, and the theme
of the physician, strong in the play, runs as strongly through
the ode. *P.* 1 supremely states Zeus's harmony through the
imagery of music.   Though Typhos is still unreconciled and
his outpourings from Aetna carry the undertone of violence
which haunts the poems to Hieron, the wonderful image of
the eagle asleep on Zeus's staff gives in a line the meaning of
the trilogy.   The eagle is enchanted to sleep by the singing
of Apollo and the Muses, figures of beauty and healing;
even Ares is softened, and anger drops away from Olympus.
This is the language of that peace which Prometheus likewise finds with the death of the eagle and the end of warfare.   "Those that Zeus loves not flee over land and the restless sea at the sound of the Pierides' singing." (*P.* 1. 13-14)
Movement and restlessness are the opposite of this peace,
but whereas in *P.* 1 Zeus is himself the order which the
Muses apprehend, in the play he is still in a state of intense
movement and his effect on Io is to drive her over the earth.
Similarly Prometheus' lonely rock is the sign of a quiet which
he hates to accept; his mind keeps the restlessness which his
body has lost.   Quietude, Hesychia, the spirit invoked at the
start of *P.* 8, expresses a repose that is visible not only in
music but in friendship and wisdom.   She suggests that harmony of feeling by which Cyrene and Evadne find completion, not conflict, in Apollo and which certifies that creativity
is not out of tune with earth and nature.

But all these evidences of similar feeling apply to the
solution of the trilogy rather than to the first play.   The
creativity of Athens destroyed for Aeschylus any sense of

initial repose, and Pindar's Thebes can represent an older society which kept its poise by avoiding challenge. If our play stood alone, the dreadful possibility would be raised that intelligence and the will to justice are at odds with the world. That Aeschylus could thus conceive Zeus as force and Prometheus in chains shows what opposition he felt surrounding Athens. The range of the myth is such that this opposition can also appear as within Athens, in an intractability which resists creative change and hence forces advocates of change, however generous, into a mood of partial hate. The myth can then become still more interior, allying this hate with creativity itself. It is notable even so that Aeschylus did not question the Promethean mood of progress. The Oceanids' sympathy for Prometheus seems to make companions of mind and sensitiveness and to state that the world as beauty is akin to the world as thought.[130] It is the very optimism of this faith which steels the creative mind against opposition and thus contradictorily leads to hate. Yet the Oceanids, in this guise of the beauty of the world, contain the means of Prometheus' salvation. The choral ode in which they state mankind's lament for Prometheus is followed by two odes in which they shrink from conflict and seek a life of inner joy. They announce a theme which Earth certainly took up in the second play and which became dominant in the third. Though Aeschylus could entertain the fearful suspicion that intelligence and sentience are at odds with the world and end in hatred for the world's intractability, he finally escaped the ghastly thought. His means of escape was to see the limits of intellect. In its own terms intellect can hardly reach forgiveness, since those who oppose it seem merely brutish. It is only when intellect perceives states of being beyond itself that it sees its own partiality, hence is ready to forgive. The solution of the trilogy follows from Aeschylus' sense of this wider being. The mind's harmony with the world, prefigured in the sympathy of the Oceanids, ultimately frees the mind from its isolation, returning it to understanding of the whole.   The Athenian creativity, which at first seemed to shatter the older ideal of harmony, in the end appeared barren without it.

THE *SEVEN AGAINST THEBES*

THE line which divided the excellence from the evil of heroism was narrow for Aeschylus. His sympathy for Prometheus verged toward hatred of Zeus, toward a state of mind, that is, so sensitive to the nobility of intellect and courage that any limit to them could appear malign. Yet the logical consequence of such creativity as Prometheus' was to dim the concept of the state and to strain the quiet bonds with earth, the source of creativity. Neither a harmony which lacked the flash of the heroic nor a heroism which violated harmony was finally admirable to him, but only their accord. Politically speaking, this accord was the just and inclusive idea of the state which he felt in Athens. Religiously speaking, it was the vision of the Olympians, not as an assertive dynasty destined like its predecessors to be overthrown, but as the timeless rule of pure being. Inwardly speaking, it was a state beyond simple activism, when pain had taught freedom by distilling the creativity from the heat of self. Yet this high view hardly matched the rough demands of action. It is significant that the sense of space and distance (which is to say, the sense of the mind's freedom) is least felt in the opaque and heavily-woven *Seven Against Thebes,* and the play concludes its trilogy at a stage of half-injustice and half-defeat with which the other trilogies begin. It attests a sheer recalcitrance in things which cramps ideal solutions and leaves victory imperfect. Taken by itself, it is not a darker play than the *Choephoroe,* but whereas Orestes' terrible choice leads on to his own and his city's salvation, Eteocles' similar choice brings no such end. It is itself the end, and though he saves his city, he does so not by inaugurating a better future but by ending a worse past. All the exaltation and the failure of heroism are in

him.   As the third in the tough-grained line of Laius and
Oedipus (in *P. 4.* 263-269, Oedipus compares himself to an
oak), he has their dominating force.   He even stands towards them as Orestes stands towards Atreus and Agamemnon, as a juster figure in whom the ancestral wilfulness is
ebbing.   Hence his native power is directed more than theirs
to the good of the state, and he has almost the civic strength
of the Athenians in the *Persians.*   Yet the crisis in which
he shows his strength is partly of his own making, the attack
on Thebes led by his exiled brother Polyneices.   The only
way by which he can in fact save his city is to die and, by
dying, rid it of the burden of his heroic line.   The play shows
a mood of desperation in which the best that could be hoped
from effort is the canceling of evil, not the attainment of
good.   Aeschylus' epitaph stating that he fought at Marathon is often cited as illustrative of his mind, and in the dark
year of 405 Aristophanes looked back in the *Frogs* on the
fighting vigor of the *Septem.*   But the spirit of stubborn
courage in the play is not so much in the famous description
of the seven antagonists as in a willingness to contemplate
the imperfect nature of heroism itself.   The *Septem* would
resemble the *Prometheus* if the *Prometheus* stood alone, and
as such it shares Sophocles' feeling for the tough validity of
heroism even in its darkness and imperfection.

The play has been said with some justice to fall into two
parts corresponding to the two sides of the Theban legend.[131]
The tradition of an Argive attack on Thebes reflects the in-
testine wars of the Mycenaean age as the Trojan legend
reflects its foreign adventures.   This story dominates the first
two-thirds of the play, and as the champion of land and city
Eteocles there carries all the associations with which Aeschylus sees civic duty.   But the legend of the Argive attack was
interwoven with that of the Labdacids, and from the moment when Eteocles names himself as the seventh champion
and is paired against his brother, the former theme yields to

the latter. Little remains of the first plays of the trilogy, the *Laius* and the *Oedipus,* but their import appears from the choral ode just following Eteocles' decision. (vv. 720-791) The chorus of Theban girls go back in thought to Laius' original disobedience of Apollo, who three times warned him that he could save his city only by dying without offspring. But he yielded to his desire and begot Oedipus, who killed him and married Jocasta. "What man," they ask in lines very like the great chorus of Sophocles' *Oedipus,*[132] "did gods and fellow hearthsmen of his city and his wide-nurtured generation so admire, as they admired Oedipus when he freed his country of the man-snatching spirit?" (vv. 772-777) His intelligence in answering the riddle of the sphinx was not unlike Prometheus' and he was similarly honored for it. "But when, disastrous man, he understood his bitter marriage, with unhinged heart and chafing at his pain he did two evil acts. With his parricidal hand he quit his eyes, and bitter at his sons for their aging care, he spoke, alas, the stinging curse that they one day divide his wealth with swords." (vv. 778-790) Oedipus cursed his sons for a driving desire in them, like his own, for achievement and place. Each generation overthrew but could not escape its predecessor. Laius' wish for a son was his wish to perpetuate himself and his power, and Oedipus' brilliant merits reveal his father's force. But as Laius' wish was deceived and he died by Oedipus, so Oedipus was neglected by his sons and cursed them. Jocasta was Laius' shadow over Oedipus, as the curse was Oedipus' shadow over Eteocles and Polyneices. Other lines further describe the curse: iron, the Chalyb, the Scythian stranger, will be the executor of his wealth, and the sons will inherit only so much land as they will lie in. (vv. 727-733) The Theban legend seems to contain a further motif of conflict between the earth-descended Spartoi, progeny of the men who sprang from the dragon's teeth, and the Labdacids, whose rule shows equally in Oedi-

pus' achievements and in his disasters. Two of the Spartoi
are named by Eteocles as Theban champions, and they embody the ancient tie with earth and place which gives strength
to the Theban cause. (vv. 412, 474) Eteocles at the start
of the play identifies himself fully with this cause, yet at the
end cannot escape something in himself and his past which
does violence to it. Laius' will and Oedipus' intellect leave
the heritage of a breach with nature analogous to the breach
which was in Prometheus' achievements. The motif of the
Spartoi is minor, but what is quite clear is that the opening
theme of attack evokes the sacredness and beneficence of
the city's rooted life, with which Eteocles, for all his desire,
cannot identify himself except by dying. The curse contains
the legacy of something hostile to the corporate earth and
city which must be expiated and subsumed before they are
again at rest. The two sides of the legend meet in this expiation, and if Eteocles' death leads to no such higher solution as appears in the other trilogies, he nevertheless saves
the city, which henceforth will contain his high example. He
resembles Oedipus as both a savior and accursed. That he
only half-resembles Orestes in winning his city's salvation
but not his own is a commentary on the age of the heroes:
their dominating virtues must die to create the new community.

The words 'save the city' (v. 749) which Apollo spoke
in warning Laius against offspring are thus the refrain of the
play. Eteocles' opening speech wholly looks to them, and
the messenger's first statement when he returns near the end
to announce the outcome of the duels is that the city is at
rest. (v. 793) The play has to do with how this idea of salvation is to be understood. Eteocles, as we have seen, appears at last against the shadow of his inheritance. Polyneices is this inheritance, and the hatred between the brothers
is the clinging evil that descends from the past. Wealth is
increasingly mentioned toward the end. For all their abil-

ity and achievements the Labdacids were dogged by the price which they demanded for leadership. This price was prefigured in Laius' preference of a son to the good of the city, and the son himself, in spite of his saving act against the Sphinx, was unable to reconcile the good of the city with his continuing kingship. Hence the road to salvation cannot lie through Eteocles but only through his death: which is to say, through the abandonment of glory and power as the price of leadership. It is in this sense that the play, like all the plays, finds heroism of the old Homeric kind inadequate. But Eteocles does not appear only against the shadow of his inheritance but in two other positions, as against the chorus of Theban women and as against the Argive champions. The deep suggestiveness of the play draws also from these relationships, notably from the former, though it is much the darker and more ambiguous. The Argive champions are clear enough. They are contemners of the gods carrying on their shields emblazoned assertions of their will to win against any denial. They express a pitch of heroic pride compared to which the Labdacids' is mild, and when Eteocles matches them with Theban champions who breathe obligation to city and gods, the contrast of the *Persians* between blind pride and conscious responsibility is repeated. So long as he is seen in this setting, Eteocles shares the Theban spirit of control and reverence, and the shadow of his inheritance is absent. The contrast of champions occupies a third of the play, and as they successively appear with a certain archaic self-containment, at once slightly stiff and intensely alive, all Aeschylus' feeling for fighting masculine courage is apparent. This is the part of the play that Aristophanes remembered, and justly so. But were the play only this scene, it would be much simpler than it is. Eteocles would lack the vestige of affinity to these reckless Argives which he has through his ancestry, and he would not feel the tension towards the Theban women which expresses

Aeschylus' sense of conflict between earth and achievement, community and heroism. The command 'save the city' is not answered by masculine power alone but by a tempering of it. The Argive warriors express a pure extreme of self-regarding assertiveness, from some likeness to which Eteocles must find escape.

"To speak in season, Cadmus' citizens, is task of him that keeps the city's stern, guiding the helm, his lids untouched by sleep. If we succeed, god is the origin. If, what heaven forfend, disaster fall, Eteocles only will be bruited loud in rising overtures of lamentation throughout the state — from which Averting Zeus, I pray, prove rightly named for the Cadmeans." (vv. 1-9)   In these opening lines Eteocles distinguishes between a victory which will come from Zeus and a defeat which will come from himself. The scene is very like that at the start of the *Oedipus King,* and after reminding the gathered citizens of their duty to city, native gods, children, and nurturing earth, he sends them to the walls. He is alone when the messenger enters to announce that seven Argive champions have drawn lots for the seven gates of Thebes and are making sacrifice and leaving memorials for their children at home before attacking. Only then does he invoke his father's curse. "O Zeus and Earth and city-keeping gods and Curse, you strong Erinys from my father, never tear out in ruin from the roots this city captive, speaking the tongue of Greece, and all our hearths and homes." (vv. 69-73) He invokes the curse as a spirit of vengeance against Polyneices, but the speech stands in curious contrast to the prayer which he had made openly before the crowd. Then victory was to be a gift of god; now it will follow partly from ancestral hate. Actually it will follow from both, in that the gods will reject the Argive pride and Eteocles will be driven by hate to meet his brother. This working of the gods through the curse gives unity to the play. But in the light of the second prayer the first prayer takes on irony. The gods who protect the city will do so in a way not quite foreseen by Eteocles. He is in the position of his grandfather in wanting the safety of the city to be compatible with himself and his line, and in that of Sophocles' Oedipus who in the similar first scene thinks that he can survive as king while rooting out the pestilence. But whereas Laius, when pressed, consciously preferred a son to the good of the city, Eteocles in the end prefers the city to himself. This is the slow process of amendment that moves through the trilogy. Yet even at the end when he leaves to fight his brother, his motives are mixed, and he acts partly through hate, partly through honor. The chorus tries to restrain him. "Passion too raw compels you to the harsh-fruited letting of blood that is unlawful." But he will not be stopped. "My foe from my own father, the black curse, with dry unweeping eyes stands by my side, telling me first my gain and then my death." (vv. 692-697) His gain will be his vengeance, which he prefers to life. They appeal to him on the grounds that restraint is honorable. "God also honors the inglorious conquest." He now replies rather from courage than from hate. "That is advice no soldier will accept." The scene ends with a statement of both motives. "Will you then take your very brother's blood?" "When gods give evils there is no escape." (vv. 716-719) As he had said at the start, the gods in fact save the city but by means now of the curse that he had first conceived as including only his brother, not himself. He is not driven into this fate automatically but, like all Aeschylus' heroes, grasps it of his own choice. The motives of honor and reverence which distinguish the Theban from the Argive champions work in him coinciding with those of his hatred, and the latter became canceled in his death, leaving only the former. Legend held that the sons of the present champions, including those of Eteocles and Polyneices, later renewed the conflict with opposite results, but Aeschylus evidently rejects this tradition, calling the brothers childless. (v. 828) The family will end with them, and the curse will at last work good because Eteocles will have seen it, if partly through hate, as working salvation for the city. "Since the gods urgently compel the event, let the whole Phoebus-hated breed of Laius drift with the wind down to Cocytus' wave. — We are long since forgotten by the gods. The grace required of us is our destruction. Why linger then upon the final act?" (vv. 689-691, 702-704)

The women carry complex suggestions of those in other plays, chiefly of the Danaids, Atossa, and Iphigeneia. They first appear just after the messenger's account of the Argive preparations for attack. As the Argives show the pitch of male violence, so the women show extremest agitation. The repeated figure of the protective bird before the violent snake describes them. (vv. 292-294, 381, 503) They run from image to image of the gods, and the crash of missiles speeds their prayers. Eteocles in his impatience can only be described as railing at them when he says that he would cheerfully be rid of women altogether, who are intolerable in security and disastrous in danger. A kind of debate follows, he asserting that salvation lies in discipline. "It does," they agree, "but god's strength is higher yet. In disasters it often lifts the helpless out of the bitter pain of clouds that veil their eyes." (vv. 226-229) Their position towards Eteocles resembles that of the Danaids toward Pelasgus. Their agitation is excessive, yet they have a deeper sense than Eteocles of the divine will. Without them he could fall into something like Pelasgus' position of believing life soluble to prudence and courage. As he himself grasps at the end, the gods in fact work, but not as he had at first imagined. In the same way, the Danaids' agitation will be brought home to Pelasgus when he dies in the second play. A recent writer has seen in the chorus a certain archaic excessiveness which the nascent fifth-century ideal of classic restraint rejected.[133] The chorus in their way are as violent as the Argive champions in theirs. The two are the extremes of which Eteocles is the mean or, more correctly, becomes the mean when he realizes that the gods in fact work through his fate. The classic restraint would be shallow if it expressed only rational self-reliance, and Aeschylus means no such thing. Eteocles' restraint ultimately changes to an intensity of feeling at least as great as the chorus's. Then the positions are reversed. They try to calm him as he had calmed them. But, in the exchange already quoted, he will not be calmed but knows that in a way seen by the gods his and Polyneices' deaths are necessary if the city is to be saved. It is generally accepted that the present end of the play introducing Antigone and Ismene is a later addition and that the trilogy ended with the women lamenting the brothers.[134] They share Atossa's sorrow for necessity, an awareness of what the gods have demanded of the Labdacids. There is curiously little differentiation of the brothers at the end. A will greater than either's has been shown in them, and if Eteocles' dedication to land and city has been validated through the victory of the Thebans, his traits of courage and honor are more than ever felt as rooted in the gods.

The women thus have the final word on Eteocles. Two passages express the contrast between peace and war which underlies their contrast to him. The first is the superb choral ode on the fate of a captured city which is sung just before the pairing of the champions. It begins with the imagery of bird and snake and with questions to the gods, what springs they could prefer to the sweet waters of Dirce. From this vision of home and peace, they pass to the hectic possibility of destruction. "There are crashes through the town; against it a towering net. A man dies on another's spear. Wails the hurt cry newly-born of babes at the breast. The pillage of running bands makes kinship. The taker meets the taker, the empty-handed calls the empty-handed, seeking partners but wanting not the same nor less. What can be guessed from this? Stores of all kind strewn on the ground give chancing pain, sight bitter to the housewife. The earth's abundant gifts roll fouled in worthless streams. Captive girls fresh to the sorrow of their war-won bed are his who takes them as their hated lord. They can expect the nightly act to come, increment to their tears." (vv. 346-368) The lines describe a state of horror which is the obverse of masculine heroism, the violence which heroism does to the settled order of peace. The women state the theme which reappears in the *Agamemnon* in Artemis' hatred for the eagle that kills the pregnant hare and in Agamemnon's sacrifice of Iphigeneia. This is the evil of war as such. The women here stand in clearest contrast to the frenetic Argive champions, but their opposition extends to Eteocles also. His and his family's greatness has led to war, and the terrible picture of the ode is the logical end of their pretensions. It describes a violation of nature analogous to Oedipus' union with his mother. The ode may be taken with the odes in which the Danaids pour out blessings on Argos and the Eumenides on Athens.[135] It is the exact reverse of these, and the women in all three odes stand for a state of peace, in the light of which the destructive side of heroism becomes impious. The women stand toward Eteocles as his mother Earth stands towards Prometheus, urging transcendence of the hate which is implied in creativity.

Their position is strengthened by the memorable and affecting portrayal of Amphiaraus, the one Argive champion who disapproves the war. (vv. 568-596) He rebukes Tydeus for his fury and asks Polyneices how he can conceive an attack on his native city to be acceptable to the gods. As a prophet, he foresees his own death at Thebes and welcomes the oracular role that awaits him after death. He is the sixth Argive champion, and his opposition to the preceding five prepares the mind for the seventh pair, Eteocles and

Polyneices. Eteocles resembles Amphiaraus as Polyneices resembles the other Argives. Both Eteocles and Amphiaraus are involved in the evil of war and ambition which the chorus have described. Both disapprove it but, being involved, will find no way out except through death. As Amphiaraus will find posthumous glory as a prophet, so Eteocles will have the glory of living in the city's memory. Aeschylus would transmute the irresponsibility of male strength into reverence for earth and gods. The classic temperance of his Theban warriors ends by including Eteocles. The women's dirge over the brothers is a lament for the brightness of the old heroism, destructive though it was. Because he realizes his imperfection and accepts its consequences, Eteocles inaugurates a juster state than the assertive Labdacids had known. "The earth's abundant gifts roll fouled in worthless streams." (vv. 360-362) The women's hectic vision of waste and desecration is not fulfilled. The Argive Capaneus' threat to sack the city, god willing or unwilling, was only the extremest statement of the heroic mind. This mind is checked, against their will in Capaneus and the other Argives, consciously and of their own choice in Eteocles and Amphiaraus. This return from the delusive freedom of heroic assertiveness to the bonds of earth, community, and true freedom creates a final accord between Eteocles and the women.

With the *Septem* Aeschylus achieves a grasp of tragedy which takes him far from Pindar. The order of the plays is by no means certain, and the *Prometheus,* as noted, has lately been placed among the latest instead of before the *Septem.* If one were to argue for the earlier date, it would be on the ground that the Promethean trilogy ends in reconciliation. So of course does the *Oresteia,* but after the deepest conceivable sense of intransigence in the family of Atreus and after sufferings by Orestes which amount to a second birth. The *Septem,* as several times observed, ends at a stage preceding this rebirth, and Eteocles is an Orestes who dies to make atonement. Without arguing the date of the *Prometheus,* which admittedly shows something of the same intransigence, one can only feel that with the *Septem* Aeschylus reaches a new and terrible sense of the incompleteness even of virtue. This deeply tragic sense divides him increasingly from Pindar. In *N.* 10 Polydeuces cries out in anguish at his brother Castor's death, and he sacrifices half his immortality to redeem him. Yet they end by sharing Olympus and a grave beneath Therapne, and their bond deeply expresses that between earth and gods. In Pindar this harmony is not so deeply shaken as to stand in doubt. But tragedy is precisely the vision of such a doubt, the fearful apperception of something so wrong with things that even nobility is colored with disaster. The width of separation of the women in the *Septem* from Eteocles betrays how far the world is from repose. Aeschylus seems to have drifted from the confidence which united Hypermnestra with Lynceus at the end of the Danaid trilogy, declaring a Pindaric harmony. He regains this harmony in the *Oresteia,* but through Athens, hardly through the legendary heroes. Life as hitherto known did not escape the tragic imperfection, and only the better hope of Athens finally remained. To Pindar the gamut that led from victors to heroes to gods expressed the continuing possibility of momentary perfection, and if in the last poems he too feels tragedy and imperfection and introduces evil among the heroes, his brighter vision did not wholly fade. In *P.* 8 Amphiaraus watching the young Alcmaeon from the grave feels only the beauty of his heroism though he knows him destined to die. Eteocles' beauty in the *Septem* is more clouded, and the dry eyes of the Labdacid curse watching beside him declare a human inheritance from which peace is far removed.

THE *ORESTEIA*

ALL the great Aeschylean themes culminate in the *Oresteia*, partly as the only extant trilogy, hence the only example of his themes in full sweep, partly as a work of his last years and highest powers. The conflict of the *Suppliants* between scope and commitment returns in the spectacle of Agamemnon's wide conquests which yet disrupt the family and the community, and this conflict is phrased again in the language of the sexes. Like the Danaids, Clytaemnestra resorts to an act which pollutes place and earth, and Orestes' recapturing of innocence is harder than Hypermnestra's. If the *Persians* is simpler than the *Oresteia* because Xerxes' attack on Greece lacks the half-justice of Agamemnon's on Troy, the vision of Athens in the *Persians* adumbrates the marvelous close of the *Eumenides*. The latter play states more profoundly, but not in essence differently, Aeschylus' positive vision, at once moral and political, of a justice which alone is freedom and power, and which endows human fixity with a scope of the divine. The doctrine of learning by suffering necessarily postpones this spectacle of full and affirmative freedom. The plays move in the twilight of confining error into which Aeschylus' wide style brings suggestions of the freedom of day. The *Persians* and the *Eumenides* alone emerge into this day, the former retrospectively at Salamis, the latter prospectively in the free working of institutions harmonious with both earth and gods. The Promethean trilogy stated this same evolution, from a creativity which includes strife and therefore half-injustice to a truer creativity drawn from more self-forgetting sympathies and leading to a fuller harmony. As noted earlier, the problem of date remains troublesome. The Promethean trilogy has been held among the latest, partly on linguistic grounds, but chiefly because it applies to the gods themselves the principles of evolution which are applied in the *Oresteia* to human history.[136] Yet it can also be held, in the conventional way, earlier than the *Septem* because it lacks the perception of final intransigence in the heroes which breathes through the Theban play. This perception in any case supplies a deep bond between the *Oresteia* and the *Septem*, relatively stiff and archaic though the *Septem* appears by comparison. The lines of Atreus and of Laius have in common a tough will to dominate which clearly enough explains their achievements but shows as clearly in their disasters. In both trilogies Aeschylus constates a rocky core in human nature which will not yield to death itself. That Orestes surmounts this intransigeance is his difference from Eteocles. Yet in the account of Orestes' escape from his past, Aeschylus makes a visionary leap which carries him beyond history. Orestes abruptly drops out as a character when he is cleared of his mother's murder, and the solution of the trilogy comes less in his regained innocence, as inwardly and personally felt by him, than through the city and court which declare it. Aeschylus evidently did not wholly feel Orestes' new state of freedom but leapt instead to the vision of an ideal freedom. On the surface the trilogy shows an historical evolution from the patriarchal family to the free community, and in Athens this change seems complete. But on second thought this purely historical tone is less convincing. For perfect innocence would demand a freedom in Orestes greater and fuller than Agamemnon's, a sense of personal release which alone could reconcile creativity and community and thereby create the ideal city. In fact this ideal is stated in terms as visionary as any in Pindar, as a mystic harmony of earth and gods. This harmony rather touches than springs from Athens, and Aeschylus has moved to a religious plane beyond history.

The three steps of the trilogy resemble the three stages

of the *Divine Comedy*. The plays move from the vitality
and violence of error, through the wasting strain of the attempt to cleanse error, to the lucent serenity of freedom. As
with the *Divine Comedy*, it is unclear whether this progress
is chiefly conveyed through the action or through the
imagery. Three great images unite the plays, of light, of
law, and of earth, and minor images, of the eagle, the net,
the axe, riches, the snake, and the seed cross and relieve the
major themes. Running throughout is the antithesis between
creativity and earth, which is variously seen as the conflict
between achievement and community, male and female,
Olympian and chthonic gods. When the conflict is resolved,
the sexes are at last in harmony, the brilliance of the Olympians no longer threatens but lights and enlarges the ancient
ties of nature, and achievement rises from rather than violates community. Light is the chief symbol: announced in
the watchman's opening sight of the beacon that tells the fall
of Troy, proved deceptive when the flashing triumph of
Agamemnon's return is darkened in his murder, quenched
during Orestes' exile and shrouded even in his revenge, waking again at Delphi in the figure of the bright Apollo,
radiant at the end when the dark Furies are changed into
figures of light and are guided to their new shrine in Athens
with torches. Light is associated with creativity, the male
sex, and the Olympians. When the light fails in the first
play, it is because Agamemnon's heroic and military greatness and the brilliance of his wealth do not coincide with justice, hence are a delusive light. His creativity did not therefore reveal the Olympian creativity, though, unlike Xerxes',
it was not wholly alien from it. Only as Agamemnon dies
and partly lives again in the purgatorial sufferings of
Orestes, is the Olympian strain in his heroism freed of dis-
figurement. The Olympian creativity then becomes the
Olympian justice, and the male will to achievement ends its
quarrel with female continuity and process.

The figures of law and of earth concern this same change. Agamemnon is originally Priam's prosecutor; he is the eagle who avenges the despoiling of its nest (the theft of Helen by Paris); he is the agent of Zeus's retributive hammer which destroys injustice. Yet the very choruses which thus describe him show him also in an opposite role, as the eagle who kills the innocent hare and as the conqueror who, through war the gold-changer, sends back ashes in place of men. It follows that he himself shall fall victim to such a stroke as that which he dealt Troy, and that the net which he threw about Troy shall become the fatal robe with which Clytaemnestra entraps him. He is executed by the law of half-justice which he dealt out, and this imperfect law descends to Clytaemnestra and Orestes, until it is made perfect by the judgment of Athene in the Areopagus. The figures of earth and seed express atonement for the imperfect. Orestes and Electra cry to their father for the reflowering of the ancient seed. Their revenge first seems to them the promised flowering, but when Clytaemnestra is dead and the Furies pursue Orestes, the concepts of seed and earth take on a deeper meaning than he had grasped. He himself becomes an atonement for the family's violation of natural sanctities, and being afflicted by spirits of earth and night, he enters their darkness. Apollo had threatened him with corrupting diseases, mark of nature out of joint, if he failed to avenge his father, and now his entrance into darkness is the promise of reborn health. When the Furies in the end yield to Athene, Orestes' salvation is the flowering of the earth in a new innocence, and the blessings which the Furies, changed at last to the Eumenides, pour out on Athens express the fruitful union of earth with light.

The thrilling interplay of the action with this symbolism gives the *Oresteia* its force. Aeschylus has cast off the archaic formality which, for all its charm, slightly dimmed his earlier characters as men and women, and the humanity

of his portraiture now foretells Sophocles. Yet this gain in
clarity could have brought a loss in scope, had the merging
of action and symbolism not given the characters a significance beyond themselves. The way in which Aeschylus leaps
at the end from Orestes' regeneration to that of society
shows the burden of symbolic meaning which his characters
held for him. The marvel of the trilogy is the tenseness of
the interplay between the characters as people and as stages
in a moral process. Sophocles' verisimilitude was held in
check by a like feeling for characters as simultaneously themselves and more than themselves. The Greek classic is precisely this momentous balance of human shape with impersonal law, which further weight to either side would disturb.
To advance further towards verisimilitude would be to over-
weight humanity by too exact representation. To withdraw
further toward abstraction would be to dim the faith that
the divine relationships are visible among men. Aeschylus'
characterization in the *Oresteia* is in many ways more exact
than that which Sophocles' idealizing manner was to allow.
The minor figures such as the watchman and herald in the
Agamemnon and the nurse in the *Choephoroe* show an individuality, even an idiosyncrasy, which is in keeping with the
highly complex portrayal of the king and queen. But this
subtlety of characterization is joined at each step with an
outpouring of image and symbol which surrounds the characters, exactly conceived as they are, with much wider meaning. The two forces noted earlier of the late archaic style
are at their pitch in the *Oresteia*: intense attraction to the
variegation and color of the world, yet equal awareness of
powers beyond the world which check its play and hedge its
pretentions. If Pindar instinctively seeks a point of connection between these two forces and in *N*. 6 can see in man's
great mind and form a mark of kinship to the Olympians,
Aeschylus tends to keep the two forces apart. The tension
of the plays, and of the *Oresteia* above all, resides in this

separation of the characters, seen in their full and sharp individuality, from the operative will that surrounds them. Aeschylus' intense attraction to the world speaks in the uniqueness of his characters; his opposite sense of powers beyond the world speaks in the outpouring of his symbolism and culminates in the divine figures of the *Eumenides*. Whereas Sophocles blends his human figures with his sense of law in such a way that each seems to imply the other, Aeschylus, by keeping the two elements apart until the end, expresses both a profusion and a simplicity. The profusion is the sparkling and vivid life of his characters; the simplicity is the working of the laws to which their actions tend. The world as sense and will struggles with the world as mind and order.

The old servant lying like a watchdog on the roof of the palace at Mycenae, scanning the stars and waiting for the beacon from Troy, opens the trilogy ambiguously. His fatigue expresses the length of the siege and the dimming of once clear hopes; his guardedness concerning Clytaemnestra conveys the dubious effect of years on life at home; his sudden joy at the beacon and hope of touching Agamemnon's hand again are yet joined with a secrecy which hints at the king's involvement in these changes of a decade. Though the watchman's cry rouses fires of celebration, neither these nor the beacon dispel the surrounding darkness, and the light of rejoicing at Mycenae is not that of dawn. The entering song and three following odes of the chorus of old men may be the most celebrated passages of Aeschylus. They resemble each other in starting with the justice of Agamemnon's claims against Troy, yet in passing insensibly to an injustice which attended his justice. Presented as the judge, the king subtly becomes the judged. That the opening chorus goes back to the scene of the army's departure for Troy ten years before confirms the sense of time's obscuring progress which was in the watchman's speech, and the backward movement prepares for the forward movement of purgation that awaits. Time thus becomes the discoverer of the king's moral ambiguity, as it will also become the healer of the family and the state.

Yet the ten years of the wars did not of themselves bring guilt; they only made an initial guilt more patent. The old men begin with the previously mentioned images of the prosecutor and the eagles. (vv. 40-71) Agamemnon and Menelaus are mighty and punitive birds wheeling in the sky, crying just vengeance for the despoiling of their nest, and a god hears their cry. But as the chorus live again the moment of the army's departure, they presently recall another act by eagles, the devouring of a pregnant hare before the gates of the palace. The prophet Calchas, they say, foresaw from the portent that Agamemnon would indeed seek Troy, but that Artemis, the protectress of young and innocent things, would resent the eagles' act. (vv. 104-158) Eduard Fraenkel has well stated that Aeschylus seems intentionally to overlook any previous offense of Agamemnon against Artemis which might explain her anger.[137] This anger is soon felt in adverse winds which hold the chafing fleet at Aulis, and the seer Calchas makes a second prophecy, that the winds will die only as Agamemnon sacrifices his daughter Iphigeneia. Artemis, the hare, and Iphigeneia are associated figures, like in their sex and their innocence, and contrasting to the warlike eagles, the Atreidae, and the army. In the absence of previous offense by the king against the goddess, his offense becomes the act of war itself. Aeschylus is not saying that, because the eagles devoured the hare, Artemis held the fleet at Aulis and offered Agamemnon his terrible choice. Rather, the devouring of the hare by the eagles expresses his act of choice itself. The seeming sequence from the eagles to Iphigeneia's death is less a set of causal steps than a mythological statement of implicit meaning. Agamemnon's final and decisive act of guilt was in

killing his daughter, but the choice followed from his decision for war. By destroying the calm and fruitful order of
peace, war commits an offense against nature, and this offense is portrayed in the eagles' devouring of the hare. The
maiden Artemis is herself the innocence of peace. Despite
the justice of his claim against Paris, Agamemnon is touched
by the evil to which he consents. His choice is in fact between the calm and quiet sequence of the family and the
glory of conquest. It accordingly harbors a conflict between
female and male, family and army, and the relationship between just kingship and the peace which it should foster is
broken in a father's act of killing his daughter. To the logical mind Artemis' anger is rather a consequence than a cause
of this terrifying cleft in nature. But to the mythological
mind the goddess stands first in the sequence because the gods
are inresident in our acts, revealing what already is.

The old men describe with sympathy the king's plight at
Aulis. He strikes his staff on the ground in the anguish of
his choice, yet decides for the army. (vv. 202-204) As the
chorus reach this moment, they break into an impassioned
cry to Zeus which, as noted earlier, resembles in position and
language the Danaids' bewildered cry in the *Suppliants*.[138]
"Zeus, who'er he be and if he gladly be so hailed, I hail him.
Pondering all I cannot find conjecture, save only Zeus, to
empty from my soul its hollow weight. He who before was
great, in matchless boldness waxing, shall not be counted
even to have been. And he who followed, finding overthrow, is gone. To cry from the full heart the victor's song
to Zeus is wisdom's all — who guides men to sobriety, makes
sovereign learning by suffering. There steeps from sleep
before the heart the burden of remembered pain. Even the
loath arrive at modesty. The mercy of the gods is done with
force, who keep their austere thrones." (vv. 160-183) The
verses on Zeus's predecessors describe a progression in
heaven from Ouranos and Kronos to himself, but with him

the progression has ended, yielding to changeless being. Men, in the same way, initially involved in the change and succession of evil, learn by chastisement the repose of righteousness. The fine verse on the pain which steeps from sleep conveys the inescapability of the divine teaching and suggests the nature of the true repose, which is not sleep but justice. The Danaids, caught in a like dilemma between their just flight from Egypt and their coming act of murder prefigured in the nightingale's lament, similarly cried in bewilderment towards Zeus's unseeable solution. Agamemnon, for all his regret, now solves his still crueller dilemma by sacrificing Iphigeneia, and the evil which from then on haunts him and his family allows no rest until it is purged by Zeus's gift of instruction through pain. The onward life of the family is comparable to the troubled sleep in which suffering is renewed. The chorus clearly mark the moment of Agamemnon's choice. "When he took necessity's proffered bridle, a godless, guilty, polluted wind in his heart blowing, he veered to think the final unrestraint. A man grows harsh with evil-hinting madness, the dire first source of grief." (vv. 218-223) The Persian elders recalled a like turn in Xerxes when he resolved on his expedition (*Pers.* 107-114), and the Theban women saw Eteocles' frenzy against his brother as such a maddening shift. (*Sept.* 686-688) The nearly unbearable scene which follows, of Iphigeneia's innocent approach to the stony princes and of her seizure, gagging, and death, completes the change in Agamemnon. The punitive eagle of justice has merged with the predacious eagle that rends the innocence of peace, and a corruption has touched the king, the war, the army, and heroic achievement itself of which only the unplumbed mind of Zeus can see an end.

The two following episodes and odes expound this involvement of justice with injustice. Clytaemnestra's high description of the flaming course of the beacon from Troy ostensibly expresses the brilliance of the triumph, but the flame which she welcomes carries also the hectic light of her own maturing plans. Her vision of the sack of Troy more expressly casts shadow on the victory, which she sees, almost with the eyes of the women of the *Septem,* as an act of horror. Similarly the messenger who returns from the army in the second episode chiefly recalls the sufferings of the dreadful decade, and his account of the storm that has scattered the returning flood takes force from Clytaemnestra's warning that divine anger would follow the conquerors' desecrations. (vv. 341-347) In all these speeches there is a mixed feeling that the king's glory is marred by the cost which it exacted and by something inherently corrupting in conquest. The chorus hint to the messenger of comparable contagions at home (vv. 615-616), but the joy of the reunion drowns these suggestions in a mood of relief. The old men shrink from pressing their fears, and the messenger from hearing. This mood, partly of satisfaction that the war is over, partly of doubt how to regard it (since it had, but outran, justification), speaks in the two odes that close these episodes. As noted, they carry forward the inner contradiction of the opening ode. They again begin with the crime of Paris and proclaim the justice of his punishment; yet presently direct back on Agamemnon the guilt which he claimed to be punishing. It is not easy to fix the precise distinction between these complex and deeply troubled outpourings. If the opening ode had to do with the mixed greatness and guilt of the king's heroic enterprise, the second ode concerns the state of mind from which such an undertaking could spring, and the third connects this state of mind with wealth.

The sack of Troy which Clytaemnestra had described first appears to the old men as the net of Zeus closing on Paris and as the blow from Zeus which foolish men think will never fall. (vv. 355-380) With thoughts which anticipate the third ode, they ascribe these men's delusion to their wealth. "Nowhere stands there a bulwark of wealth for the man in his surfeit who spurns Justice's altar high into obscurity." (vv. 381-384) But until the blow falls a man thinks himself free. He listens to the persuasions of his desire and is a child following a bird. The figure of the unattainable bird then glides into that of Helen, who for Paris represents the delusion of perfect freedom and for Troy becomes its consequences. But the loss of Helen brings as potentially dangerous a mood to Menelaus. He sits in his silent house with his silenter pain. "The grace of fair-formed statues is hateful to him; in his eyes' penury Aphrodite is quite flown." (vv. 416-419) Yet when the army follows him to Troy, his sorrow becomes the sorrow of all the houses in Greece. "Whom they sent away they knew, but in their place urns and ash to each man's house return. Ares, the gold-trafficker of bodies, who sets his balance in the battle-spear, sends back from Troy a heavy lamentable dust refined by fire, freighting his well-turned urns with ash that once was man. They praise one man for skill in war, another for his honorable death, but silently add, 'dead for another's wife.'" (vv. 438-449) These mutterings rise at the end into a people's curse against their kings; "the gods' eyes do not leave the killers." (vv. 461-462) The circle is complete. The ode has moved from Zeus' retributive net and blow, through Paris's insouciant heedlessness, to a like heedlessness in the Atreidae for sorrows not their own. Though the old men stop short of condemning their kings by name, they know that the process of retribution will not end with Troy.

The third ode moves back still another step, from men's delusion to the wealth and sense of power which inspire it. In the previous ode Helen was already both enchantment and retribution, and she is more clearly such here. Who was the prophet, they ask, who rightly named her for the ruin that she would cause? (vv. 681-690) As they describe her leaving her delicately curtained chambers and sailing with the west wind to the leafy Simois, the Ionic rhythms convey an allurement like that of the unattainable bird in the former ode. Old Troy first answered her dangerous beauty with marriage songs. She resembled Paris, the tame and fondled lion cub that grew up to show its native destructiveness. "There came at first to Ilium, I would say, a mood of windless calm, wealth's silken ornament, an arrow from soft eyes, love's flower that melts the heart." (vv. 738-743) These thoughts of wealth and charm then lead the chorus to a notable statement. It is anciently held, they say, that wealth itself breeds ruin and good luck hatches its opposite. "But I stand lone in thought apart from others. The impious act leaves a posterity resembling its breed. The course of upright halls is of happy issue." (vv. 757-762) They reject, that is, the superstitious fear of wealth itself, taking instead the strictly ethical position that only evil begets evil. Offense descends in a family; rather, evil is itself a family hatching its own offspring. This is to say that, once injustice has been committed, its consequences cannot be escaped. The outlook is at bottom social, but it has the inner corollary that a mind already touched by injustice is no longer free. For this reason only the gods are able to break in the *Eumenides* the otherwise inescapable chain of continuing evil. Yet having announced that ruin flows not from wealth but from injustice, the old men still see wealth as a temptation. "Justice shines in smoke-stained houses, heeds the man of measure. Halls gold-impasted by polluted hands she leaves with downcast eyes, seeking clean dwellings and observing not riches' praise-counterfeited power. She guides all to her goal." (vv. 773-781) Though evil acts remain the root of ruin, they come more easily to the rich and powerful. The line of thought goes back through the previous to the first ode. Both Paris and Menelaus pursued in their different ways the enchantment of the world which was Helen. She

was wealth's silken ornament, and wealth was not only riches
but the opportunity of the world and the joy of attainment.
Taken in this wider sense, wealth was even more strongly
Agamemnon's temptation, in that as king he would lead the
greatest of expeditions and reach an unmatched wealth of
heroic glory. He is therefore the true pursuer of the unattainable Helen, and in Iphigeneia he sacrificed for her the
innocence of peace and family. Though evil choice, not
wealth, remains his fault, yet the new society which rises in
the *Eumenides* will bring another concept of wealth as the
increase of family and field and the health of community.
Aeschylus sees in Agamemnon the disease of the heroic age
which Athens will transcend, the disease of unchecked will.
Insofar as the meaning of the trilogy is moral and present,
not merely historical, the sickness of the unchecked will is
not automatically escaped by Athens, but the vision of
Athens itself passes beyond history, and the remedy of learning by suffering perpetually rediscovers a new and innocent
Athens.

An ambiguity remains even after this statement by the
chorus of a man's responsibility. Are we to imagine that,
until the moment when he killed Iphigeneia, Agamemnon
was free to act innocently? Cassandra will presently describe the still darker crimes of his father Atreus, crimes
likewise committed for kingship. Aegisthus' adultery with
Clytaemnestra will similarly be seen to repeat the adultery
of his father Thyestes with Atreus' wife. Both Agamemnon
and Aegisthus perpetuate their father's infections. Did
Aeschylus conceive this process to be inevitable? The answer must be that, like Solon, he did indeed see evil as passing from generation to generation. Orestes is infected by
this inheritance, as was Eteocles in the *Septem*. Yet, unlike
Solon, Aeschylus will not willingly say that innocent men pay
for their forebears' crimes. The statement in the third ode
that only the guilty act, not wealth, begets evil, coincides

with the description of Artemis' anger in the first ode. The goddess's offense at the death of the pregnant hare, it was argued, was less a cause than a characterization of the king's criminal choice. There is no hint in the passage that Agamemnon acted otherwise than through his free choice. It is clear that Aeschylus so deeply feels a man's responsibility that he rejects the thought of evil as originating in a man's ancestors rather than in himself. Clytaemnestra later seeks to excuse her crime on the ground that she is precisely such an agent of the past, but though the chorus recognize this element in her action, they passionately refuse to deny her own responsibility. (vv. 1497-1504) Hypothetically, then, a man must be considered free to resist his inheritance, and Agamemnon could have refused to kill Iphigeneia. But actually the tie between kingship and crime, glory and transgression, is so tight that it comes close to compulsion. The fact explains Aeschylus' dislike of wealth (a feeling very different from Pindar's) as the inheritance from an unjust past. The contrast which he draws is between the humble innocent and the rich guilty. But since riches are allied in his mind with all heroic creativity, guilt extends for him to this false concept of the creative. The new community will be that which, through the gods' liberating mercy, will escape this inherited persuasion toward injustice and show the way to innocent achievement.

Agamemnon enters at the end of this ode, and the action moves implacably by the purple carpet of wealth and glory to his death. The old men assert that, though they cannot praise his acts, they genuinely welcome him (vv. 799-809), and all society's dilemma, as between recognizing imperfection yet loving it as all that there is, speaks in these touching words. In the encounter between husband and wife, the ferocity of the lioness tenacious of home and young proves fiercer than her lordly mate's. Place and scope, commitment and adventure, are locked in final opposition in this scene,

and Clytaemnestra's very masculinity expresses the toughness of the female will to home and place when it is at bay.
The king reverts to the first theme of the previous odes by
hailing the retribution of heaven that worked through him
at Troy, and he accepts the old men's loyalty with their
strictures, as if he had learned to despair of the perfect.
The queen shows her stature in the self-command with which
she welcomes her husband, but her thoughts speak in spite
of herself when she describes her recurrent dreams of his
death. (vv. 864-876) Her fulsomeness further betrays her,
and when she has her servants spread the purple carpet for
him to dismount on from his conquering chariot, he pauses.
This is the moment of decision between the two. Agamemnon seeks escape by saying that the gods will resent this show
of wealth, but she counters that Priam, had he won, would
not have refused a similar display. Nor, she adds, should
he fear common censure, the great being always envied. "I
want no altercation with a woman." (v. 940) With these
words Agamemnon is lost. He shows both fatigue of will
and ignorance of the true nature of his past choices. Previous themes converge on this moment: the length of the
war, the moral ambiguity which was increasingly evident in
it and which now weakens the king, its further character as
a war within the family between the king's impulse toward
power and the queen's toward home. Wealth, proclaimed
in the previous ode as not itself the cause of ruin but con-
ducive to the state of mind which is the cause, speaks in the
outspread carpet. When Agamemnon dismounts upon the
carpet, he is only following again the course which he followed in preferring the army to Iphigeneia: in preferring,
that is, the glory and the scope of kingship to innocence.
But whereas the partial justice of his act was then to be
crowned with victory at Troy, its partial injustice now finds
conclusion. His tired unwillingness to dispute with a woman
breathes the vain hope that only the justice, not the injustice,

of his past will be remembered. As he walks into the house, Clytaemnestra exults in the riches that can thus greet a triumph, but her words are ironical, and the path toward glory and power which Agamemnon has chosen is the path into the fatal palace. She follows him with a prayer to Zeus the completer, a prayer which, if it will complete the working of justice toward Agamemnon, will begin the working of injustice in herself.

The old men now forget what faith they once had in the justice of the Trojan expedition but veer entirely to the second theme of the opening odes. Why, they ask, are they fearful? It is ten years since the Trojan sands scattered to the prows of the Greek fleet, and they see with their own eyes the king's safe return. Yet they are in fact fearful. Lusty health, they say, is unstable, and illness is a neighbor that lives on the other side of a common wall. If a prosperous man prudently jettison his wealth in time of danger, he may recoup in better days. But there is no recouping when blood has been shed. (vv. 975-1034) Knowledge of this law is the cause of the old men's fear; they are repeating with new terror what they had said in the last ode of the relationship of conducing wealth to guilty act. At this moment when the old men have acknowledged their fear, yet still cannot see how soon it will be confirmed (like Agamemnon, they do not know consciously what they know subconsciously) Cassandra, hitherto silent, comes forward. Addressed first smoothly, then harshly by Clytaemnestra, she waits until the queen has returned to the palace, then breaks her silence in obscure divinations. By comparison with the common procedure of Greek tragedies, she replaces through her gift of second sight the messenger who reports a catastrophe off-stage. But she is more than an announcer. Relatively to Agamemnon, she is the reward of that will to conquest which drew him to Troy; she is his counterpart of the unattainable Helen, but a counterpart which, when gained, proves disturbed and dire. Relatively to herself, she is the fit sister of Paris, having received a divine gift but at a disastrous price, not unconnected with weakness in herself. She describes how she broke her promise of union with Apollo after receiving from him her prophetic powers, and how she suffered in consequence the penalty that her prophecies would not be heeded. (vv. 1206-1212) Like all the great figures of the play, she attests to a dislocation between gods and men, a disastrous cleft by which the due bond is broken. Her unwillingness to accept union with Apollo recalls the Danaids' mood of flight and uncommitment. She was unable to square her lofty gifts with the feminine traits of her nature; she is the obverse of Clytaemnestra, in whom these latter traits have turned obsessive. She accordingly inveighs against Apollo as the cause of her ruin (vv. 1269-1278), the same Apollo who in the *Eumenides* will help recreate through Orestes the harmony now lost between earth and gods. Finally, relatively to the family of Atreus, she is the first to set its present corruption in a true light. She cries in horror as by her gift she sees in the palace Thyestes' adultery against his brother Atreus and Atreus' inhuman vengeance on Thyestes' children. As Aegisthus later says (vv. 1583-1586), the struggle between the brothers was for kingship and Agamemnon fell heir to the fruits of Atreus' success. In his act towards Iphigeneia, he corrupted nature for kingship as his father had done, and Cassandra is the rediscoverer of this evil in kingship which persuades to crime. As the old men slowly grasp the meaning of her words, first opaque, then quite clear, their intuitive fears grow tangible, and the law of retribution which they had proclaimed without certainty as to the time and manner of its working is enacted with only the palace wall between.

When Cassandra has entered the palace to her own death and just before Agamemnon's dying cry is heard, the old men at last grasp clearly what they had groped toward in the previous odes. "Prosperity is an insatiate state in men. Yet none dissuading warns from eminent halls, crying out 'do not go in.' To Agamemnon the blessed ones gave to take Priam's city, and he comes home god-honored. If now he shall pay for blood long shed and, to the dead dying, wake retribution of other deaths, what man on hearing this shall boast to be born to a vengeanceless fate?" (vv. 1331-1342) The palace which Agamemnon has entered has become the world-wide palace of ambition, which no one has the wit to shun. Though his victory at Troy has the splendor of the divine, its involvement with evil-doing haunts the final triumph. This is Aeschylus' indictment of the old heroism. The train of thought parallels that of the *Septem* and the *Prometheia*. As the family of Laius could not 'save the city' while simultaneously pursuing its own ambition, and as Prometheus' creativity contained at first a self-assertion which conceived the world as warfare, so Agamemnon like his father was willing to buy glory with bloodshed. The final vision of the *Eumenides*, like that of the *Prometheia*, is of a mind in which achievement pays no such price of hate. The tragic process is toward the sight of such an innocence. The present ode, like the culminating chorus in the *Oedipus King* (vv. 1186-1222), sees the obliterating side of this vision, that which shows the imperfection of high achievement. If Sophocles does not there go farther but constates Oedipus' new state of purged and inner achievement only in the *Oedipus at Colonus*, Aeschylus in this trilogy conceives the whole process. The close of the *Eumenides* will augment the present destructive vision by the affirmative vision which lies beyond it, and suffering will have taught a guiltless creativity. But now retribution looks not only to Iphigeneia but, since Cassandra's revelations, to the crimes of Atreus. The halls of ambition from which no one warns opened to them both. As the ode closes, the cry is heard from the house, "Oh I am struck an inner deathly blow." (v. 1343) Agamemnon's

cry fulfills a process which in the opening lines of the ode
is applied potentially to all men (since none refuse the palace
of ambition) and which is to be escaped, if at all, only by
the divine chastisement.

Before the old men can think what to do, Clytaemnestra
appears above the body of Agamemnon. In the passionate
interchange which follows she ironically retravels the track
of half-justice which Agamemnon had traversed, and she
ends like him with the tired hope that the evil of the past
will somehow stop with her. The rain of his blood, she
says, was as grateful to her as the flower-bringing rain of
spring. (vv. 1389-1392) Similarly Aegisthus on entering
salutes the light of a new day. (v. 1577) But this springtime and this light, which will come with Orestes' healing,
are no more for them than they were for Agamemnon. She
conceals to the chorus what degree of motive she felt from
Aegisthus and asserts only her vengeance for Iphigeneia. In
the same way Agamemnon had suppressed his own motive of
glory and its reward in Cassandra, holding forth only his justice in punishing Paris. She rebukes the chorus for despising
her as a woman (v. 1401), and this assertion of sex constates the claims of family as Agamemnon's conquest asserted the counterclaims of male achievement. When the
old men recall the ancient evil that has haunted Mycenae,
she eagerly reaches for exoneration by saying that she was
in fact only the vengeance for it. But as noted earlier, the
chorus will not agree. (vv. 1505-1506) They recognize a
compulsion deriving from the past, but refuse to declare innocent her embracing of it. As the play closes, the tone
grows increasingly political. The chorus revert to their
reverence for Agamemnon as king, and when Aegisthus sees
his part in the murder as an act of vengeance for the political losses of his father Thyestes, the old men apply to him
the name of tyrant. The history of Greece is retraveled, as
legitimate monarchy, corrupt though it was to Aeschylus'

eyes, is overthrown by a usurper, and Aegisthus' call to his
bodyguards and threat to imprison the old men are the acts
of a tyrant. (vv. 1633-1642) Clytaemnestra wearily quiets
the growing struggle. She even, in one line (1655), regrets
the blood so far shed, and though she quickly reminds herself that it was necessary, she at least would have no more.
But the old men have already invoked Orestes. As they
knew that the retribution which Agamemnon visited on Troy
would not stop there, so they know that Clytaemnestra's
vengeance for Iphigeneia will not be the end. "Reproach
rises out of reproach. Decision is a bitter war. The spoiler
is despoiled; the killer pays. Yet while Zeus on his throne
abides, abides that to the doer shall be done. For this is
law." (vv. 1560-1564)

The steps of the *Oresteia* were earlier compared to the
stages of the *Divine Comedy*. Actually the divisions do not
neatly correspond, and Orestes' purgatorial sufferings extend
into the third play. The parallel, faulty in many ways, was
intended to evoke the emphasis of the three plays. It was
noted of Cassandra that her divine gift of prophecy lacked
connection with common life; her unwillingness to accept union with Apollo after she had received her prophetic gifts on
promise to do so implied some failure to adapt the gods to
earth. This failure marks the *Agamemnon* generally. All
the chief characters, including Paris and Helen as they appear in the opening odes, have a counterpart of Cassandra's
divine gift which they in some way misuse. The similarity
to the *Inferno* consists in the violence with which they assert
their personal wills. And as the *Inferno* has a vividness
greater than that of the two following parts, so has the
Agamemnon. Strength of will diffracts into the lurid colors
of the world, and these colors express Aeschylus' extreme
impressionability to the sweep and flow of events. A mind
as optimistic as his, as hopeful of change and evolution,
must inevitably respond thus vividly to the movement of the

world, which is not for it the mere outward show of some deeper reality beyond but itself partakes of this reality. Yet the disease of the heroic world of the *Agamemnon* was precisely its excessive surrender to desire and glory. Desire was the unattainable Helen; glory was the palace before which no one cries 'do not go in.' The *Choephoroe,* as a second, purgatorial stage in understanding marks a curbing of the ancient wilfulness. Politically considered, it describes the assassination of the usurper and the attempt to restore the legitimate monarchy. But since the monarchy was itself defective, those motives in Orestes which express desire for his father's place and wealth are likewise defective. Atreus and Agamemnon had not shrunk from murder as the price of kingship, and Orestes does not shrink. But a subtle change has taken place in him, not unconnected with his youthful exile and abstention from wealth. His motives are only in part toward kingship, chiefly toward justice. To the degree that this latter impulse is dominant, it transforms his crime against nature into a fulfillment of nature. Justice, to Aeschylus, is more than retribution; it is the discovery of an innocence which reintroduces the divine harmony into mortal life and makes possible true creativity. Something of this creativity was seen in the *Persians* in the Athenians' high performance at Salamis, also in the close of the Argive trilogy in Aphrodite's fragmentary speech on the marriage of earth and heaven. Insofar as Orestes, unlike Agamemnon and Clytaemnestra, from the first chiefly sought justice, his sufferings are the sloughing off of his secondary desires for wealth and kingship which were his corrupt inheritance. The state of innocence to which he finally attains through Apollo and Athene closes the heroic age, the age of wilfulness. Corrupt kingship will have passed, through a still corrupter tyranny, into the free community which, seen negatively, is the community of law, seen positively, is the community of free creation. This political meaning merges with a moral meaning. In the latter sense, Orestes' emergence into justice is the will's new sense of freedom through its regained harmony with the divine laws.

As the watchman's cry heralds the events of the *Agamemnon,* so does Clytaemnestra's cry those of the *Choephoroe.* She dreamed that she gave birth to a snake which she wrapped in swaddling clothes and put to her breast. When she did so, it drew blood mixed with milk, and waking with a shriek she called for light. At daybreak she sent Electra together with maidservants of the palace to Agamemon's grave to placate his ghost, the ghastly dream having seemed to announce a new smoldering of his anger. Atossa in the *Persians,* disturbed by a similar dream, sought the same recourse of offerings to earth, but though like her in feeling for family, Clytaemnestra is more disturbed and her dream is more terrible because the ties of family, the root of her being, are more damaged. Her cry for light rises from blackest darkness, and the dawn which the watchman deludedly greeted in the beacon fire and which Aegisthus thought to have found is far removed. The play opens beside Agamemnon's grave to which Orestes, now a man, has returned from Delphi. An unknown number of verses seems to have fallen out from the beginning, and these may have contained some intimation of light from the healing Delphian god by whose commands Orestes is present. His youthful figure making offering to his father in the early morning, like the similar figure at the start of Sophocles' *Electra* and in *P.* 11, in any case implicitly expresses a saving promise. Standing aside with his friend Pylades, he sees Electra and the women approach with their offerings, hears the account of the dream, and listens as they lament, in the spirit of the Persian elders, the loss of majesty from Mycenae. The servants augment the judgment of the old men in the first play by saying that two crimes cannot be washed out, adultery as well as bloodshed (vv. 66-74), and this new emphasis describes the play, which has to do less with glory than with family, less with husband than with wife.

Electra states her uncertainty whether to make these offerings as from Clytaemnestra, which she feels to be impious, or to ask requital from her father not for these gifts but for his death, or simply to turn away. The chorus feel no such hesitation, and when they urge her to ask for vengeance, she prays to that effect, adding a prayer that the absent Orestes may return to kindle light in the house. (vv. 123-151) The vengeful law of an eye for an eye breathes through this scene and through the play. It is in fact the punitive side of justice and continues to be honored in Orestes' sufferings. Yet in itself it brings no advance. The chorus are notably more confident of the law than are Orestes and Electra, whom here and later they whip on to execute it. The weakness of the law is that, being executed by mortal hands, it stains the judge with the evil that he punishes. This is perhaps to say that he cannot himself be wholly disinterested, as Agamemnon was not in his punishment of Paris and as Orestes will not be in his vengeance on his mother. If this stain of incomplete disinterestedness clings to the law of vengeance, the law will only produce further vengeance, and an endless chain of guilt and punishment will stretch forward, much as in the *Prometheia* the prospect of strong gods overthrown by stronger sons harbors a future of perpetual warfare. At some point the chain of vengeance must be broken if justice is to exist in its positive rather than in its punitive form. Similarly in the *Prometheia* the concept of god must change from perpetual becoming to full and present being. The punitive law, without being discredited, must merge with a mercy which will include the judged, as Orestes will be included in Athens, and which because it includes him will heal the judge also. This mercy, the product of community, expresses the inclusive bounty of nurturing earth and sky. Since it comes healingly from natural sources, it is the gift of the gods, who can alone break the ancient chain of vengeance. It speaks well of Electra and Orestes that they hesitate at revenge and need the chorus to lash them on. Stained though she is, Clytaemnestra contains an element of the true community of mercy, and Orestes' plight is that he must reject this vestige because of its corruptions, in the hope of a higher state of justice beyond.

As Electra sees the lock of hair which Orestes had laid at the grave, she leaps to the hope that he has returned, and when he steps forward and convinces her who he is, their joy is boundless. They join their prayers to Zeus rather than their father, calling themselves the defenceless young of the eagle that had died by the snake. (vv. 246-249) The words are ambiguous; for the eagle, if royal and of Zeus, is also the predacious eagle of the former play, and the snake, if proper to the coils in which Clytaemnestra had entrapped her husband, is also the nightmare snake. These ambiguities well describe Orestes' position. Yet he also faces Apollo's command. (vv. 269-296) He relates the wasting illness and leprous decay with which the god had threatened him if he should fail of his duty. A line on the nightly torments of the disobedient man, who "blazingly sees though he moves his brow in shadow" (285), recalls that remembered pain which in the *Agamemnon* is said to steep in sleep before the heart. Were he to disobey the god, Orestes' life would take on the quality of nightmare that Clytaemnestra's life now has. Even as it is, though the bright Apollo stands by with promise of waking, the troubled dream of his inheritance still claims him, and the snake which Clytaemnestra dreamed will become the Furies. It will be recalled of the *Suppliants* that the Argives were threatened with a like wasting and decay if they rejected the Danaids' appeal for safety, and, as there, the threat expresses the impossibility of lingering in an outworn state. For the Argives this state was their once happy isolation from history, their removal from the

onward moving will of Zeus as it was revealed in Io and
her descendants; for Orestes it is the now lost adequacy of
the family. He must break the ties that had been shown
defective in his parents, and by this act discover a wider
community in which the family, by regaining its true place,
will recover its fruitfulness.

In the dreadful following appeal to Agamemnon for
ghostly support, Orestes and Electra gradually take on the
ferocity of the chorus, only to have the chorus turn fearful
at the end when they themselves are resolved. Thus they
end quite alone, and this loneliness transmits itself to Orestes
as he moves forward to his vengeance and punishment. The
servants repeat the old men's warning of the former play,
"To the doer shall be done, so speaks the thrice-old warning" (vv. 313-314), but the children linger with fantasies
of the glory that would have remained, had Agamemnon
died at Troy. As the chorus recall them by chanting their
hate, the law of vengeance, and Agamemnon's final indigni-
ties, the children steadily breathe in their father's wrath, to
emerge as agents of the thrice-old warning. In this spirit
Orestes does not hesitate to apply to himself the snake of
his mother's dream. (vv. 540-550) The term expresses his
stealth and his underearthly prompting but does not yet convey its further and full meaning. Dominated as they are by
their mood of hate, the chorus rehearse in the least moving
ode of the trilogy the past crimes of passionate women.
Clytaemnestra's monstrosity fills their minds, and Agamemnon as a warrior seems guiltless by comparison with the
home-keeping Aegisthus. If the play stood by itself, one
could hardly have conceived another time and mood when
Agamemnon's crime similarly filled the mind, and it is this
frenetic and hypnotized absorption with Clytaemnestra's evil
that creates so deep a shock when Orestes finally confronts
her. Actually, he sees her once before the final encounter,
when in an ironic scene he seeks admission to the house with

news of his own death. Night is coming on, he says, and it were better that he spoke with a man. (vv. 660-667) She greets the false news with a lament of which she herself can hardly know how far it is pretended, how far genuine, but when Orestes has entered (in a manner opposite to Agamemnon, since he is now the deceiver as Agamemnon was the deceived), she makes clear that, having Aegisthus, she is less bereft than she had said. (vv. 716-718) An almost Shakespearian scene of half-comic relief follows, as Orestes' old nurse emerges to summon Aegisthus and his bodyguards but is persuaded by the woman to omit the part of the message having to do with the guards. In the old woman's garrulous talk of Orestes' infancy and of her lost labors of washing and feeding there is a curious suggestion of the final outcome. The nurse expresses in her simplicity the riches of nature of which the Eumenides will sing at the end. As the messenger from Troy stated in the first play the common sufferings of the army which were the obverse of Agamemnon's ambition, so the nurse states the goodness of family which is the obverse of Clytaemnestra's passion. But the chorus return to their hate. They see Orestes as Perseus about to face Medusa; when she cries "child," they say, reply "my father's." (vv. 829-831) Aegisthus returns, suspicious of womanly credence in the story of Orestes' death; most ironically, since he has himself been tricked by the nurse and the chorus to return without his guards. His suspicion sits curiously on a man whose whole career has been through women, and this irony well describes the present impossible state when family, as apart from kingship — Clytaemnestra as apart from Agamemnon — has been made the ruling principle. His dying cry is presently heard from the house, and the servant who rushes out for help ends by saying that things are beyond help.

The fearful moment is at hand. When Clytaemnestra appears in answer to the cries, she is told, "the dead destroy

the living." (v. 886)   But the words could as well mean,
"the living man destroys the dead," and the two sides of
Orestes' act, as vengeance and as redemption, are in these
intertwined meanings. The queen calls for a man-killing
axe and, as Orestes is shown above Aegisthus, she at last
faces him. It is of the essence of the scene that that side of
her which was expressed in the axe suddenly falls away and,
with it, Orestes' hypnotized confidence in his own justice.
She becomes simply his mother and, as she bares her breast,
the nightmare of the snake is reënacted. Orestes, grasping
now the true character of his act, cries in anguish to Pylades,
"what shall I do?" (v. 899)   In his reply Pylades, as friend
and as Delphian, becomes almost Apollo; "deem all your
enemy sooner than the god." (v. 902)   This is the turning-
point of the trilogy, the moment when the divine illumination enters mortal action. That it enters at this terrible
moment recalls the scene of Dante's turning; it is from a
present Hell that Orestes cleaves to Apollo. When his
mother calls herself an agent of Fate, he replies that then
he too is such an agent. When she disclaims responsibility
for his exile and asks to be shown what price she had for
him, he says that he is ashamed to state. He means Aegisthus, and when she recalls her ancient loneliness and isolation, he counters with the labors of men away from home.
The male principle, guilty in Agamemnon, begins its exoneration in these words. (v. 921)   Yet Orestes, though shaken
from his previous confidence, is not yet free of the mood
which the old men rebuked in Clytaemnestra in the first play.
He asserts himself simply as the agent of justice and, in so
doing, neglects his own guilt. As a subtle change took place
in the *Agamemnon* from the king's to the queen's guilt, so
now a change begins from the queen's to her son's. Her
last words are to identify him with the snake, and as he
drives her from the stage, he approves the prophetic dream.
"You murdered whom you should not; suffer now what

should not be." (v. 930)   Only in this statement is there
hope.   By admitting the evil with the necessity of his act,
Orestes at last shows a moral awareness of what he is doing, a freedom from the automatism of hurt and counter-
hurt.   Though in the final scene he exposes the ancient blood-
stained robe in which his father died and casts back on his
mother the name of snake, the tone of his self-exoneration
differs from hers in the first play.   He knows that his act is
one of atonement as well as of vengeance, and the Furies
whom he now begins to see do not come to him quite against
his will or by surprise.   He had not, like his parents, sought
chiefly his own good but the end of evil.   Though the chorus
ask to what this third disaster leads, they have already urged
Orestes to Delphi, and his cry to the god is a statement that
his motive was in essence new.

   The length of the solution in the *Eumenides* shows how
deeply rooted in Greek life were the ties of place and family.   E. R. Dodds' previously mentioned theory of tragedy
took account of this feeling when it represented the tragic
act as at once great in its liberating courage, yet guilty in its
disruption of old ties.[139]   When in the *Eumenides* Apollo
first confronts the Furies, who have pursued Orestes to
Delphi, the dispute between them comes finally to the question of blood-relationship, the Furies holding that the bonds
of marriage, because free of consanguinity, are less sacred
than those between mother and child, Apollo holding the opposite.   He defends his view, much in the spirit of Aphrodite in the Argive trilogy, by seeing in marriage the earthly
counterpart of Zeus's and Hera's union and the pledge of
Aphrodite's favoring presence. (vv. 213-218)   In defending marriage, the Olympians defend freely chosen compacts,
and the issue between Apollo and the Furies comes down to
trust in the creative will.   The Furies conceive men as bound
to their inherited past; Apollo asserts the free light of mind
and choice.   Pindar, it was repeatedly noted, felt no such

conflict between heritage and creation, and the birth of Iamus in the half-dark, half-golden light of violets was taken to express the happy mingling of earthly and Olympian strains. The *Oresteia* will end by asserting a similar mingling. But for Aeschylus the path to this desired state is far harder than for Pindar, evidently because the revolutionary forces at work in Athens during his lifetime enhanced the cleft between heritage and novelty. The statement of each was forced to extremes. Agamemnon's huge vitality, like that of Prometheus and the Labdacids, contained an innovating force of masculine will and mind which was capable at once of extending and of violating the ancient limits. Clytaemnestra, rooted in these limits, has a vigor proportionate to her husband's because she must, if she is to protect her competing right. Each of the two positions is forced to tragic and guilty overstatement, and the possibility of the harmony that Pindar dared believe in is remote. The *Eumenides* treads a road which, in one sense, leads back to a harmony lost through guilty excess, but which is more truly a road forward to a new harmony. Politically speaking, this new harmony transcends those ties of family which gave sanction to kingship; it therefore brings a new concept of the community. In this respect, Agamemnon's impulse of fidelity to the army, half-guilty though it was, is enlarged and confirmed. But since the new community is itself rooted in place and past, Clytaemnestra's fidelity to these is also sanctioned, and the change of the punitive Furies into favoring Eumenides expresses what was benign in her. That Orestes must tread alone the dreadful path to this solution signifies a part of it which is not political. He travels toward a purity of personal motive which will at last escape the self-assertive legacy of his royal forebears and in that escape will discover the character of freedom.

It has been noted that each of the former plays shows a progressive change of emphasis, the *Agamemnon* from the

king's to the queen's guilt, the *Choephoroe* from the queen's
to Orestes'. A like change takes place in the final play, but
more complexly because the solution is now at hand and the
conflicting forces are to merge. The dire and snake-haired
Furies at first inspire only horror, but as they presently state
their age-old descent from Night and assert society's dependence on them, they grow less forbidding because more
comprehensible. Not that they may stay unchanged, since
then the future could claim no freedom from the past; yet
it grows clear that they must not change beyond recognition,
since nature would then lose its punitive force. The problem of the play is to assert the sanctions of the past and of
nature, yet in such way as to leave place for freedom, which
must therefore be freedom, not to destroy, but to include and
to transform. As in the *Agamemnon*, an interval of time
elapses within the play. Orestes is first seen at Delphi, with
bloody sword and hands yet wet from murder, with the
Furies about him, though asleep in this moment of his safety
beneath Apollo's care. When the god sends him into the
world to seek purification by time, travel, and men's acceptance, and the ghost of Clytaemnestra rouses the Furies to
pursue him, a period of his wandering intervenes before he
seeks trial before the Areopagus in Athens. At Athens he
is seen in three successive moments: alone with the Furies
still upon him, under Athene's eyes as she appears in answer
to his cry and listens with Olympian lucidity to both him and
his pursuers, and in his trial and exoneration. These four
stages, of fresh crime, of living with it, of the first vision of
release, and of actual and present release, are the steps in
Orestes' salvation. Since the jury is divided and Athene
casts the deciding vote, the narrow outcome attests the
strength of the Furies' position. The history of the family
of Atreus ends as Orestes leaves, and the final solution involves Athene and the Furies alone. The trial having hinged
on the relative rights of father and of mother, she has de-

cided for the former and, by so doing, has asserted the right
of freely chosen compacts as against the old authority of
mere inheritance. The weight of her lucid spirit has been
for freedom and mind. Her task is accordingly to win by
mind, which is to say, by persuasion, Peitho, the ancient figures of night to share her open day. Were she to win by
force, something like the dilemma of the *Prometheus* would
be repeated, and the rancor of the past would smolder into
the future. That she is able to persuade them is the final
step in their progressive transformation. In effect, they
change as Orestes changes; their presence in the world is the
presence in it of such guilt as his. As Athene's Olympian
reason is a kind of sky opening above him, so, in spite of
their momentary bitterness in defeat, is it above them. The
Eumenides, the Benignant Ones, were worshiped in Athens
as deities of fertility and family, and their awesome presence
was felt in the court of the Areopagus. When the Furies
become the Eumenides, it is a sign that ancient powers of
Earth and Night share without conflict the lucent life of
Athene's city. An order is established which, unlike the
heroic monarchy and the tyranny which followed it, works
through reason and consent. The orderly process of Orestes'
trial and the principle of equity which it sanctioned remain
the political model, and if the Areopagus keeps the threat of
force, the threat attends on reason. The belief in reason
which Pericles in the Funeral Oration makes the foundation
of democracy speaks in the change, as does Socrates' faith
that the soul will follow where reason leads. As previously
noted, the change is also from the family to the community
as the frame and setting of life. But since, even so, men are
bound to earth as the gods are not and mortal reason cannot
stand clear of place, the Eumenides remain as operative
among men, or nearly so, as are the Olympians. Men's freedom is not something absolute and unconfined. It is rather
the capacity so to live with nature as to find in it a favoring

force that guides to full activity. The wide Aeschylean style
expresses this dimension toward which place and fixity look.
Freedom is the inresidence of potentiality in the fixed. The
final friendship between Athene and the Eumenides expresses
this union of creativity with heritage, of scope with commitment.

Themes and figures of the two previous plays now recur
in a new light. The priestess who in the opening scene describes the succession of gods at Delphi, from primal earth
and her daughters Themis and Phoebe to their descendant
and Zeus's son Phoebus (vv. 1-8), gives the divine model
for earthly evolution. When she staggers from the temple
in horror at the Furies, it is as if she had recognized with
shock an unsuspected residue in the world which had not
shared this evolution. In rousing the Furies, who growl in
their sleep like dogs, the ghost of Clytaemnestra continues
the theme of nightmare from the former plays, and the
theme now connects itself with this dark and untamed residue. The Furies should live, says Apollo, where men are
tortured or in the bloody caves of lions. (vv. 186-195) The
heroic lion of Homer's similes has degenerated, like Agamemnon himself, from a figure of courage to a figure of violence, which must be left behind. The net which Agamemnon threw about Troy and which Clytaemnestra threw about
him awaits Orestes at the hands of the Furies (v. 147), and
it contains the grip of the past. Yet Apollo's insulting bitterness toward the Furies is excessive; it holds no promise
of healing and clashes with his title as the remedial god of
prophecy. Between them and him the conflict is open and
sharp between old and new, and though he is Orestes' champion and his advocate at the trial, Orestes' true healer is
Athene. The fine scene of his first moments at Athens when
his crime is already old but before Athene has appeared to
him shows him with the Furies still at his heels. They
threaten to make him "bloodless, the prey of ghostly powers,

a shadow" (v. 302), and they sing over him what they call a binding spell. These threats and the song express the self-doubt which lingers beside his growing sense of freedom. He is still in the state when, though conscious of right motives, he is uncertain of their power to transform the future. Yet mere time has led toward healing. As the old Oedipus of Sophocles' last play says that the years have lifted his first burden of guilt, so Orestes has moved toward sanity by time alone, and Apollo's support may be seen as the ray of faith which guided him from the first. Suffering has been a further healer. As Prometheus in the second play has lost his will to conflict, so Orestes' first words at Athens, that he is "taught through evils" (v. 276), recall the old men's prayer to Zeus at the start of the *Agamemnon,* "who guides men to sobriety, makes sovereign learning by suffering." (*Ag.* 176-178) But it is only through Athene that time and suffering at last pass over into freedom. Her effect as of light has already been mentioned. Unlike Apollo, she is notably fair to the Furies, out of respect, she says, for their antiquity, but evidently also from a quality of spirit in herself. For the first time in the trilogy there enters with her a tone of shining reason, which is not free of emotion (she speaks kindly to the Furies and lovingly of Athens) but before which the harsher emotions fade.

The change which she brings, as of lifting skies and widening views, affects not only Orestes but the Furies. The ode which they now sing is not, like the binding song, essentially negative and repressive, nor is it directed largely against Orestes, but toward society and in a positive spirit. Where will be redress for injustice, they ask, if the new gods wholly triumph; on whom will injured parents call? "At times 'tis well that terror dwell; as the heart's watchman it must sit enthroned. There's gain to learn sobriety by groaning. What man whose heart holds nothing in the light, what city of mankind will still revere the gods? Praise an ex-

istence neither enslaved nor lawless. To every mean god
gives the victory, though various his sight. In tune with
which I tell you: violence is impiety's true child, from the
heart's health springs men's beloved and prayed-for bliss."
(vv. 517-537) The Furies have rounded to the position
of the old men in the *Agamemnon*, who looked with suspicion on wealth and power and with horror on the injustice
which pursuit of these fosters. They have become in
effect the voice of a changed community and of a mind which
finds freedom through restraint. As such, they come near
representing Orestes' new mind. He and they had in fact
never been far apart; as a snake, he had been to his mother
what they have been to him. Both have expressed justice
in the negative and punitive sense, and the darkness in which
both have moved has not been so much the presence of evil
as the absence of the bright, creative face of justice. Apollo
and Athene assert this latter side, the former as hope, the
latter as realization. With it the male principle is finally
vindicated. The decisive argument at the trial concerns
who is the true parent, the father or the mother, and Aeschylus adduces a contemporary medical theory to the effect that
the father is the essential creator, the mother the recipient
and nurse of the implanted seed. (vv. 657-673) Athene accepts this view, she says, because she herself sprang from her
father without intermediary. Apollo had earlier claimed to
speak the mind of Zeus in prompting and protecting Orestes
(vv. 616-621), and when Athene in turn invokes Zeus as
reason for her support, the united weight of the Olympians
is for the male. The chorus of the *Choephoroe* had already
seen in Agamemnon's murder the collapse of civil authority,
and Apollo returns to this view when he says that a mother's
death is not the same thing as that of a king who holds the
Zeus-given sceptre. The male principle which the Olympians
thus defend is that of government and, as such, of a range
of activity beyond that of the family alone. The court of

the Areopagus which Athene here founds remains as a pledge
of this wider scope of corporate life.   In retrospect, Agamemnon's crime against Iphigeneia appears as an inner contradiction in a bygone society where kingship, founded on
family, must assert itself by violating family.   Further, the
public goals of society were corrupted for private ends, and
Menelaus' loss was no worthy cause for the death of fighting men.   The point of view closely resembles that of the
Persians, where Xerxes, even more clearly than Agamemnon,
damaged the state for personal ends.   But the vision of positive justice now revealed through the Olympians has resolved
this ancient contradiction.   The free community of law and
reason, by including the family within itself, has at once
healed the family and won creative scope.   The trilogy has
traced the emergence of democracy from its troubled ante-
cedents. History has been the working of instruction through
pain.   The male principle of freedom, like that which shone
in the sunlight of Salamis, wins its creativity by taking into
itself the lessons of the past.   From being chastening, these
lessons have become liberating, and in the change appears
the Olympian rule of reason.

Orestes leaves with the promise of his city's lasting fidelity to Athens. (vv. 762-777)   The civic tone of the conclusion speaks in these words, and, as suggested earlier, one
misses in them a statement by Orestes of his inner and personal freedom.   Perhaps only the generation of Socrates
was to discover this language of inner affirmation, which appears also in the old Oedipus' sense of spiritual release and
oneness with the gods.   But the whole end of the play is in
effect a circumlocution for this state of regained peace and
joy.   Here Aeschylus and Pindar are most nearly at one.
As Pindar found in the figures of heroes the means of stating
the mind's sight of joy and meaning in the world, so does
Aeschylus now in the conversion of the Furies.   Bitter and
threatening in the moment of their defeat, they yield to

Athene's persistent smiling persuasion, to outdo her at last in their outpoured blessings. "I shall accept joint residence with Pallas nor shall disprize the city which conquering Zeus and Ares mark the fort of gods, shrine-guarding ornament of divinities Greek." (vv. 916-920) Here speaks the heroic energy of Agamemnon, now purged of that violence which desecrated Troy, transformed, rather, into the defensive ardor of Salamis. To this masculine energy the Eumenides add the fertile blessings of field and flock. "Let no tree-blighting injury blow (I speak it as my gift), nor heat that blinds the blossoms of the plants trespass these bounds, nor fruitless withering plague come on; but prospering flocks let Pan with double young increase in season due, and rich earth's offspring yield its heaven-sent find." (vv. 937-948) With gifts of field go those of family. "Gone be the plights that cut men early down; to lovely girls give lives with husbands matched, o final gods and goddess Fates, my sisters, spirits just, who share in every house, on all times weigh, to righteous company most honored powers." (vv. 956-967) As in N. 7, the Fates are goddesses, among much else, of birth and childhood, and they stand here with Zeus and Hera as guardians of family. Like the Danaids, the Eumenides include prayers against faction and civil war, and they end by invoking the concord of mind which is a people's salvation. This is still not entirely the language of inner and personal peace, but no more is it the language of mere history. It is rather the mystical expression of a harmony which embraces both the state and the mind, outer history and inner history. The reconciliation of the new gods with the old changes each. If the new gods sanction the free light of creative reason, they do so in no hostile spirit. On the contrary, freedom is itself seen as flowering from rooted community and ancient earth. The mind does not assert its creativity against earth, one part against the other, but Zeus himself has become inclusive being. Those parts of the tril-

ogy that have seemed to express a purely historical evolution
have been caught up in a higher evolution, from a world of
strife and becoming to a world of harmony, and which, like
that of Pindar's highest sight, is simultaneously bright, at
rest, and alive.

CONCLUSION

THE judgment of Eduard Meyer mentioned at the start, that Pindar speaks for a vanishing, Aeschylus for an emergent age, is correct but incomplete. It has been argued that Aeschylus' sense of conflict and of time contains the experience of a revolutionary generation, confident of its gains and aware of having brought novelty into the world. If his vehicle of the trilogy owes something to the sweep of epic and even of Stesichorus' lyric narrative, it owes much more to this contemporary exaltation. The trilogy as a form expresses time's creative working. The *Iliad* and *Odyssey* had described no such process. They showed final limits toward which the heroic spirit mounts in its desire for completeness. The gods who inspire the heroes impart this flame and fullness of being, and if the heroes when alone reveal their own stubborn courage, their final gain is to have felt the gods' heightening presence. Thus both Achilles and Odysseus at the end look back with cleared eyes on the world that they have seen. They have not changed the world; it is their sight of it which has been changed. Aeschylus sees the world made new, and no poet breathes a higher ardor for liberating change. This ardor taught him his view of creative time, his single most revolutionary insight. It further made vivid and present to him the mind's responsibility for choice and consequent conflict with the past. The tragic dilemma of his heroes springs from this double awareness. Being responsible for its choices, the mind is face to face, not with unpredictable visitations of gods, but with itself; yet it is simultaneously conscious of a prior order which also has claims and to disturb which involves deepest self-searching. Agamemnon's anguish at Aulis and Orestes' before his mother show at once this urgency and this doubt of de-

cision. Yet the choice must be made and the guilt of break
with the past incurred, if time is to beget its possible gain.
A further concept of healing then reveals itself within the
idea of time. Prometheus' long pain and the danger which
Hypermnestra incurred for Lynceus resemble Orestes' suffering as instruments of time's healing course. Conflict,
choice, and healing all take their place in the idea of creative
time, and the doctrine of learning by suffering contains the
promise of the goal.

These are the fit ideas of the generation that created the
democracy, fought Marathon and Salamis, and founded the
Aegean League. That all of them did not continue to be
held in their pristine force, as the aging democracy moved
on to struggles within itself and abroad, did not erase them
from the Greek mind. As previously noted, the idea of
progress speaks in a famous ode of the *Antigone,* in the so-
called Archaeology and Pentecontaetia of Thucydides and
in the Funeral Oration, in the Periclean figure of Theseus
in Euripides' *Suppliants,* in contemporary medical writings,
in the sophist Protagoras as Plato represents him, and, more
dimly, in Isocrates.[140] But it was not the idea of progress
which chiefly remained; it lost its strength by the end of the
fifth century. The Attic trait which, if present in Solon,
first brilliantly shines in Aeschylus is faith in the moral
cogency of reason. The spirit of his luminous Athene of the
Eumenides descends to Pericles, Socrates, Plato, and Aristotle.

What is meant is the assumption that reason can so guide
and unite the faculties as to redirect both the individual life
and that of society. Democracy was born from this assumption that all can share in the city's enlightening life with gain
to it and to themselves. A like faith inspires Socrates' view
that no one willingly pursues evil, hence that to know the
good is to follow it, and this faith speaks also in Aristotle's
description of virtue as lying in right choice. It is no acci-

dent that, as the prophet of democracy, Aeschylus is also the prophet of reason. As the product of suffering and time, reason is not to him the analytical faculty that it later became, but it is reason nevertheless and shows its fruits in a lucidity of spirit which resolves conflicts, not by assertive will, but by generous and inclusive understanding. This, as observed at the start, is equivalent to Aristotle's purging of the soul as applied to a whole society. It is in this sense that Eduard Meyer's judgment is correct. The future of the West was on the side of Aeschylus. His belief that experience can issue in enlightenment and that enlightenment can advance society has made him notably accessible to centuries since the Renaissance. Even the abruptness of his language has not kept him from standing with Socrates as the Athenian of Athenians.

Yet this high faith in redemptive reason has proved perishable, chiefly because it can degenerate into faith in merely analytical reason and, as such, can lose grip on experience. Aeschylus was in no danger of this attrition. His mind was filled with the shapes of gods and heroes through whom he saw reality. He was accordingly free to unfold his visionary progress without suspecting that this progress could endanger the directness of experience on which he relied. What is involved seems the flash and mystery of the world, the sense of it as alive with moving forces which speak at once to the senses and to the mind, therefore to the whole being. When reason is understood simply as intellection, something remains over, the search for which may seem in defiance of mind, as eluding or transcending it. As early as a generation after Aeschylus, Sophocles abandoned the Aeschylean view of progress for an Homeric reliance on the heroic will, and he fitly also abandoned the trilogy for single plays showing moments when the will is laid bare. His heroes have the deep instinct to respond worthily to the world whether or not it yields reasonable meaning. To them the momentous-ness and beauty of experience defy immediate understanding, though they may ultimately be seen to include it. It is at this point that the relationship of Pindar to Aeschylus takes on importance. Certainly Pindar lacked any hope of social progress or desire for it, and he correspondingly lacked the sense of evolutionary reason. Yet the future cannot be said to have been against him. On the contrary, poetry as the mysterious record of Protean meaning has come into existence chiefly by means like his. It has not found, that is, its validation in historical gain, and when, as with Dante, it has been allied with analytical reason, it has taken reason into itself to give it living shape. Pindar's sense of revelation from the fitful flash of the world reflects the working of the total consciousness. To heed this state is to assert reason as part of a more complex, inclusive whole, and it is because Pindar relies quite simply on this undivided state of spirit that he stands beyond change.

But this antithesis looks too much to the future. If it is true that Attic reason had its prophet in Aeschylus, he stood at the edge of the promised land, which offered the more golden prospect from that distance. What has been repeatedly described as the common ground between him and Pindar is their feeling for final harmony. The struggle toward it was for Aeschylus the struggle of history toward a new order. Yet the solution which he finally sees is beyond history, a mystical reconciliation of the aspiring, creative mind with earth and past. In this vision the two men are at one. It might be rewarding to pursue by what steps the Greeks discovered a language to express spiritual states. These states cannot of course be conveyed independently of image, but there is a difference whether a man is conscious of using images as the spirit's language or, on the contrary, gropes intuitively to express spirit by the myths and images in which it seems embedded. Mythology, which through the heroes passed over also into history, gave the Greeks a set of shapes which ambiguously expressed both history and spirit. It has been noted that the release and joy which are the true end of Orestes' sufferings are not, as such, expressed by him; they are implicit, rather, in the concord of the Olympians with the Eumenides in the Attic future. Yet what Aeschylus is quite clearly describing is a new state of spirit. In the same way the reconciliation of Prometheus with Zeus expresses a change of understanding, from creativity as strife and hence as partial exclusion, to creativity as peace and therefore as inclusion. The change was further described as from becoming to being. Pindar finds in the acts of gods and heroes a like circumlocution for inward states. The divine music before which in *P.* 1 the eagle's eyelids droop describes a final harmony like that between Prometheus and Zeus. Though the two men's emphasis is different and Pindar waits on the gods for the illumination toward which Aeschylus' characters energetically struggle, their final goal of peace is similar, as is the method by which it is stated. The method is the incompletely metaphorical manner of the late archaic style. A fully metaphorical method would imply awareness that what is being said of the gods or heroes is simultaneously being said of the mind. But whereas both men tend to this awareness and their metaphorical styles constate the relevance of divine or heroic acts to conscious spirit, they at the same time live so fully in mythological events that these have a reality of their own. The result is a tension between the color and vividness of events and their revelation of meaning, and in this tension is the power of the late archaic. Perhaps the very vividness of the world, as they knew it, created its counterpoise in the desire for transcendent harmony. Heraclitus' judgment of life as a bow speaks in the tense bowman of the Aeginetan pediment, and not less in Pindar's and Aeschylus' styles. The figure they both draw of the eagle catches their soaring or plummeting energy. Yet beyond this energy, and in a mysterious way allied with it, is their peace. Pindar sees it the more steadily: in the joy of the procession at Orchomenos in *O*. 14, in the mercy that crowns Polydeuces' act of heroic faith in *N*. 10, and more serenely, in the calm deities that guide from birth to manhood in *N*. 7 and *N*. 8, in the stately figure of Quietude in *P*. 8, in the likeness of men to gods in *N*. 6, in the music of *P*. 1. As has been repeatedly said, he felt no deep conflict between earth and gods. His Iamus lying in the golden and dark violets is the sign of a bright harmony shining from the dark earth. But however sharp the original tension which Aeschylus feels between place and creativity, female and male, earth-born and Olympian gods, he too resolves it. Agamemnon and Clytaemnestra survive amended in Orestes, whose healing is the sight of the divine radiance.

NOTES

NOTES

Poems and fragments of Pindar are cited from the text of C. M. Bowra (2nd ed., Oxford, 1937); scholia and Eustathius' essay on Pindar from A. B. Drachmann's *Scholia Vetera in Pindari Carmina* (3 vols., Leipzig, 1903-27).

Reference is often made to:

L. R. Farnell, *The Works of Pindar* (3 vols., London, 1932)

U. v. Wilamowitz-Moellendorf, *Pindaros* (Berlin, 1932)

G. Norwood, *Pindar* (Berkeley, 1945)

W. Schadewaldt, 'Der Aufbau des Pindarischen Epinikion' (*Schr. d. Königsb. Gel. Ges.* 5 [1928] 259-343)

L. Illig, *Zur Form der Pindarischen Erzählung* (Berlin, 1932)

W. Theiler, 'Die Zwei Zeitstufen in Pindars Stil und Vers' (*Schr. d. Königsb. Gel. Ges.* 7 [1941] 255-289)

C. M. Bowra, 'Pindar, Pythian II' (*H.S.C.P.* 48 [1937] 1-28 = *Problems in Greek Poetry* [Oxford, 1953] 66-92)

C. M. Bowra, 'Pindar, Pythian xi' (*C.Q.* 30 [1936] 129-141)

J. H. Finley, Jr., 'The Date of Paean 6 and Nemean 7' (*H.S.C.P.* 60 [1951] 61-80)

1. Eustathius 28 (Drachmann III 300); Wilamowitz, *Pindaros* 88-114. He composed *P.* 7 in 486 for Megacles and, according to the scholiast on v. 18 (Drachmann II 204), a threnos for Megacles' father Hippocrates, brother of Cleisthenes.

2. Farnell (*Works of Pindar* II 201 and 'Pindar, Athens and Thebes: Pyth. ix 151-170,' *C.Q.* 9 [1915] 193-200) interprets *P.* 9 to show Pindar in 474 answering criticism at Thebes for recent praise of Athens. This praise is most naturally connected with his famous dithyramb, fgs. 64 and 65, on Athens' performance in the second Persian war. The same period seems to fit the story that a fine was levied on him at Thebes which the Athenians paid. (The sum is given as 1000 drachmas by Eustathius 28, Drachmann III 300, as 10,000 drachmas by Isocrates XV 166. A bronze statue in Athens of Pindar seated and with his lyre beside him, not mentioned by Isocrates and presumably from after his time, is described by pseudo-Aeschines, *Epist.* 4.3 and Pausanias, I 8.4. Cf. Wilamowitz, *Pindaros* 273, and for discrepancies of statement on where the statue stood, J. G. Frazer, *Pausanias's Description of Greece* [London, 1913] II 92). A further tie with Athens is reflected in the poem to Pan, fg. 85, the opening line of which is taken from the Attic skolion, 4. (C. M. Bowra, *Greek Lyric Poetry* [Oxford, 1936] 426-428.) This poem too may fall in the period of the 470's. At least Pindar speaks in *P.* 3. 78 of a shrine to Pan which tradition held that he himself built near his house in Thebes (Pausanias IX 25. 3), on the profits, Wilamowitz thought, of his Sicilian visit (*Pindaros* 270). These lines of evidence suggest that his estrangement from Athens did not occur until the 460's.

3. *Vita* from Suidas, 7 (printed in Murray's edition of the plays). A. W. Smyth, *Aeschylus* (Loeb Library: New York, 1922) I xxiv.

4. *Vita Ambrosiana*, Drachmann I 3.

5. *Geschichte des Altertums* (3rd ed., Stuttgart, 1939) IV 423-433.

6. 'How to Read' (in *Polite Essays* [London, 1937] 174). *The Letters of Ezra Pound* (New York, 1950) 55, 91, 295.

7. W. Schadewaldt, 'Der Aufbau des Pindarischen Epinikion,' 275, 307.

8. *Les Voix de Silence* (Paris, 1952) 72-78, 233.

9. *Principes de la Philosophie de l'Histoire*, trans. J. Michelet (Brussels, 1835), Axioms 49-53, pp. 103-105.

10. *The Laws of Civilization and Decay* (New York, 1895) esp. 290-295.

11. Xenophon, *Memorabilia* II 1. 21-34.

12. A. Lord, 'Homer, Parry, and Huso' (*A.J.A.*, 52 [1948] 34-44), which contains a bibliography of Parry.

13. S. K. Langer, *Philosophy in a New Key* (Cambridge, 1942), especially ch. IV, 'Discursive and Presentational Forms,' 78-102.

14. C. M. Bowra, *Greek Lyric Poetry* 173.

15. H. Fränkel, *Dichtung und Philosophie des Frühen Griechentums* (*Philological Monographs of the Amer. Philol. Assoc.* XII New York, 1951) 60-64.

16. *Eth. Nic.* VI 7, 1141a 24.

17. D. L. Page, *Corinna* (*Soc. for the Promotion of Hellenic Studies, Supplementary Paper* 6, 1953).

18. W. W. Jaeger, *Theology of the Early Greek Philosophers* (Oxford, 1947) 115.

19. W. Schadewaldt, 'Der Aufbau des Pindarischen Epinikion.'

20. With the exception of *N.* 7, on which see Farnell, *Works of Pindar* II 289.

21. Farnell, *ibid.*, II 217. Simonides' poem on the infant Perseus (fg. 13, Diehl) may have been composed for a Thessalian audience (C. M. Bowra, *Greek Lyric Poetry* 351).

22. W. Theiler, *Die Zwei Zeitstufen in Pindars Stil und Vers*.

23. *O.1.11*; *N.1.19-20*. So Wilamowitz, *Pindaros* 233.

24. Fg. 80. Probably but not certainly a prosodion. Wilamowitz, *ibid.* 274-75; cf. A Turyn, *Pindari Carmina* (Cambridge, 1952) fg. 155.

25. *C.Q.* 30 (1936) 129-141.

26. These three periods are more fully discussed, *H.S.C.P.* 60 (1951) 61-80.

27. W. Theiler, 'Die Zwei Zeitstufen in Pindars Stil und Vers.' H. Gundert, 'Der Alte Pindar' (*Mnemosynon Theodor Wiegand* [Munich, 1938]) 1-13.

28. E. Havelock, *The Crucifixion of Intellectual Man* (Boston, 1950).

29. W. Theiler 'Die Zwei Zeitstufen in Pindars Stil und Vers.' Farnell, *Works of Pindar* II 274.

30. Prof. Eduard Frankel has kindly caused me to see how finely W. v. Humboldt grasped Pindar's feeling for gold as expression of the divine brilliance in the world. (*Gesammelte Schriften*, Berlin 1903, I 411-29, esp. p. 422).

31. Scholium on 1a (Drachmann I 16-17). C. M. Bowra, *Problems in Greek Poetry* 77.

32. G. Norwood, *Pindar,* chs. V-VI.

33. Scholium on 29c (Drachmann I 68).

34. E. R. Dodds, *The Greeks and the Irrational* (Berkeley, 1951), ch. V.

35. Wilamowitz, *Pindaros* 250.

36. Scholium on 157a (Drachmann I 99).

37. G. Norwood, *Pindar* 172-74.

38. Pausanias VI 7. 1-2.

39. Cicero, *Tusc.* I 46. 111.

40. Drachmann I 195, 197-8.

41. Wilamowitz, *Pindaros* 361. Farnell, *Works of Pindar* I 40.

42. L. Illig, *Zur Form der Pindarischen Erzählung.*

43. Wilamowitz, *Pindaros* 362.

44. H. J. Rose, 'Pindar and the Tragedians,' *C.R.* 61 (1947) 43-45.

45. *Iliad* 3. 219, 2. 671-75.

46. Fg. 19. 8 (Diehl).

47. W. Theiler, 'Die Zwei Zeitstufen in Pindars Stil und Vers.'

48. *Eth. Nic.* VII 11-14, esp. 1153a 12-15.

49. *Philebus* 16c, 52c, 63d — end.

50. Fg. 1 (Diehl).

51. I 70, II 63, VI 18, 87. H. T. Wade-Gery, 'Thucydides The Son of Milesias.' *J.H.S.* 52 (1932) 224-25. J. H. Finley, Jr., *Thucydides* (Cambridge, 1942) 122-28. V. Ehrenberg, 'Polypragmosyne: A Study in Greek Politics,' *J.H.S.* 67 (1947) 46-67.

52. W. W. Jaeger, *Paideia* (Eng. transl. by G. Highet [Oxford, 1939]) I 23, 193.

53. The date and much of the interpretation here adopted for *P.* 2 follow from C. M. Bowra's admirable 'Pindar, Pythian II.'

54. Bowra, *ibid.* (*Problems in Greek Poetry* 75).

55. So B. L. Gildersleeve (*Pindar, The Olympian and Pythian Odes* [New York, 1885]) and Farnell.

56. For the view here taken of the date of *N.* 7, see *H.S.C.P.* 60 (1951) 61-80.

57. Herodotus VIII 122.

58. So Schadewaldt, 'Der Aufbau des Pindarischen Epinikion,' 311-13.

59. Respectively, Farnell *Works of Pindar* II 296, Finley *H.S.C.P.* 60 (1951) 77, Schadewaldt, 'Der Aufbau,' 313, of whom Schadewaldt seems correct.

60. *N.* 4. 81, *I* 4. 75.

61. H. T. Wade-Gery 'Thucydides The Son of Melesias,' *J.H.S.* 52 (1932) 211.

62. The view here adopted of the difficult passage, 76-96, is that of Farnell (*Works of Pindar* II 201-202, 205-206 and 'Pindar, Athens, and Thebes: Pythian IX. 151-170,' *C.Q.* 9 [1915] 193-200).

63. See above n. 2.

64. L. Illig, *Zur Form der Pindarischen Erzählung* 33.

65. Scholium on 165 (Drachmann I 193).

66. W. Theiler, 'Die Zwei Zeitstufen in Pindars Stil und Vers.'

67. Thucydides I 108. 3.

68. Herodotus I 23, Thucydides I 13.2.

69. L. Illig, *Zur Form der Pindarischen Erzählung* 20-25.

70. Farnell, *Works of Pindar* II 316-317.

71. *Iliad* 16. 432-438, 666-684; 22. 167-176; 24. 64-76.

72. In Proclus' summary, *Homeri Opera* (Oxford: T. W. Allen, 1891) V 103.

73. Eustathius 34 (Drachmann III 303. 9-11).

74. Fg. 1 (Diels, *Fragmente der Vorsokratiker*).

75. See above n. 2.

76. A. Severyns, *Bacchylide* (Paris, 1933) 117-132.

77. Wilamowitz, *Pindaros* 393.

78. *Rep.* VI 507d-509d.

79. Farnell, *Works of Pindar* II 425-27.

80. Fg. 1 (Diehl) 39ff., where the singular is steadily used.

81. So Wilamowitz, *Pindaros* 436-37.

82. *De Demosthene* 39 (Usner-Radermacher I 213. 18-19).

83. *De Sublimitate* 9. 11-15.

84. So Wilamowitz, *Pindaros* 168-169; Farnell, *Works of Pindar* 274.

85. W. Theiler, 'Die Zwei Zeitstufen in Pindars Stil und Vers.'

86. C. Gaspar, *Essai de Chronologie Pindarique* (Brussells, 1900) 62. Farnell, *Works of Pindar* II 274.

87. Thuc. I 105-108. A. W. Gomme, *A Historical Commentary on Thucydides* (Oxford, 1945) I 307-19.

88. Wilamowitz, *Pindaros* 410-11. Farnell, *Works of Pindar* II 303.

89. N. O. Brown, 'Pindar, Sophocles, and the Thirty Years' Peace,' *T.A.P.A.* 82 (1951) 1-28.

90. C. H. Whitman, *Sophocles* (Cambridge, Massachusetts, 1951) 42-46.

91. *Ajax* 1102. C. M. Bowra *Sophoclean Tragedy* (Oxford, 1944) 52.

92. Scholium on 1a (Drachmann III 140). So Wiliamowitz, *Pindaros* 410.

93. *Rep.* II 366 c, VI 492a.

94. See the article on Moira, S. Eitrem, *R.E.* 30 (1932) 2485-2486.

95. Scholium on 23a (Drachmann III 264).

96. The translation follows Farnell's text in omitting a period at the end of line 39b.

97. C. M. Bowra, 'Pindar, Pythian XI.'

98. Fg. 44, vv. 35, 43.

99. Farnell, *Works of Pindar* II 224.

100. C. M. Bowra, 'Pindar, Pythian XI.'

101. Fg. 44.2; fg. 40.12.

102. Wilamowitz, *Pindaros* 263.

103. C. M. Bowra, 'Pindar, Pythian XI.'

104. Thuc. I 113-115.1, II 21.1.

105. Thuc. I 70, VI 18.2. Euripides, *Suppliants* 320-325, 509, 576-577. See above n. 51.

106. The translation follows Farnell's reading of line 68 (*Works of Pindar* II 196-97).

107. *Poetics* 8 1451a 22.

108. Athenaeus VIII 347e.

109. *The Discovery of the Mind* Eng. trans. by T. G. Rosenmeyer (Cambridge, 1953) 1-22.

110. *Iliad* 16. 527-31, 1. 197-200. *Odyssey* 3. 25-28.

111. *Iliad* 22. 294-305.

112. B. Snell, *Aischylos und Das Handeln in Drama* (*Philologus*, Supplementband xx, 1928) 20, 33.

113. *The Greeks and the Irrational* (Berkeley, 1951) 28-63.

114. The plays are cited from the edition of Gilbert Murray (Oxford, 1937).

115. G. Thomson, *Aeschylus, The Prometheus Unbound* (Cambridge, 1932) 38-46.

116. E. Lobel, E. P. Wegener, C. H. Roberts, *The Oxyrinchus Papyri* (London, 1952) XVI 2256, fg. 4. E. C. Yorke, 'The Date of the *Supplices* of Aeschylus,' *C.R.*, New Series, 4 (1954) 10-11.

117. F. Stoessl (*Die Trilogie der Aeschylus* [Baden bei Wien, 1937] 102-114) would place the appearance of Aphrodite in the second play of the trilogy. H. W. Smyth (*Aeschylean Tragedy* [Berkeley, 1924] 44) lends strength to the older view by adducing *Prometheus* 853-870, where the Titan describes to Io three successive actions by her descendants: the Danaids' flight, their murder of their cousins, and Hypermnestra's refusal to take part in the murder. These actions seem to represent the three steps in the trilogy.

118. G. Thomson, *Aeschylus and Athens* (London, 1941) 304.

119. G. Murray, *Aeschylus* (Oxford, 1940) 112-14.

120. In an unpublished paper by the gifted Japanese Hellenist, Masaaki Kubo.

121. Herodotus VII 144.

122. F. Solmsen, *Hesiod and Aeschylus* (Ithaca, 1949) 133-37.

123. *Theogony* 507-616, *Works and Days* 50-105.

124. *Antigone* 332-75, Thucydides I 1-19, II 36-46, *Suppliants* 195-249, *Protagoras* 320d-328c.

125. *I* 8. 37-38. *P.V.* 922-23. Farnell, *Works of Pindar* II 379-80.

126. G. Thomson, *Aeschylus, The Prometheus Bound* 18-32.
127. Fg. 202. Athenaeus XV 674d.
128. *O.C.* 56 and scholium.
129. Preface to the *Prometheus Unbound.*
130. E. Havelock, *The Crucifixion of Intellectual Man* 208-210.
131. Wilamowitz, *Aischylos* (Berlin, 1914) 67.
132. *Ibid.* 60. *O.T.* 1186-1222.
133. B. Snell, *Aeschylus* 81-82.
134. Wilamowitz, *Aischylos* 88-95.
135. *Suppliants* 625-709. *Eumenides* 956-1020.
136. G. Thomson, *Aeschylus, The Prometheus Bound* 46.
137. E. Fraenkel, Aeschylus *Agamemnon* (Oxford, 1950) II 96-99.
138. *Suppliants* 86-103.
139. *The Greeks and the Irrational* 44-50.
140. See above n. 105.

INDEX

INDEX